In Search of Our Ancient Ancestors

In Search of Our Ancient Ancestors

From the Big Bang to Modern Britain, in Science & Myth

Anthony Adolph

Pen & Sword
FAMILY HISTORY

First published in Great Britain in 2015 by
Pen & Sword Family History
an imprint of
Pen & Sword Books Ltd
47 Church Street
Barnsley
South Yorkshire
S70 2AS

ISBN 978 1 47384 921 1

A CIP catalogue record for this book is available from the British
Library

Typeset in Ehrhardt by
Mac Style Ltd, Bridlington, East Yorkshire
Printed and bound in the UK by CPI Group (UK) Ltd,
Croydon, CRO 4YY

Pen & Sword Books Ltd incorporates the imprints of Pen & Sword
Archaeology, Atlas, Aviation, Battleground, Discovery, Family History,
History, Maritime, Military, Naval, Politics, Railways, Select, Transport,
True Crime, and Fiction, Frontline Books, Leo Cooper, Praetorian
Press, Seaforth Publishing and Wharncliffe.

For a complete list of Pen & Sword titles please contact
PEN & SWORD BOOKS LIMITED
47 Church Street, Barnsley, South Yorkshire, S70 2AS, England
E-mail: enquiries@pen-and-sword.co.uk
Website: www.pen-and-sword.co.uk

Contents

Introduction   vii

Part One: Book of Life   1

Chapter 1   Tracing the Family Tree of Life   3

Chapter 2   Starting with a Bang   13

Chapter 3   In the Primal Seas   18

Chapter 4   First Steps on Dry Land   25

Chapter 5   Meet the Synapsids   31

Part Two: Book of Man   39

Chapter 6   The Southern Ape-Men   41

Chapter 7   Of Habilis and Hobbits   47

Chapter 8   The Neanderthals of Oldbury Hill   52

Chapter 9   'Thinking Man'   59

Chapter 10   The Genetic Adam and Eve   64

Chapter 11   Out of Africa   71

Chapter 12   My Great-grandfather, the Neanderthal   74

Part Three: Book of Ice   83

Chapter 13   Our Crô-Magnon Family Tree   85

Chapter 14   How to Visualise a Flying Rhinoceros   93

Chapter 15   The People of the Lion Man   98

Chapter 16   The Reindeer Hunters of Creswell Crags   103

Chapter 17   Leading the High Life at La Madeleine   110

Chapter 18   Voices from the Caves   120

Part Four: Book of Grain   127

Chapter 19   The False Spring   129

Chapter 20   The Stag Dancers of Star Carr   133

Chapter 21   From the City of Plastered Skulls   138

Chapter 22   The Heroes from the Sea   144

Chapter 23   Our Ancestors in the Age of Troy   151

Chapter 24   '... And All That'   159

Part Five: Book of Myths   165

Chapter 25   Looking Back in Wonder   167

Chapter 26   Out of the Chasm   173

Chapter 27   'Upon the Face of the Waters'   178

Chapter 28   The World Shapers   185

Chapter 29   The Birth of Mankind   190

Chapter 30   The Great Flood   198

Chapter 31   An Origin Myth for Britain?   205

Chapter 32   Tendrils from the Past   210

Chapter 33   Creation, Evolution or Aliens?   220

Epilogue: How You Fit Into the Story   224
Acknowledgements   236
Select Bibliography   237
Index   239

Introduction

It is of changes of shape and new forms that I am inspired to speak. Oh gods…
spin out for me in one continuous poem a thread of words, from the world's
beginning down to my own life!

Ovid, Metamorphoses, 1, 1–4

It is written 'Hypocrene' in English, but the Greeks pronounce it more earthily, *Ip-o-kree-nee*, so that you can almost hear the sharp crack in the rock as the winged horse Pegasus stamped his hoof down on the spine of Mount Helikon, causing a narrow fissure to open below, out of which bubbled fresh, cooling water. Hesiod knew the Hypocrene spring and the mythology that explained its existence and mentioned it 2,700 years ago at the beginning of his *Theogony*. He must have climbed that far up the tree-dotted scree of the mountain countless times, tending his goats and keeping them safe from wolves. Without the spring's water his musings up there would have been far less fertile.

I had little idea who Hesiod was until I began to research this book, eleven years ago. Until then, like most genealogists, I had contented myself with tracing family lines back as far as oral history and surviving records would allow. In Britain this usually means going back to somewhere between the early 1800s and the 1500s, when parish registers started being kept. Some lines can go back further, especially when the families concerned held land. For those who can make a link back to royal lines then sometimes it is possible to trace back to the last few centuries BC before the trail goes cold. But aside from the hard, scientific evidence of original records there existed older pedigrees that seemed to connect real people with mythological characters such as Adam and Eve and the Greek gods, and that put me onto studying origin myths from around the world. Hesiod's name kept cropping up, so when I found a second-hand copy of his *Theogony* for sale in a North London bookshop, I bought it and it changed my life. For what it contained was a family tree like no other: a continuous narrative that started with the birth of Gaia, Mother Earth, out of a primal chasm at the beginning of the world, and then came down to all her descendants, Uranos the deity of the starry heavens, the Titans, Zeus and the rest of the Olympian gods and everything else – including Hesiod himself for, like many Greeks, he claimed direct descent from Zeus.

Eventually we went to Askri, not far to the east of Delphi, and found the ruins of the village where Hesiod had lived. We liked it so much that we went back again a few years later to search for the Hypocrene spring. It entailed a three-hour scramble up the loose rocks, following a series of red dots spray-painted on the boulders to mark the path, and we almost missed the spring itself when we reached the top, but in the end we found it. The continuous shifting of the Earth's continental plates, which forced up Greece's mountains in the first place, has led to many rivers changing their courses, so it is not unusual to find that the springs associated with Classical temples and ancient cities have run dry. But when we lowered the black plastic bucket down on its thin chain, it came back up brimming with water. Goats' bells still clang across the valleys and they still have shepherds to guide them and protect them from wolves, which we heard howling sometimes at night. Much time has passed, but gratifyingly little here has changed.

Hesiod attributed his inspiration to the nine Muses who haunted the mountain 'and dance on their soft feet around the violet-dark spring'. But back down in the valley, looking up at the looming bulk of Helikon, I wondered whether the mountain itself might have been the *Theogony*'s greater inspiration. Above broods the Greek sky and below the mountain sprawls out like a recumbent woman, or goddess. The union of Gaia and Uranos gave rise to an enormous family of spirits, deities and, ultimately, their human descendants, spreading out just like the mountain's slopes down which the Muses danced, so Hesiod decided to write a narrative starting with sky and earth and then working down, generation by generation. His inspiration was brilliant: nobody had created a genealogical narrative like it before. It is, arguably, the third oldest surviving piece of Western literature (after Homer's *Iliad* and *Odyssey*, which could be up to a century older). Scholars consider that its genealogical structure influenced the writing of the biblical *Book of Genesis*. It makes Hesiod the earliest genealogist whose name we know anywhere in the world. His work is the ancestor, so to speak, of my profession.

Like all genealogists, Hesiod's perennial desire was to understand who he was and where he came from. He wrote of gods, Muses and mountains because they were his nearest points of reference. Had he been alive now he would probably have written a book like this and had I lived then I would, I feel sure, have attempted to write a theogony.

Something has changed between Hesiod's time and ours, because now there are some very different points of reference: to the old, mythological views of our origins has been added a new, scientific one. Another factor that compelled me to research this book was the plethora of television programmes about different points in our history that identify people in the past as 'our ancestors' but without explaining how you get from them to us, and the numerous press reports of new finds of 'missing links' in our evolutionary story, but again without describing the fossil chain from which the connecting finds had previously been absent. A further factor still was the arrival of commercially accessible genetic testing in the late 1990s. At first most genealogists regarded it with contempt, for of course such jiggery-pokery with test tubes could never replace traditional genealogical records. Yet geneticists kept insisting that this was exactly what it could do, or at least that their findings could compliment the traditional methods, and after a while I goaded myself to learn this new subject (and persuaded the geneticists to explain it to me clearly) and soon appreciated just how important it was likely to become. Now, in 2015, genealogical research clothes the more recent generations of our family trees with names, dates and other details, but the bigger picture – our individual places within the greater family tree of humanity – comes from genetic testing. Genetics has even supplied a 'Genetic Adam' and 'Mitochondrial Eve', to supercede, in scientists' eyes, at any rate, the biblical ones.

Science and the origin myths embodied in religion seem to contradict each other at every turn. Perhaps, then, I should have flung away my dog-eared copy of Hesiod's *Theogony*, and the Bible for that matter, and written a book based solely on the findings of these new, white-robed priests of the microscope and periodic table. Their arguments are certainly persuasive: as far as I can tell they seem true and they certainly occupy centre-stage in mainstream Western culture. But science has yet to stop us dying, and until it does so religion will not go away and, while it remains part of many people's lives, so too will the ancient origin myths with which its holy books tend to begin.

My own experience of both worlds is perhaps not untypical: I was brought up in a Catholic school where I was taught that we were all descended from Adam and Eve. Evolution did not impinge much on my consciousness until David Attenborough's *Life on Earth* was broadcast in 1979, when I was twelve. Modern children have readier access to information on both fields now but the two contradictory narratives remain, nonetheless. But they share in common an inate, human desire to know and understand our origins. There are plenty of books about origin myths and many more about evolution, but I wanted to approach both subjects as a genealogist and try to work out what each could really tell us about our origins, and what our ancestors thought about themselves. We are taught as genealogists, you see, to be relentlessly critical and sceptical of everything, to hold fire on accepting connections between generations until we can be absolutely sure they are right, and to seek out the lines of descent that we know must run through the past like spring water through cracks in the rock. That is why, though neither a scientist nor a theologian, I felt I stood some chance of success in completing this project, despite complex variants within different versions of the same origin myths and the shifting sands of scientific understanding, which have compelled me to rewrite whole sections of this book several times over as new discoveries have been made.

Hesiod, musing on Mount Helikon 2,700 years ago, shared with me a burning desire to understand who we are and where we come from. His head was full of gods and muses, but science now suggests that the pressing need to invent higher, spiritual powers to rationalise the human condition was the by-product of the human mind's evolution during the Ice Age, the period during which most of the main elements of human civilisation were established, in order to enable our ancestors to survive in conditions far harsher than even those on the rocky slopes of Helikon. Before Hesiod's ancestors had evolved into humans, they had had much simpler brains, not so different to those of his goats. Both he and his goats were descended from earlier, smaller mammals and further back they shared a common, wriggling ancestor with the flies that buzzed about them constantly during the summer months. Earlier still, their single-celled forebears were also the ancestors of the tufts of grass that his goats nibbled and the pine trees that clothed the lower slopes of the mountain. Everything, from Hesiod to his goats and the plants dotting the mountainside, was composed of chemical elements, no different to those that composed the water in the Hippocrene spring and the mountain rock and the air all around them. The heat of the Sun above animated all: its heat and all the building blocks of the elements go back, not to Hesiod's chasm but, say the scientists, to the Big Bang. But if Hesiod was alive now, he'd probably have called his chasm 'the Big Bang' in any case.

But now, before we travel back in time to encounter the Big Bang, what was the genesis of the scientific view of our ancestral roots that so upset the older, Hesiodic and biblical views of the world? How and why did our more recent ancestors ever embark on this giddying journey back in time, to discover our origins amongst the dust of stars?

Part One

Book of Life

Chapter 1

Tracing the Family Tree of Life

Breaking with tradition

The efforts of science to understand the world are not normally seen as a colossal act of genealogical research, but in many ways that's exactly what they are. As we follow through the story of our evolution, from single-celled life forms down to the appearance of modern humans, we will also follow the story of our developing brains. These developed, we presume, to help us survive, but they also precipitated an unexpected leap forward to a human intelligence that compels us to ponder ourselves and our origins.

We hear of Ancient Greek philosophers who used their rational minds to conceive a world view that seems in some aspects – such as the Earth being round, not flat – to be remarkably modern; of Arab mathematicians skilled in the numerology that underpins modern science; of Medieval monks who risked the wrath of the Catholic Church by conducting alchemical experiments, thus laying the foundations of modern chemistry. But the momentum that led to the unlocking of our true origins began in sixteenth-century Britain.

It was a time of extraordinary religious, social and intellectual upheaval. A new, city-based middle class had arisen which, like its counterparts in the trade-fuelled cities of Renaissance Italy, had ambitions to think for itself and not simply in the manner dictated by the Church. The Protestant Reformation in Europe, which started with Martin Luther's protest against Catholicism in 1517, created an atmosphere in which old religious certainties started being questioned. As the Protestant Reformation gathered momentum, Henry VIII broke with the Catholic Church, forming the Protestant Church of England in 1534.

That year also saw the publication of the *Anglica Historia*, written by the Renaissance humanist scholar, Polydore Vergil. This new history of England was a fine example of fresh, Renaissance thinking that left none of the old assumptions unchallenged.

By the sixteenth century Britain had accrued a venerable mythology, rooted in the Bible and the old myths of Troy. This traced a line of kings back via King Arthur to Brutus of Troy, who was imagined to have led the first human settlers to Britain about 1130 BC. Brutus was a great-grandson of Aeneas, the hero of Virgil's *Aeneid*, who was also one of the Trojan heroes of Homer's *Iliad*. Aeneas, said Homer, was descended from Dardanos, the founder of the Trojan race, who was a son of Zeus (the Roman Jupiter). These were purely Classical characters, but by the AD 800s a fabulous new pedigree had been made up for them, claiming that Zeus had been merely a powerful ancient king who was worshipped as if he had been a god, and a plausible pedigree had been fabricated tracing him further back to Japheth, son of Noah, who had survived the Great Flood. This made Brutus not only the mythical ancestor of the British, but also the gateway ancestor who connected them back, very comfortingly, through Noah to Adam and Eve.

When Polydore Vergil sought hard evidence for Brutus, however, he found none, for there was none to be found. Accordingly, he pronounced Britain's Trojan myth 'a silly fiction' and was highly dismissive of the kings believed to have been his successors too. None of this constituted a major challenge to the orthodoxy of *Genesis*, but it did create an intellectual atmosphere in which all the old certainties about Britain's past seemed suddenly far less definite.

Most discussions of the birth of science focus on the excitement of new discoveries that would benefit mankind, the eagerness of its early practitioners to rectify the apparent wrong thinking of the past and their anger at the Church's restrictive stranglehold on human knowledge. All that may be true, but the early scientists also came from a society experiencing a sense of deep psychological uncertainty. The family tree that had linked the people of sixteenth-century Britain back to Noah suddenly had a howling great gap in it. It was to try to plug this gap that Britain's new voyage of discovery started, as antiquarians began exploring archaeological remains and interrogating old coins and texts to try to reconstruct a fresh picture of the past based on hard evidence. Natural Science started almost as a sideshow to this, with the direct observations made of nature by Sir Francis Bacon (1561–1626, see plate 2).

Climbing the tree of life

They were like ants on a beach, those early scientists. Each day the ants would build up great castles of sand and each evening the tide would wash almost everything away. Only a tiny mound would remain, on which the next day's ants would labour. But over time the residual mound grew larger, until the day came when the tide could not wash over it: and from that point it grew into an island, and then a continent, and eventually an entire world of new belief. In the vacuum caused by the loss of the Trojan myth, Natural Scientists sought to learn afresh our place within the greater scheme of things as posited by *Genesis*. The focus shifted rapidly, however, because soon their discoveries called into question what that greater scheme might be at all.

Initially, their work revived Classical Greek ideas that had lain largely dormant for almost two millennia. Aristotle, wandering by the lagoons of Lesvos in the 300s BC, had recognised the many differences between different forms of life. He attempted to organise these into a *scala naturae*, or ladder of life, with the simplest and least animate things on the bottom rungs, increasing in complexity through plants to animals and humans, with the Olympian gods at the top of the ladder. The concept survived into the Middle Ages, when it was used mainly for the classification of the ranks of angels, who were believed to occupy the rungs of the ladder between humans and God.

In the eighteenth century the Swedish scientist Carl Linnaeus (1707–1778, see plate 3) built on Aristotle's idea through taxonomy, the identification of living things (species, such as types of mole) and their arrangement in different groups (genuses, such as *Talpa*). He then worked out how those different groups might belong to similar, wider groupings (orders, such as *Soricomorpha*, which includes moles and shrews, and above them classes, such as *Mammalia*). Instead of considering insects, for example, as occupants of a lower step of the ladder of life, below that of mammals, Linnaeus's method opened up the possibility that there existed many separate forms of life, each as developed in their different ways as the rest.

But like Aristotle's *scala naturae*, Linnaeus's system was initially a static one. It might all have been created that way by God, right at the beginning. Yet the connection it suggested between humans and apes was disturbing. Writing to the German naturalist Johann Gmelin in 1747, Linnaeus admitted there was so little physical difference between men and apes that, were it not for the Church, he would have classed men and apes together.

So what had started as an innocent attempt to reconstruct the history of the world since the Creation now seemed to challenge *Genesis*'s assertion that humans and animals were completely distinct. Fortunately for those who felt uneasy at this, analysis of human and ape skulls revealed a small but psychologically important difference: apes had an intermaxillary bone sitting between the two halves of the upper jaw, and we didn't. Those who wanted to retain the established view of the world breathed a sigh of relief.

But Johann von Goethe (1749–1832), author of *Faust*, had the nerve to probe further. A keen anatomist, he knew what to look for and, dissecting a human body, he found a suture or joint that must be a vestige of the intermaxillary bone. In 1784, Goethe declared, 'What I have found makes me unspeakably happy – the *os intermaxillare* in man! … It is like the keystone,' he added, prophetically, 'of mankind.'

The age of the Earth

At the same time as our true connection to the animal world was dawning on us, an assault was being made on the age of the Earth itself. Back in the sixteenth century, James Ussher, Archbishop of Armagh (1581–1656) had worked out that the world must have begun in 4004 BC. This was a rather conservative revision of two earlier dates – 5508 BC and 5490 BC – that had been worked out by Orthodox Christians in Constantinople, and the early Christians of Syria, respectively. All such calculations were made by adding up the ages of the people in the biblical genealogy that stretched back from Jesus to Adam, and on which the Bible is based. Later, John Lightfoot (1601–1675), Vice Chancellor of Cambridge University, honed Ussher's calculation yet more finely and announced that the world had started on 23 October 4004 BC. Five days later, on the sixth day of Creation, God created Adam and Eve, the ancestors of every single human being alive today. John Lightfoot's calculation that the world had started on 23 October 4004 BC was the prevailing seventeenth-century view, and any disagreement was simply within a few hundred years of that figure. All was rooted in biblical scholarship.

The observations being made by Natural Science suggested that the Earth must be far older than this, but many of the early Natural Scientists were religious men who chose not to interpret their findings thus. Athanasius Kircher (1602–1680), a Jesuit, recognised that woolly mammoth bones were extremely old, yet interpreted them as the remains of giant men whom God had destroyed in the Great Flood. Even when the greater antiquity of fossils was appreciated, many people argued that God had simply made them *seem* old deliberately, as a test of our faith.

But in the eighteenth century more realistic views began to prevail, albeit still tempered by religion. The Abbé Moro (1687–1750) proposed the Plutonist or Vulcanist theory, which held that the Earth was formed from molten rock that had then been shaped by volcanic activity and overlaid by sedimentary rocks deposited by water, particularly during the Great Flood. In opposition to this was Neptunism, the brainchild of Abraham Gottlob Werner (1749–1817). Based on his study of fossils and the effects of erosion, Werner's theory held that the solid Earth had crystallised slowly out of a great ball of mineral-rich water.

Many thinkers now realised that the world was far older than had previously been imagined. Voltaire (1694–1778) questioned how so many diverse languages and skin colours could have arisen within mankind in the short time since 4004 BC, arguing that our human story must go back much further. By studying the time it took for large spherical objects such as iron balls (and, by extension, planets) to cool, the Comte de Buffon (1707–1788) proposed, in *Les Époques de la Nature* (1778), that the Earth must be 75,000 years old at the very least.

James Hutton (1726–1797), studying the erosion and deposit of rocks by water, took this theory further in his *Theory of the Earth* (1788). He proposed that the world might be locked into an eternal process of erosion and deposit, with 'no vestige of a beginning, –no prospect of an end'. That was too extreme: but in the nineteenth century Plutonism (or Vulcanism) was generally accepted as being broadly correct, but with the date of the Earth's birth being pushed ever further back into the past to the tune not of thousands, but of millions of years.

These developments unsettled the religiously minded because of the implied challenge to *Genesis*. My own great-great-great-grandfather, William Adolph (1810–1868), was a staunch Catholic whose work as a dye importer in London required a detailed understanding of modern science. He wrote *The Simplicity of Creation* (1856) as an attempt to reconcile the worlds of science and religion, arguing that the seven phases of creation asserted in the Bible may have taken aeons, but were but seven days to God. He argued that our universe was a tiny thing that God held 'upon his hand like a precious pearl', and beyond this was an 'exterior ... filled by God ... from eternity to eternity'. Everything within the Universe could be explained, Adolph hoped, by the workings of electricity, which was much under investigation at the time. Electricity was, he believed, the mechanism by which God had animated his creation and which powered the laws of nature. Thus, by arguing that *Genesis* was an allegory, my ancestor thought he had saved religion from any further assault by science. He presumably took it for granted that God had created man as an entity quite separate from animals: how his faith withstood the challenge from what came next I can only imagine.

The antiquity of man

The process of discovering our planet's great age created a giddying realisation of a world that had existed for vastly longer than we had ever thought – or wanted to think – was possible. But the idea opened up new possibilities for our own human story, because the further back the Earth's age was pushed, the longer life itself may have existed.

In 1802, Buffon's pupil the Chevalier de Lamarck (1744–1829) proposed that the forms of life in the *scala naturae*, or as classified by Linnaeus, may not have been created individually in the forms they have now. Instead, Lamarck suggested that the more complex forms of life had developed out of simpler ones. He suggested that different species 'pass into one another, proceeding from simple Infusoria [microscopic organisms] right up to man', and postulated how a tree-dwelling creature might, on leaving the trees, learn to walk upright. But Lamarck's idea that all life progressed upwards towards perfection still owed a huge amount to the old views that placed humanity just below the level of angels and gods. He did not appreciate that, whilst we are highly developed, so too are ladybirds and oak trees. Yet his idea was an essential step towards realising the truth.

Although the overwhelming majority of people still clung to the belief that humans had been created by God, it was now possible for men of science to think of humanity as having existed for much longer than 6,000 years. Ancient human bones had been found, of course, but they had always been interpreted as dating from after the time of Adam. By the 1850s, however, the rigorous science of geology enabled new discoveries to be dated within a stratified system that went back millions of years. In that same decade, Jacques Boucher de Crèvecœur de Perthes, who had devoted thirty years to seeking what he called 'Adam's ancestors', found hand-worked flints in north-western France in soil strata that were palpably many tens of thousands of years old. Almost simultaneously, William Pengelly, excavating in Kent's Cavern at Brixham, Devon, discovered flint tools mingled with bones of long-extinct mammoths and woolly rhinoceroses. It seemed suddenly very obvious that our human lineage was a very ancient one indeed. As Sir Charles Lyell (1797–1875) put it in 1859, humans were 'old enough to have co-existed … with the Siberian mammoth'.

A further step was taken when human bones were found in the Neander Valley, Germany, in 1856. Rudolf Virchow, a great medical authority of the time, claimed these were the bones of a modern man who had suffered from rickets. Another leading specialist thought the curved thigh bones denoted a Cossack in the Russian Army, which had passed that way in 1814. But the president of the local naturalists' society, Johann Carl Fuhlrott, realised that the bones belonged to 'a typical very ancient individual of the human race'. He was right: for these were the bones of Neanderthals.

'Man is but a worm'

Three years later, in 1859, Charles Darwin (1809–1882) published his book *On the Origin of Species*. He championed the idea of evolution, the idea that modern animals and plants had developed slowly out of earlier and ultimately much simpler forms. He built on the ideas of Linnaeus, Lamarck and also of his own grandfather, Erasmus Darwin (1731–1802), and of Robert Chambers. Back in 1844, Chambers had advocated a theory of evolution in *Vestiges of the Natural History of Creation*, but he was attacked savagely because of his lack of evidence. Darwin's contribution was not in fact the idea of evolution, but the discovery of – and evidence for – the mechanism by which it might work: natural selection.

If groups of creatures seemed similar, and there was a general trend from simple to complex, then the connection must be a genealogical one. Darwin's genius lay

Charles Robert Darwin. *From Sarah K. Bolton,* Famous Men of Science *(New York, 1889) / Wikimedia Commons*

in explaining how such a genealogy could possibly have come about – by evolution driven by natural selection. In the course of breeding, living things produce offspring that differ subtly from each other. Those less suited to their environment die, and those best suited to their surroundings have the best chance of breeding. Over long periods of time, and especially in isolated locations such as the remote Galapagos Islands, which Darwin visited during the voyage of the *Beagle* in the 1830s, the most advanced survivors of one species might evolve into a new species. Over a vast period of time, a great genealogical tree might spread out, at the ends of whose branches are all the different groups of plants and animals that Linnaeus had identified as being alive now.

Darwin saw clearly that we humans must belong to this genealogy of life too, but he did not say so, because he did not want to upset the deeply held religious views of many of his contemporaries, including his wife. Indeed, he had much sympathy for their views. If the religious basis for morals, honour, decency and duty were swept aside by a dog-eat-dog philosophy like natural selection, could society survive at all? (How society regulates itself in a secular age is an ongoing experiment, but one view, advanced by Richard Dawkins, is that it has forced us all to grow up, and that this has done us very little harm at all.)

Most Victorians wanted to see mankind the way Michaelangelo had painted Adam on the ceiling of the Sistine Chapel, only a finger's touch away from God. Apes, in Victorian England, were depicted as clownlike metaphors for lewd savagery. Thus, when *Punch's Almanack* published a cartoon in 1882 lampooning Darwinism, entitled 'man is but a worm', it showed a whirlpool of life, with writhing worms morphing into grotesque apes who then passed through a series of hideous cartoons of early man, ending with a Victorian gentleman wearing a top hat, the whole circus being presided over by a godlike caricature of Darwin himself.

Such prejudices remain. In 1961, Nikos Kazantzakis recalled (in *Report to Greco*) how news of evolution clashed with his Greek Orthodox Christian upbringing: could it be true, he wondered, that God had not made him with his own hands and breathed the breath of life into his nostrils? Was his genesis due simply to the transfer of sperm from a male monkey to a female one? Was he in fact the son, not of God, he wondered, but of an ape?

This, but in much gentler terms, is exactly what Darwin's friends Thomas Huxley (1825–1895) and Lyell spelled out in 1863, in *Man's Place in Nature* and *The Antiquity of Man* respectively. And over the twelve years following 1859, Darwin devoted himself to studying our animal-like characteristics, such as our wisdom teeth and appendixes, the fine covering of hair we have as six-month old foetuses in the womb, and the rudimentary tails we all retain under the skin at the base of our backbones. In *The Descent of Man* (1871), Darwin spelled out his own belief that our ancestors were apelike, but that 'we must not fall into the error of supposing that the early progenitor of the whole simian stock, including man, was identical with, or even closely resembled, any existing ape or monkey.' Trying to ameliorate the bruised feelings of his contemporaries (and of himself) he added that 'Man may be excused for feeling some pride in having risen … to the very summit of the organic scale', a fact that 'may give him hope for a still higher destiny in the distant future.'

But if one could overcome any initial revulsion over the direct ancestral link between man and apes, it was a splendid discovery. Back in 1863, Darwin praised Lyell, writing, 'What a fine long pedigree you have given the human race.' But in reality the praise goes to Darwin himself.

Decoding *Genesis*

The same burning desire for knowledge about our ancestry that had engendered these discoveries enervated the study of history and archaeology too. Napoleon's 1798–1801 invasion of Egypt started a craze for the rediscovery of ancient civilisation there. This in turn inspired archaeologists to start looking for the lost Middle Eastern civilisations of Mesopotamia, in what is now Iraq. Most of what we now know about those ancient empires was dug up during the nineteenth and early twentieth centuries.

Amongst the Mesopotamian clay cuneiform tablets that were excavated and translated were versions of the epic of Gilgamesh, in which the ancient, semi-mythical king of Ur went on a long journey to meet Uta-Napishtim, his ancestor who had survived a great flood sent from Heaven to wipe out humanity.

It was in 1872 that George Smith (1840–1876) of the British Museum translated the passage in which Uta-Napishtim tells Gilgamesh about the flood itself. As his Ark floated on the seemingly endless waters, Uta-Napishtim sent out a dove, then a swallow and finally a raven to seek dry land. In *Genesis*, Noah sends out both a dove and a raven and the details here were so similar that they seemed beyond coincidence. For the first time scholars realised that the flood story in *Genesis* might be a reworking of older, Mesopotamian stories.

It was a literary nail in the coffin of the credibility of *Genesis*, to accompany the growing body of scientific evidence that suggested that the story of the Creation might not be entirely correct – a nail that subsequent generations of believers have tried to ignore, but which could never truly be prized out of public consciousness.

Haeckel's family tree

In his 1874 book *Anthropogenie oder Entwicklungsgeschichte des Menschen*, Ernst Haeckel drew a pedigree like the one Lyell and Darwin had envisaged: a genuine Tree of Life for the animal kingdom (see plate 6). Copying the way genealogies were sometimes presented for aristocratic families, Haeckel drew a gnarled tree trunk with sprouting branches in which he located the different orders of living creatures. Where the tree rose to its apex, he placed the apes and, above all else, 'Menschen', men. This tree was an inspiration for generations of anthropologists, geologists and biologists who came after, and it was certainly an inspiration for this book.

The creation of a genealogical tree showing how different groups of animals are related to each other is not particularly difficult. The main stem on Haeckel's tree leads up from 'Moneren', or single-celled organisms, towards the higher forms of life. Haeckel imagined a progression from worms to simple fish and up to amphibians: then, reptiles branched off and next in our direct line he placed *Promammalia* – in other words, creatures that were not mammals, but which would one day evolve into them, though he did not have much idea of what these *Promammalia* might actually have been like. As Haeckel found, knowing *exactly* which creatures to put on the tree trunk representing the direct line between single-celled organisms and us – identifying, in other words, our direct ancestors – is a much harder problem, and one with which science is still wrestling to this day.

Scientists are often at pains to remind us that we are not the pinnacle of all earthly life. All the branches of the Tree of Life have been evolving side by side. Each living creature now is the pinnacle of its own personal twig. We may be the best humans, but near us on the evolutionary tree is the pinnacle of chimpanzee evolution, and the epitome of gorilla evolution, and so on. Yet for all that, our journey of discovery did not start, and does not really continue, as a fully objective effort to learn the true nature of the Universe. The real quest is to discover our own place within the Universe – and thus our own ancestral story. In the handful of generations since Darwin, we have felt more isolated, perhaps, than ever before, from both the earlier generations who did not have to face up to such an immense past, and from future ones, too, who we now realise might never be born if nuclear wars, or the arbitrary laws of nature, turn against us. This sense of isolation has further stimulated our human quest for knowledge. We seek now, more than ever before, to predict the future through science and to explore every possible future scenario through science fiction. And we have also intensified the search for our origins, from the boom in tracing personal family history, right up to our scientists' quest for the truth about the Big Bang, that mysterious genesis from which all else flows.

Chapter 2

Starting with a Bang

The Big Bang

'From the Helikonian Muses let us begin to sing.' With such an invocation of the Muses of Mount Helikon, Hesiod, the earliest genealogist whose identity we know, began his *Theogony* (see plate 1). Composed about the 700s BC on the slopes of Helikon, 60 miles north-west of Athens (and just east of Delphi), Hesiod's *Theogony* goes on to describe a primal chasm, from which emerged Eros, the Underworld and Gaia, the 'wide-bosomed Earth'. Gaia then gave birth to the starry heavens, 'to cover her on every side'. From Gaia and her progeny, Hesiod traced the descent of all the gods, nymphs, muses and monsters of Greek mythology in a single genealogical narrative. Because the rulers and peoples of Greece already claimed descent either from these gods, nymphs, muses and monsters, or directly from Gaia herself, and attributed the origins of other rulers and peoples beyond Greece to such sources too, Hesiod's *Theogony* rooted all humans in the dramatic story of the beginning of the world.

Now, science suggests a more complex explanation for the start of our story in the Big Bang, that mysterious starting point for the Universe some 13,770 million years ago. The Big Bang theory first appeared in 1931 as the 'hypothesis of the primaeval atom', the work of a Catholic priest, Georges Lemaître, basing his work in Einsten's 1916 general theory of relativity and the earlier observations of astronomers who had realised that the Universe was in a state of flux. The theory was first termed 'Big Bang' by the astronomer Fred Hoyle in 1949. As with Hesiod's chasm for the Ancient Greeks, the Big Bang is as far back as we know now.

We can theorise, but never know for sure, what, if anything, could possibly have existed before the Big Bang, or what caused the 'bang' itself. One view is that the Big Bang resulted from an immensely dense 'singularity', which appeared out of nowhere. Or, others have theorised recently, the Big Bang was in fact a collision between two older universes, whose destruction heralded the birth of ours. In such a vision, our whole universe might be a mere chapter in an eternal cycle of universes. But some physicists and mathematicians hypothesise that it may all have started with numbers. If, at the very start of everything, the time, matter and space that came into existence followed physical laws that obey abstract mathematical formulae, then did those numerical formulae, or at least the potential for them, exist already? Perhaps, it has been suggested, the Universe as we perceive it is merely a physical manifestation of an underlying, abstract mathematical reality that is truly eternal.

For all practical purposes, the Big Bang is the point from which we, now, can begin to sing the story of our origins. Immediately after the bang, an explosion of dense, hot matter expanded to start filling what became the Universe. As expansion continued, and still within the first few minutes of this extraordinary event, energy formed the first protons, neutrons and electrons, and the protons and neutrons combined to create the first atomic nuclei. Thousands of years later, electrons combined with these original nuclei to create the first atoms, the earliest being atoms of hydrogen, helium and lithium. Everything, in one sense, is a leftover from the Big Bang. From the fabric of our world, to the substance of our bodies and the air we breathe, the basic building blocks of all matter were formed in those turbulent moments at the beginning of the Universe. One observable, direct residue of this violent beginning is cosmic microwave background radiation. Another is the continued outward expansion of the galaxies, all resulting from the initial, outward momentum of the Big Bang. This is what we are told by the scientists and in the absence of any better explanation it seems sensible enough to believe them.

Knowing how the world began also means that we can theorise how it will end. In a hundred trillion years' time, they tell us, the last sun will die and the lifeless Universe will be enveloped in eternal darkness. That is a bleak thought, but fortunately our concern here is not with endings, but with beginnings. That is one of the reasons why genealogy is so popular.

The birth of the Earth

The physical world that surrounds us formed out of gasses that coalesced gradually into clouds and grouped themselves into spinning clusters. These became the galaxies, including our own, the Milky Way, which had appeared about 13,200 million years ago. It is a disk of up to 400 billion stars, about 120,000 light years wide with a dense black hole at its centre, all spinning at about 1,440,000 miles an hour.

Our planet is about two thirds of the way out from the centre of the Milky Way, on the Orion-Cygnus Arm. Looking back in towards the centre, the flattened disk of the spinning galaxy looks to us like a broad band of stars in the sky, arching overhead: it is impossible to see it from cities because of all the light pollution caused by street lights, but when viewed from the countryside it is an extraordinary sight. The Greeks called it *galaxías kýklos*, 'milky circle' (so the word 'galaxy' comes from the Greek word from 'milky'). It is explained in Classical mythology as a stream of milk that shot out of the breast of the goddess Hera when she suckled the infant Hercules, and was the bridge used by the gods to reach Olympos.

The fact that the Milky Way is composed of stars was first confirmed by Galileo in 1610, using his newly invented telescope. The discovery that it is but one of many galaxies was demonstrated by Edwin Hubble with his own newly improved telescope in the 1920s. We now know that our galaxy belongs to a group of galaxies called the 'Local Group', which is in turn part of the Virgo Supercluster. The Virgo Supercluster is 110 million light years wide, and is itself one of millions of such superclusters, which together comprise the Universe.

Each star of our Milky Way galaxy started as a cloud of particles. Our own cloud, composed mostly of hydrogen and helium, spun as it travelled around the outer edge of the Milky Way. As the cloud spun, gasses concentrated in its centre. These gasses grew ever more compressed until they collapsed into a dense body, the Sun. The power of the collapse initiated a fusion reaction at its heart, igniting it and turning it into a ball of burning gas, releasing light – light that was the ultimate product of the primal energy released in the Big Bang itself.

Our cloud also contained more complex elements, including atoms of iron, silicon and carbon, that essential building block of life. This carbon had been created by the nuclear fusion of helium with hydrogen inside ancient stars, which then exploded into supernovas, releasing their carbon to form, ultimately, a small percentage of our cloud. While the Sun was forming, other gasses and elements from the original cloud slowly formed into rings around it. These rings started coalescing into ever larger objects, termed protoplanets. These then collided together to create the great planets that we know today, and their moons and satellites.

Our Earth probably took about 10–20 million years to form, about 4,600 million years ago. Gravity pulled heavier elements, especially iron, into our planet's centre, where it remains as our molten iron core. Clouds of silicon condensed to form solid rocks on the surface.

Thus was born our solar system. Most of the original cloud that was not absorbed by the Sun and the planets was blown away by the Sun's solar wind.

Earth shared its orbit with a small planet known to science as Theia, named after the Titaness in Greek mythology who gave birth to Selene, the Moon. About 4,530 million years ago, we collided with Theia, absorbing most of its molten mass into the Earth. The impact gave us our small orbital tilt. Instead of the axis around which our planet rotates remaining the same throughout the year, it wobbles slightly, so that the northern hemisphere tilts slightly towards the

Sun for half the year and slightly away from the Sun for the other half – causing summer and winter respectively.

Meanwhile, rock from both crusts, thrown into space by the momentous impact of Earth and Theia, coalesced to form our moon, whose gravitational pull perpetuated and regularised our lopsided spinning. Much later, once there was water on Earth, the gravitational pull of the Moon also caused the tides. The combination of seasons and tides keeps our planet in a constant but regular state of flux and this may have been an essential factor in stimulating life to evolve, and maybe even in kick-starting life in the first place.

But at first there was no water, and no life. Volcanic violence raged across the planet's wracked surface. Vast numbers of icy comets containing nitrogen, carbon dioxide, methane and ammonia came hurtling down. It is the phase of Earth's history we call the Hadean eon (4,600–4,000 million years ago).

The naming of planets and time periods – and, later, of continents and creatures – using Ancient Greek words, lends a wonderful air of mystery to the past. Yet whilst science uses names derived from Greek mythology, it is a world seemingly devoid of gods. Instead, our world's story seems to have been driven by the unthinking forces of nature – the blazing of the Sun; the spinning of the Earth; the advance and retreat of glaciers; the ebb and surge of sea levels and the explosions of volcanos. But what a story it is.

Naming time

It's easy to imagine science and religion as being totally separate from each other, but it's useful to remember that science grew out of religion, and religion, through its myths, tried to do what science is doing now – to explain the world around us.

Five thousand years ago, when the inhabitants of ancient Mesopotamia (modern Iraq) dared contemplate the distant past before the Great Flood, which they believed marked the start of the modern era, they imagined a series of ten, named, pre-Diluvian (pre-Flood) kings, whose extremely long lifespans totalled just under half a million years. They imagined these kings so that they could divide up this great span of time into more manageable chunks. By naming these kings they named the spans of time during which they lived. Time was humanised.

As modern science developed during the seventeenth and eighteenth centuries, it became clear to many that the world must be vastly older then the Bible had suggested, and considerably more ancient than even the Mesopotamians had imagined. Faced with such terrifyingly immense spans of time, those pioneering scientists sought to gain their own psychological grip on the past by doing exactly what the Mesopotamians had done – naming it.

The new, scientific equivalent version of the Mesopotamian King List divides the Earth's history up into four named geological eons. Each eon is divided into eras, each comprising several hundred million years, divided further into periods. Each period is subdivided into epochs and those epochs into ages. Science has invented names for all of these. We live in the Holocene epoch of the Quaternary period in the Cenozoic era of the fourth, Phanerozoic, eon. Our age alone seems nameless – a good name might be the Oil Age.

This system for naming the geological time spans in which our remote ancestors lived was invented by Abraham Gottlob Werner (1749–1817). Because of the high antiquity they represent, the names of these eons, periods and epochs have taken on a sonorous quality. But the choices of the names of the geological periods, unlike the naming of T.S. Elliott's cats, was not a difficult matter and was undertaken with seemingly casual randomness. The Carboniferous period is so-called simply because carbon-rich coal was formed then, for example, and the evocatively named Jurassic period has its name just because Alexander von Humboldt (1769–1859) first discovered rocks from that time in Switzerland's Jura Mountains.

But for that first, long, tortured phase of the Earth's history, from its very beginning about 4,600 million years ago up to 4,000 million years ago, the scientific namers of time thought back to their education, which was primarily rooted in the works of Homer and Hesiod. They likened the broiling surface of the Earth to the Ancient Greeks' vision of the Underworld. So they named it the Hadean eon, after the Greeks' mythological king of the primordial underworld.

Chapter 3

In the Primal Seas

Signs of life

Following on from the Hadean eon comes the Archaean eon (4,000–2,500 million years ago). Its name holds particular significance for us, because *archaea* is Greek for 'ancient life'. This is when the chemical elements, whose own building blocks go back to the Big Bang, first combined to form life. It is when our family tree begins.

At the start of this eon, Earth's surface started to cool and gasses formed an atmosphere. Clouds began to appear in the sky, and out of these precipitated rain to soothe the tortured furrows of the world. Before long, seas spread across the Earth, filling up the deepest valleys and stretching far over the broad surface of the planet.

It was probably quite early on in the Archaean eon, perhaps about 3,500 million years ago, that life appeared. Our first ancestors probably appeared around hot, volcanic vents, deep in the oceans. Here, the vast amount of energy locked in the Earth's core comes bubbling up into the sea in the form of hydrogen protons. That flow of protons, as Brian Cox put it once, was probably the first, true 'spark of life' because the availability of this energy, combined with the congregation of chemicals around the vents, is thought to have triggered the creation of the first amino acids, the so-called 'building blocks of life'.

Another theory is that our earliest ancestors came hurtling here through space, hidden deep in the icy fissures of a meteorite. Amino acids have been found in meteorites that have struck Earth and when the Philae probe landed on comet 67P/Churyumov-Gerasimenko in November 2014 it detected organic compounds containing carbon. It has been theorised (and proved, as far as genuine proof is possible, in laboratory experiments) that such acids could have been created within the nebulae of dying stars. If so – and it is a fine theory yet to be disproved – then life did not begin on Earth at all, but is common, in its 'building block' stage at least, to the whole Universe.

We do not know which of these options for our origins is correct. The possibility that our ancestors were aliens, albeit of a sub-cellular nature, and that our origins lie somewhere out there in the stars, remains seductively intriguing. But scientists are veering back towards believing that life began here, on Earth.

If so, instead of thinking of life just happening to have appeared on Earth, maybe we should think of living things, including ourselves, as the life *of* the planet. And maybe we humans are not so much an intelligent life form that lives on this planet, but the intelligent life *of* the Earth.

Is life an extraordinary phenomenon, a miracle? Or is it no more than one might expect from a planet rich in water and carbon, spinning around an energy giving sun, far enough away not to be fried yet not so far out as to be frozen? We are certainly here thanks to those circumstances, miraculous or not. All else that follows seems to have been determined by very basic causes too, such as the natural behaviour of water, light and gravity. The size of the chemical elements, for example, dictates how small living things can be, whilst gravity places a natural check on how large creatures can become. Nothing really seems to have happened by pure accident at all.

Our earliest ancestor

Whatever its origins, and however it really happened, the combination of amino acids led to what scientists have dubbed the 'Latest Universal Common Ancestor' (LUCA) or 'Cenancestor'. This was a cell able to extract energy from its surroundings, which could replicate itself by cellular division. All later life is derived from LUCA. These early cellular life forms lacked nuclei, so are termed prokaryotes. Each time they replicated themselves, their genes were copied, but not always perfectly. It was due to such mutations that the cells evolved: those less suited to where they lived were victims of natural selection and died, whilst those better suited multiplied. In the first billion years of life on Earth, there was probably much promiscuous swapping of genes between prokaryotes, so it is impossible to identify a branch to which we belong: we are descended, generally, from all the early prokaryotes.

All around our cell membrane pressed the briny water, enclosing us and transmitting nutrients, warmth or cold, light or dark and the occasional prodding, indifferent presence of others of our own kind. Slowly, elegantly and with no external stimuli whatever we divided ourselves, parting without emotion from our other halves, ever alone amidst the primal seas.

At length, however, branches emerged from the prokaryote stem. One branch were the archaea, who were our ancestors, whilst another branch became the bacteria. Viruses might have evolved from bacteria, or from plasmids (which are pieces of DNA that can move between cells), though some scientists argue that viruses are not truly alive at all – or that viruses are 'alien' invaders who really did come here on meteorites.

About 2,400 million years ago in the bacteria branch of the family tree, cyanobacteria started practising oxygenic photosynthesis: they used energy from the Sun to break water down into hydrogen and oxygen and then to combine elements of both with carbon, in order to create sugar. It is a highly complex process that probably developed only once. All green plants, from seaweed to oak trees, use cyanobacteria in their cells to photosynthesise, and all of this cyanobacteria is in turn descended from the same original ancestor in which that process started.

Cyanobacteria is also termed 'blue-green algae', though it is not technically an algae at all. It bloomed across the oceans and its oxygenic photosynthesis produced and released excess oxygen into the oceans. This oxygen was a poison to most of that other major branch of the family tree, the archaea, our ancestors. Most of us were wiped out. Some survived as 'extremophiles', living far away from oxygen in sulphurous caves, or in ice, or around the boiling vents of deep-sea volcanoes – and they remain living in these hostile environments to this very day.

A tiny number of archaea, however, neither died out nor retreated. We not only learned to absorb the poisonous oxygen, but thrived on it, multiplying prolifically. By about 2,100 million years ago, during the Proterozoic eon (2500–542 million years ago), we had evolved into eukaryotes, cells with an internal pouch, or nucleus, which contained our genes.

For two thirds of our entire existence as living creatures, we floated through the oceans as single-celled eukaryotic protozoa. Hesiod had been correct in thinking that Eros was one of the most primal of entities, because from about 1,200 million years ago, we started enjoying sexual reproduction, recombining the genes from our nucleuses with partners. This speeded up the process of change, giving each generation much greater potential than before to be slightly better than the last.

It was at this point in our ancestry that the male Y chromosomes and female X chromosomes became distinct. They have remained so ever since. If you trace your family tree back up your direct male line, father-to-father, and also trace back through your mother, mother-to-mother, those two lines will not meet up until you reach our pre-sexual ancestors in the primal seas, just over 1,200 million years ago.

Multicellular life

Having one cell imposed limits on what we could become. Admittedly, some eukaryote protozoan cells such as nummulites can grow up to 2 inches in diameter. But a better way of developing was to combine. About 900 million years ago, some eukaryotes began to combine, initially as loose coalitions. Such loose groupings still exist today: we call them choanoflagellates.

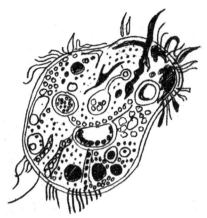

Protozoa.

It took a savage stimulus for matters to develop further. About 700 million years ago, our ancestors endured the deepest ever Ice Age, termed 'Snowball Earth'. Ice covered the land even on the Equator and the surface of the oceans froze solid. Our ancestors only just survived, far below the frozen surface. When volcanic activity eventually started to thaw the ice on land, mineral-rich meltwater poured into the warming oceans, providing rich food for those few life forms that had clung on in the depths. Cyanobacteria started pumping fresh supplies of oxygen into the atmosphere and eukaryote cells now started evolving rapidly – and combining in a manner not seen before. As they did so, different lineages emerged. Scientists are still not entirely certain of the details but there seems to be a general consensus (qualified by the usual question marks and quibbles), as follows.

One line of eukaryotes, which happened to contain photosynthesising cyanobacteria *within* their cells, started combining to form multi-cellular slime moulds, which were the eventual ancestors of true algaes, including seaweed, and of all plants.

Combination of cells started taking place in another eukaryotes too, who lacked cyanobacteria in our cells, and were forced to take our nutrition directly from the environment. Some of these were the ancestors of the amoeba; others were the ancestors of fungi, resulting eventually in mushrooms and toadstools (so we are more closely related to fungi than we are to plants). A further branch used the new supplies of oxygen to produce collagens – sticky strands of protein that helped them stick together. The results were sea sponges, which remain to this day as loose coalitions of largely independent cells. Then, by at least 579 million years ago, some of these spongy coalitions became true metazoans, our ancestors. These were what we are now, multi-cellular life forms in which different cells take on particular functions, interdependent on each other, all working for the greater good of the whole.

Such early animal life went largely unnoticed until the discovery of the fossil of a fernlike animal, *Charnia masoni*, in Leicestershire in 1957. Fossils are the remains of living things preserved in mud or volcanic ash and thus turned into stone. Usually only hard bones become fossils, whilst soft tissue rots away, leaving nothing to be fossilised. Yet, miraculously, the rocks of the Charnwood Forest in Leicestershire and of Mistaken Point, Newfoundland, are full of fossils of early soft-tissued creatures, including charnias, some several feet long. There are many other creatures too, perfectly preserved in the rocks – silent witnesses to the colourless world that had wriggled and squirmed in the dark depths of the primeval seas.

The naming of life

The naming of now extinct plants and creatures known only from their fossils follows the system devised by Linnaeus, in which species are grouped into genuses (meaning 'families'), which are in turn grouped into orders and then broad classes, such as reptiles or mammals. Each species has two names, the first being its genus name, akin to a surname, and the second identifying the species itself, akin to a Christian name, sometimes derived from the name of its discoverer. Thus, *Charnia masoni*'s name was created by naming the genus to which it belonged, *Charnia*, after the Charnwood Forest in whose rocks it was found, whilst its particular, species name, *masoni*, honours its discoverer, Roger Mason, who happens to have been a friend of David Attenborough's.

Naming creatures after their discoverers can lead to some amusing outcomes. A Pliosaur species, known from its 155 million-year-old skull found on Dorset's Jurassic Coast in 2003, was discovered by an amateur fossil hunter called Kevan Sheehan, so was named *Pliosaurus kevani*. The announcement of the name promoted an amusing newspaper cartoon, in which one dinosaur says to another 'I hope I'm not discovered by someone called Trixie Lullabell!'

Bilateral ancestors

The search for new fossil discoveries has been ongoing as a serious, scientific pursuit for the past couple of centuries and is one of the mainstays of our attempts to trace our ancient ancestry. Whenever a new find looks as if it belongs on that all-important central stem of Ernst Haeckel's Tree of Life, it is billed as a 'missing link'. The term was used originally of the transition stage between apes and humans, but it applies equally well to anything from that stem – a missing link in the chain between reptiles and amphibians, fish and worms or multi-celled and single-celled life forms like creatures from the world of the charnia.

But there is a great problem with 'missing link' labels. At best we can only say that a fossil looks like an early form of a later creature, but is it a direct ancestor of ours, or a recent offshoot from our evolutionary stem? Is it, in other words, a grandparent of ours, or a close cousin? In many cases, we simply cannot know. Of all the fossils unearthed, we may never have unearthed the fossil of a genuine many times great-grandparent. Or, on the other hand, the fossil cabinets of our museums might be chock full of them.

However, in the case of charnias, with their branching fronds, we can be confident that they were cousins, not direct ancestors. Most of these early attempts at multicellular life failed because they were based on simple, fractal structures, unable to develop further. Some survived, though, and are the ancestors of corals and sea anemones. But our ancestral branch took a different, more adaptable route, developing into bilateria, creatures that took food in at one end and expelled waste from the other. At our centre was a primitive stomach. Sensory organs developed around our mouths – the early precursors of nostrils and eyes.

Many examples of early bilateria appear in the Ediacara Hills, South Australia. They include the first true bilateral fossil, Kimberella, about 555 million years old. Similar to the modern flatworm, it had a very basic circulatory system, a simple heart and primitive gills. It could, perhaps, have been a direct ancestor of ours.

How we became fish

We writhed, 'grotesque, slimed, dumb, indifferent', as Thomas Hardy wrote about sea worms crawling over the submerged *Titanic*, into our current, Phanerozoic eon. So far, this eon has fallen into three eras: Paleozoic, Mesozoic and our present Cenozoic. The first era, the Paleozoic ('ancient animals'), lasted from 541 to 251 million years ago and started with the Cambrian period (541–505 million years ago).

Many of Britain's surface rocks north of a line stretching from Exmouth, Devon, to Hartlepool, Durham, were formed in the Paleozoic era and, of these, the Cambrian rocks of Wales – which gave the period its name – are particularly rich in fossils. But the best finds are in the Burgess Shales of British Columbia. Both reveal a diversity of life termed the 'Cambrian explosion', so rich that most of the major branches of the animal kingdom appeared at this time.

A major branch of the Tree of Life became the protostomes, which include the annelid worms, molluscs, nematode worms and arthropods (insects, arachnids and crustaceans). The early arthropods included the woodlouse-like trilobites (see plate 4), the most advanced life forms of their day, which were set to dominate the ocean floors for hundreds of millions of years to come. Their fossilised remains can be found in many places, including in the Black Country shales of Staffordshire (especially Wren's Nest nature reserve in Dudley).

Our ancestors may have looked something like this modern flatworm about 555 million years ago.

Another major branch, distinct from the protostomes, were our ancestors, the deuterostomes. An early offshoot of these were the echinoderms, ancestors of the starfish, sea cucumbers and sea urchins. Meanwhile, our deuterostome ancestors wriggled along developing ever more complex cords running down our long backs, used mainly for digesting food. We thus became protochordata, an example of which is the now vanished pikaia, which looked, one might say, like a cross between an aquatic slug and an eel. From this we became chordata, with even more developed 'spinal' chords, swimming through the oceans, sucking up food as we went. Modern descendants are lancets, sea squirts and balanoglossi. Balanoglossi look like a cross between a worm and a particularly nasty piece of tripe and you certainly wouldn't want to touch one, yet they are probably very similar to how our own ancestors looked and behaved in the Cambrian seas.

As we wriggled our way into the Ordovician period (505–438 million years ago), we developed into ostrachoderms, 'jawless fish', sucking up food from the ocean floors. By now our chords had become firm, nerve-bearing spines of hardening cartilaginous flesh, making us vertebrates, and with this came ever firmer cartilaginous cases for our brains. Some fossil ostrachoderms have been found in the Old Red Sandstone of the Brecon Beacons in South Wales, and others have turned up in rocks at Bude and Polperro, Cornwall. Lampreys and hagfish are modern survivals of this line. Below us, in the darkness, we sensed through the viscus water the scuttling feet of the sea floor predators, treading over the seething mass of trilobites. Far above us, light from the unseen sun filtered down through the plankton.

During the ensuing Silurian period (438–410 million years ago), arthropods including 8-foot long giant scorpions roamed the sea floors. Like modern lampreys and hagfish, our ancestors probably fired out jets of slime to keep such predators at bay. But we did much more than that too: we developed jaws full of sharp teeth, skulls and internal vertebrae hardening into bone, and much better developed fins, so that we could dodge away from the scorpions and the other horrors lurking on the sea bed. But no wonder each of us has an instant, instinctive reaction at the sight of a scorpion: for some 438 million years, each generation of our ancestors in turn have been frightened of them.

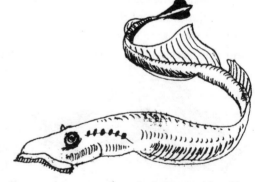

Our ancestors may have looked something like this modern lamprey about 400 million years ago.

Chapter 4

First Steps on Dry Land

The age of Coelacanths

Despite the great advances we had made, many of our ancestors succumbed to the terrifying predators of Silurian seas and died. But a few survived. During the Devonian period (410–335 million years ago), which succeeded the Silurian, our fishy forebears continued to evolve. A possible direct ancestor of ours, which lived about 415 million years ago, was *Janusiscus schultzei*. The fossilised skull of one of these, just under an inch long, was found in Siberia in 1977 and in 2015 a new study of it revealed evidence of both cartilage and bone, suggesting that it was the ancestor both of cartilaginous fish, later to evolve into sharks and rays, and of the osteichthyes, the bony fish, whose lineages diverged about 5 million years later. From our line of bony fish we evolved into the fierce, armoured placoderms, out of whom evolved all modern bony fish.

As we evolved we developed big, scaly heads, strong jaws of sharp, enamelled teeth and bodies ringed horizontally with lobed fins connected to a powerful bony girdle. Scientists call these ancestors of ours sarcopterygian ('fleshy finned'); or crossopterygian ('fringe-finned') or simply 'lobe-finned' fish. The geologist Hugh Millar found many fossils of such Devonian ancestors of ours at Achanarras, near

Our ancestors may have looked something like this modern coelacanth about 350 million years ago.

John o' Groats, Scotland, where they had died and become fossilised due to the drying up of a warm inland sea.

A survivor from this phase of our evolution is the coelacanth. For a long time coelacanths were known only from fossils, but then one was dragged up from the depths of the ocean in a fisherman's net in 1938. It was recognised as an extraordinary survival because it was virtually identical to Devonian fossils. The coelacanth is a true 'living fossil' of what we were once. If we are not directly descended from coelacanths, we certainly share a very similar ancestor in common with them.

The coelacanths remained in the dark depths of the oceans, but our own forebears gravitated, by the middle Devonian period, to estuaries and thence to rivers and freshwater swamps. We became a branch of the sarcopterygians called rhipidistians ('shore dwellers'), which included our eusthenopteron ancestors, who patrolled the shallow waters about 380 million years ago, ready to devour our prey with jaws bristling with sharp little teeth. We became used to liminal places, where water gave way to land – the edges of rivers and swamps – where there was little flow of oxygen-bearing water. As fish, we already had nostrils for smelling, but now that we spent so much time in shallow water our snouts were frequently above water. Our nostrils began slowly to admit air, while within our bodies primitive lungs evolved to absorb the oxygen it contained.

Lungfish still survive in the southern hemisphere and some types still have vestigial gills. But our ancestors were poised to take what was quite literally the next step, out onto the land – but into a world that was very different to the way it is now.

Avalonia, Gondwanaland

In 1810, Alexander von Humboldt was studying a detailed map of the world, the result of newly developed techniques in cartography. He was fascinated by the similarity of the east coast of South America to the west coast of Africa and realised suddenly that the bulge of Brazil could slot very neatly into the Gulf of Guinea. It dawned on him that the two continents must once have been joined together, but then drifted apart. From this developed the theory of continental drift, which was proved almost a century later when Ben Peach and John Horne showed that fossil trilobites in Scotland did not match those in England, but were identical to those in North America. Scotland must once have been part of North America, but continental drift had led to it becoming attached to England.

The mechanism of how such monumental drifting could have taken place eluded us until 1944, when Arthur Holmes showed that the upper layers of the Earth's crust float on molten lava. It was not until the 1960s that Tuzo Wilson worked out that the crust is divided into continental plates. As these plates drift about above the molten lava, they push together at some places, and pull apart in others – with the dreadful consequences of volcanos and earthquakes along the fault lines where two plates meet. As this science developed it was realised too that drifting had not just caused one great set of movements to create the world as it is now, but the continents had been moved and shaped many times before. So back in the Silurian period, when we were still sea dwellers, England, Wales and the southern half of Ireland were part of an archipelago, poetically named Avalonia, which lay off the northern coast of the great continent of Gondwanaland. Scotland and the northern half of Ireland, meanwhile, were attached to modern Greenland and all were part of the continent of Laurentia, which lay far to the west of Gondwanaland. Both lay in the southern hemisphere.

At the time, of course, our fishy ancestors stared at the rocky shores uncomprehendingly, and it is only science that has applied names to these continents retrospectively. Majestic though their names sound, their origins have relatively prosaic origins. Gondwanaland, for example, is named simply after Gondwana in India, whose geology first suggested the continent's existence.

Between Gondwanaland and Laurentia lay the ocean of Iapetus, named after the Greek Titan who was god of mortality, a son of Uranos and Gaia. It was in the Iapetus Ocean that some of our ancestral, fishy relatives had swum. But continental drift was drawing both the continents slowly north. As they did so they gradually moved closer together, squeezing the Iapetus Ocean dry – causing our ancestors to swim away to deeper waters elsewhere. By the start of the ensuing Devonian period the drifting of the continents caused the southern and northern parts of the British Isles to ram into each other. Where Scotland and England fused, a massive ridge was formed, along which the Emperor Hadrian later built his famous wall.

The long, slow union of England and Scotland also pushed up the mountains of the Lake District and Snowdonia. Above the weld, in southern Scotland, this same activity later created the great volcanos whose now extinct cones dominate the landscape around the Firth of Forth, including Castle Rock and Arthur's Seat in Edinburgh (see plate 7).

While these events were unfolding, the rocky landscape itself was changing. During the Silurian period, the rockscape started to come alive as arthropods such as scorpions and millipedes emerged from the sea and began to scuttle about on dry land – the first feet ever to do so. Algaes, liverworts and mosses, which had appeared in the preceding Ordovician period, spread and colonised the sea shores and the sides of rivers too, and soon these evolved into ferns to truly green the whole of the stony Earth for the first time. It was onto such a land that our Devonian ancestors first stepped.

Dawn of the tetrapods

Ours was a schizophrenic world then: below was a world of bright green weed and yellow water, and then, beyond the thick, leaf-strewn meniscus, was the universe above, in which the tops of ferns swayed out of focus against the blinding arc of the sky.

Our earliest ancestors who walked on dry land are termed tetrapods ('four feet'). It was once thought that our fins evolved into legs once we tetrapods had hauled ourselves out onto the mud, in the manner that mudskippers and climbing perches do now. But current thinking, pioneered by Jenny Clack at Cambridge University, maintains that limbs developed while we were still in the shallows, as a means of pushing our way through underwater vegetation, just as frogs and newts do today.

An early tetrapod was *Tiktaalik rosea*, whose fossilised body was found at Ellesmere Island, Canada, in 2004. About 375 million years old, its fins were already developing primitive wrists. Growing up to 9 feet long, these tiktaaliks looked, and probably behaved, rather like modern crocodiles, only they probably remained firmly in the shallows rather than coming out onto dry land.

Following tiktaaliks came a proliferation of tetrapods, including ichthyostega ('fish roof') and acanthostega ('spiny roof'), both of which lived about 365 million years ago. The first examples of both were found in the 1960s in Greenland, where Devonian rock lies on the surface. Jenny Clack tells the story of her frustration, as a young zoologist in Cambridge, at not being able to study the only known ichthyostega fossil, which was in a laboratory in Scandinavia under the jealous guard of a singularly uncooperative professor. One day she went over the road to Cambridge's geology department and asked if they had any rock samples from the part of Greenland where tetrapod fossils had been found. They had, and in one rock she was astonished to find part of an acanthostega. Clack then organised her own trip to Greenland and found many more fossils. Some, which may well be directly ancestral to us, had five digits but others, curiously, had seven or eight – evolutionary prototypes that went no further. One important discovery she made was that these tetrapods still had broad tails, suitable for swimming, and alongside their developing lungs they still had gills that worked.

But at last our limbs and lungs grew strong enough for us to emerge out of the water altogether and bask on the river banks in the late Devonian sunshine. Crawling about on the plants was a host of insects, newly evolved out of the earlier arthropods. All were, as yet, wingless – insects did not evolve their wings until the Carboniferous period – so there was plentiful and easy-to-catch food for our eager tetrapod ancestors to eat.

Without the buzzing of insects the world would have been a very quiet place, with only the wind sighing in the treelike ferns. There was nothing much to hear, so it is not surprising to learn that our earliest tetrapod ancestors had fixed stapes. It was only later that the loosening of these tiny bones in our skulls would allow their vibrations to stimulate the evolution of ears that could hear.

The labyrinthodonts

And then that early Eden came to a terrible end. Whether comets came blazing down to Earth or underwater volcanos erupted we do not know, but clouds of dust filled the skies, blocking out the Sun and plunging the Earth into darkness. Meanwhile, the proliferation of plant life on land had started breaking down rock into soil and rainfall washed many of the released nutrients into the oceans. From this resulted vast blooms of algae, which used up all the available oxygen in the water. The result was not one but two mass extinctions, called the Kellwasser and the Hangenberg events, the latter marking the border between the Devonian and Carboniferous periods (335–290 million years ago).

The real sufferers were sea creatures. Those who had adapted to life in the liminal world between water and dry land had a double chance of survival and some – maybe only a handful – of our tetrapod ancestors, perhaps ichthyostegas, survived. As the air cleared and the Sun came out again, our numbers proliferated and we evolved rapidly into labyrinthodonts ('maze tooths', see plate 5). We were genuine amphibians now, with rapidly developing lungs, long, tooth-filled snouts and broad heads with very thick skulls (hence their alternative name, stegocephalia, 'roofed head'). Labyrinthodonts ranged from several inches to 10 feet long and sometimes had a third or 'pineal' eye.

By now, all the world's drifting continents had converged. Britain, like virtually everywhere else, was part of the supercontinent of Pangea. Its name is Greek, meaning 'entire Earth', recalling the Greek deity Gaia, the personification of the Earth itself. British rocks contain a few fossil amphibians, such as the vertebra of an anthracosaur found at Lowmoor, Bradford, an almost complete *Keraterpeton galvani*, like a small salamander, from Jarrow Colliery near Kilkenny, Ireland, and the head of a crocodile-like megalocephalus from Dawley, Shropshire. All are perhaps similar to our ancestors, but all come from too late in the fossil record to be direct forebears of ours.

As we labyrinthodonts plodded about on the muddy riverbanks on our still not very strong legs, natural selection worked, silently, on our eggs. From soft, frogspawn-like eggs that needed water to develop, we started to lay better ones with leathery shells, in which embryos spent the first formative weeks of life suspended in an amniotic sack of nutritious fluid. Because of this, our labyrinthodont ancestors could lay eggs on dry land. We left the river banks to our smaller cousins, who evolved eventually into frogs and newts, and ambled away into the forests of tree ferns and giant horsetails that clothed the land. All these plants reproduced by spores – there were no flowers yet.

A horsetail is a simple plant with a central stem divided into sections, out of which emerge whorls of long, thin leaves. Remains of horsetail 'tree' stumps can be seen, petrified, at Crail, Fifeshire, together with the trails left by the giant millipedes that rumbled about amongst them. As time passed, seed-producing gymnosperms such as ginkgo trees, cycads and conifers appeared in the forests too. Their carbonised remains, squashed down – doubtless containing fossils of many of our labyrinthodont ancestors into the bargain – created much of the coal that was later to fuel the Industrial Revolution.

Above our ancestors' heads droned the earliest, giant dragonflies (but not yet flying beetles, or flies). As we pushed through the undergrowth, our scales became harder and our nervous system grew more acute. We had evolved into early reptiles, such as the cotylosaurs and the hylonomus, the 'forest-wanderer'.

Chapter 5

Meet the Synapsids

Masters of Pangea

The reptile lineage split early in its evolutionary history. Although they probably looked similar externally, some had two holes in the skull behind their eyes, making them diapsids ('double arch'), whilst our ancestors had only one hole, so are termed synapsids ('fused arch'). The first synapsid fossils were discovered by accident at Karoo, South Africa, in 1896 by Robert Broom, while he was looking for early humans. Broom had difficulty working out whether the fossils he had found were of reptiles or mammals. Then it dawned on him that they were a missing link between the two.

Almost every stage in our evolutionary story has resulted in types of creature that seem to have changed far less than us and that are still alive now. If you want to know what our ancestors were like when we were single-celled organisms, or marine worms or fish, you can go to a zoo and look at creatures that are not so very different now to what we were like then. But for the long stretch of our evolutionary story that Haeckel's 1874 Tree of Life labelled *Promammalia* (pre-mammals), the transitionary lineage between reptiles and mammals, there is nothing alive now that resembles our forebears very closely: all the (diapsid) reptiles alive now have evolved considerably from what our common ancestors looked like (see plate 6). There is not a single synapsid alive today except for the descendants of one tiny offshoot that evolved later, and beyond all recognition, into mammals like us. It is only by studying fossils, such as those found by Robert Broom, that we have learned anything about our synapsid ancestors at all.

At the time, of course, our synapsid ancestors were not a 'missing link' between anything. They were a pinnacle of the evolutionary tree in their own right and as such they dominated the world for millions of years. Early synapsids included pelycosaurs, such as the dinosaur-like dimetrodon, with vast fins of scaly flesh rising up from their backs for garnering the Sun's warmth in winter and cooling their blood in summer. Another type of synapsid were our ancestors termed therapsids ('beast arch'). We developed as therapsids throughout the Permian period (290–250 million years ago). We started to breathe almost exclusively through our nostrils, freeing up our mouths for the sole purpose of eating: and in our jaws we developed a range of differently shaped teeth, for nipping, biting and chewing.

The Permian period gained its name from the many therapsid fossils found at Perm in Russia's Ural Mountains, then part of the supercontinent of Pangea. While our therapsid ancestors quested for food on land, most of Britain was covered by warm seas whose corals and protozoa laid down layer upon layer of their chalky bodies to become the limestone of the Pennines, Cotswolds and Mendips. Some of Britain was dry land, though, and there are some Permian rocks in places such as County Durham that may have been above water, but sadly no therapsid fossils have yet been found there.

The therapsids who dominated Pangea occupied a wide range of roles that would be assumed later by dinosaurs, and after them by mammals. Our close cousins the dicynodonts were largely herbivorous and gained their name ('two dog tooth') from their two tusks. They varied from tiny molelike creatures to great lumbering giants who munched tree ferns and fir needles. Somewhere in the middle were the piglike lystrosaurs ('shovel lizards'), whose teeth enabled them to munch virtually anything, vegetable or animal. The title of an article about lystrosaurs in *The Telegraph* on 15 September 2008 put it well: 'When pigs ruled the world' – provided you can imagine not modern pigs but piglike, reptilian creatures whose legs stuck out from their shoulders, with hips like modern lizards, scaly but perhaps with a few bristles too, roaming through forests of conifers, their beady eyes and twitching nostrils constantly alert for the next meal.

Alongside these largely herbivorous cousins of ours were our own forebears, another branch of the synapsid therapsid family tree called the theriodonts ('beast tooth'). Ours was a largely carnivorous branch of the family. There were the fearsome gorgonopsians, who dominated the scene in the mid-Permian: the size of modern rhinoceroses, they had a terrifying array of teeth for devouring their hapless prey. Our own branch of the theriodont family developed into eucynodonts ('true dog tooth') and then, by the late Permian, into cynodonts, another carnivorous lineage, first named in 1861 by Richard Owen because of our doglike teeth.

Varied though we therapsids were, we shared many characteristics in common, particularly that of laying eggs in holes, and probably sleeping in such burrows too. This is suspected because casts of burrows about 251 million years old were excavated at Karoo.

This habit of burrowing would be our salvation in the apocalypse that followed, for the Permian period ended when a series of massive volcanic eruptions spewed immense quantities of dust and sulphur dioxide into the atmosphere. In the cold, dark, hellish years that ensued, 95 per cent of all species died out, including the last of the once-dominant sea-dwelling trilobites. The mighty gorgonopsians and many of the larger, fiercer cynodonts died for lack of food, but the lystrosaurs flourished on the carrion littering the blighted forests. And down in our burrows, a few of we smaller cynodonts cowered and fended as best we could.

Mesozoic dawn

The clouds cleared at the dawn of the Mesozoic era (251–6.5 million years ago), whose first period was the Triassic (251–205 million years ago). The surviving cynodonts started evolving to fill many roles that had been vacated through the mass extinction. One branch became cynognathuses ('dog jaw'), a type of cynodont like a cross between a reptilian wolf and a pit bull terrier, which rapidly came to dominate Pangea between 245 and 230 million years ago. Lurking in our holes and trying to keep out of our fierce cousins' way were much smaller cynodonts called probainognaths ('progressive jaw'), our ancestors, who stayed alive by remaining small and furtive.

For many millions of years the scales we had inherited from our reptilian forebears had been developing into fur. Perhaps most therapsids had been bristly, at least, but as the Triassic developed our cynodont ancestors became ever more furry, far advanced in our transition from reptile to mammal. We were also developing ever larger brains; teeth that occluded (they join together perfectly when our jaws close) and the ability to warm our own blood by burning food in our stomachs instead of relying on basking in sunlight like lizards. This in turn allowed us to come out at night – and thus to avoid being eaten by the cold-blooded reptiles, who could only hunt by day. We were also starting to suckle our young with milk, even though at this stage we still hatched out of eggs like our reptilian ancestors.

One type of cynodontic probainognath scurrying about the undergrowth of Pangea in the late Triassic and early Jurassic (205–135 million years ago) was the insectivorous, mouselike ictidosaur. Its name shows that it was still considered a reptile, but some of its contemporaries and near relations appear to be just mammalian enough to be considered protomammals, if not actually mammals. There were the ancestors of the now extinct allotheria, a creature vaguely similar to a large and still somewhat reptilian badger. Also scurrying about were the symmetrodonts and morganucodonts, shrewlike creatures with venomous spurs on their hind legs. Their fossilised remains have been found from China to Wales (its name means 'Morganwg [Glamorgan] tooth').

An early mammal that flourished about 195 million years ago was discovered in the Lufeng Basin, China, in 1997. Named *Hadrocodium wui*, its genus name means 'full head' and its species name commemorates its discoverer, Xiao-Chun Wu. Its

A megazostrodon, a type of morganucodont, sketched from a model in the Natural History Museum.

name written on the printed page is considerably longer than it was, for it was no bigger than a pea. But its brain, though tiny, was nonetheless proportionately bigger, compared to its body size, than anything else alive at the time, or that had ever lived before. If this tiny creature was not our direct ancestor, then it was certainly a very close cousin of ours indeed.

One of the oldest lineages of mammals are the monotremes, the group that includes duck-billed platypuses, echidnas and spiny anteaters, all of whom continue to lay eggs like reptiles, though they also suckle their young, like mammals. The genetic split between their lineage and ours seems to have been back when we were all probainognaths in the Triassic, about 220 million years ago, but they did not evolve into anything approaching what they are now until about 160 million years ago, when the earliest platypuses emerged, with echidnas appearing even later, about 100 million years ago. Amongst the platypus's vestigial reptilian features is that its body temperature is 5 degrees centigrade below the average mammal. The monotremes have only survived in Australia, where they clung on due to their tough natures: like the morganucodonts before them, platypusses and echidnas have a venomous spur on their hind legs. Platypuses can also swim to avoid danger, whilst echidnas are protected by bristling spines and can burrow down to escape from predators and fires. Both are fine examples of hardy survivors.

Unlike the monotremes, our ancestors eventually stopped laying eggs. Instead we kept our young inside soft eggs inside the womb until they were ready to be born. This way the mother was always able to defend and protect her developing babies. It was an evolutionary advantage that encouraged social behaviour and would eventually give us the edge over all others.

A second major offshoot from our ancestral line were the marsupials, who diverged during the Jurassic. They developed pouches into which their tiny babies crawled after birth and in which they were nurtured as they grew. Marsupials spread across the world, only reaching Australia about 50 million years ago. It was there that the types we know now, such as kangaroos and koalas, appeared much later; cut off by the drifting continents, they have survived solely in Australasia. But all that lay far in the future: back in the Jurassic, the ancestors of all these creatures were still tiny, very similar looking protomammals – with no guarantee of surviving any length of time at all.

The rule of the dinosaurs

The first thing my first history teacher told us was to 'put out of your mind all thoughts of cave men being chased by dinosaurs, because dinosaurs became extinct a long time before there were cave men'. That's true, but in fact, throughout the Jurassic, dinosaurs really did hunt and kill our ancestors – it's just that we hadn't evolved into cave men by then.

Ever since the early reptile lineage had divided into synapsids (who became cynodonts and then mammals), and diapsids, the synapsids had always been the dominant group. The diapsids had barely clung on at all. Some retreated back into the sea, evolving into turtles, ichthyosaurs and plesiosaurs (whose descendants are rumoured to linger to this day beneath the steely waters of Loch Ness). Other diapsids remained on land but developed into small, bipedal archosaurs, who could scuttle out of the way of our ancestors. As they ran, the archosaurs became ever faster and stronger. As the Triassic wore on, the tables began to turn as the drier environment began to favour the diapsid archosaurs. They were the ancestors of the group that burst to the fore in the Jurassic – the dinosaurs, whose name means 'terrible lizard'.

Everywhere now fearsome, carnivorous dinosaurs such as *Tyrannosaurus rex* turned the tables on their foes, battling the last packs of cynognathuses into extinction. Besides producing ever fiercer hunters, branches of the dinosaur family evolved into herbivorous sauropods such as the brontosaurus and the iguanodon, who returned to walking on all fours. A fossilised part of an iguanodon was found at Hollington, near Hastings, Sussex, one of the few areas of Britain not covered by sea at the time.

Towards the end of the Triassic, the supercontinent of Pangea had split horizontally. Gondwanaland with its dense jungles of glossopteris trees drifted south, and Laurasia drifted north. During the Jurassic, only the highest parts of Britain poked up above water, as islands off the southern coast of Laurasia. Most of the landmass of Britain lay below the warm waves. Billions of tiny protozoa, particularly foraminifera, lived in the water and when they died their tiny calcium-rich shells sunk to the bottom, laying down what would become the soft white chalk of the Chilterns, the North and South Downs (see plate 8) and the uplands of Wiltshire and Dorset. In doing so they fossilised the tightly spiralled shells of the ammonites who shared the warm seas with the sharklike ichthyosaurs and plesiosaurs, whose fossils turn up occasionally in the 'Jurassic Coast' cliffs of Lyme Regis and Weymouth, Dorset.

While the dinosaurs were dominant on land, other branches of the archosaurs flourished too. Some progressed down the evolutionary path that, by about 80 million years ago, produced the crocodiles. Others became fleet-footed pterosaurs, whose long, skin-flapped arms eventually enabled their pterodactyl descendants to fly. Other pterosaurs continued running, but developed furry feathers that, towards the end of the Jurassic, allowed them to take to the skies too as archaeopteryxes, the ancestors of birds. As they flapped through the late Jurassic skies, they looked down on the first flowering plants, such as magnolias, which had recently evolved out of gymnosperms and now unfurled their simple petals for the first time. With these first flowers evolved the pollinating insects they would need to reproduce. Then, as the Jurassic gave way to the Cretaceous period (135–65 million years ago), flowering plants became widespread on land.

Mammalian machinations

From our burrows our beady eyes processed a plethora of sights: the sudden appearance of a juicy beetle; the shadow of a bird, flapping laboriously overhead; the tree trunk of a brontosaurus's foot, which narrowly missed blocking the way out altogether.

Although dinosaurs dominated sky, sea and land, our tiny ancestors and our protomarsupial and protomonotreme cousins clung on in our burrows, hoping for better times to come. Eutheria, 'true beasts', are the branch of mammals that use plecentas to nourish our young for as long as possible within the womb. The dormouse-like eomaia, whose 125 million-year-old fossilised remains were found in China, is the earliest known type of placental mammal and may perhaps be a direct ancestor of ours. About 105 million years ago, the afrotheres branched off from our lineage. Although at that stage they were tiny and nondescript, they would evolve eventually into aardvarks, mammoths and elephants. The ancestors of the armadillos branched off about 95 million years ago. Next to branch off were the laurasiatheres, forebears of the shrews, moles, bats, horses, sheep, cattle, whales, cats, dogs and seals. About 70 million years ago another split led to the forebears of the mice and rabbits. But whilst all these branches existed, they were nothing like the wide range of creatures into which they would eventually evolve. At this stage, in the Cretaceous period, we were all still small, furry, shrewlike creatures, terrified of the dinosaurs who ruled the world, perfectly unaware of our own destinies.

The last apocalypse

Then, 65 million years ago, the tiny mammals of the world, including our own ancestors, glanced up in surprise as an 8-mile wide meteorite came blazing through the atmosphere. It pounded into Mexico, creating the 110-mile wide Chicxulub crater. About the same time, volcanos along India's Deccan plateau erupted.

Both sent vast clouds of dust and gas billowing up into the atmosphere. The air became so hot that fires burst out across the land and the world was plunged into another dreadful phase of toxic darkness. This so-called K–T or 'Cretaceous-Paleogene event' killed virtually everything. A huge swathe of sea plankton floated down lifeless to the seabed. All the dinosaurs died, either choked to death, burnt alive in the raging fires, or starved as they roamed the blasted remains of their once-fertile world.

The remains of the extinct dinosaurs lived on as fossils to overawe and astonish our ancestors. To them we owe many stories of monsters and fabulous beasts. In *The First Fossil Hunters* (2000), Adrienne Mayor showed conclusively that Greek stories of wingless, four-legged, bird-beaked griffins guarding gold in the furthest reaches of Scythia were based on genuine travellers' reports of the numerous fossilised remains of the wingless, four-legged, bird-beaked protoceratops and psittacosaurus dinosaurs that litter the Gobi desert, where gold nuggets can still be found aplenty.

But although so many living things died, there were a few survivors here and there. Each plant or animal that survived did so for a reason. Ginkgo and cynad trees, ferns and magnolias are all extremely tough plants, as any gardener will tell you. Clams, nautiluses and coelacanths survived by lurking at the bottom of the seas. Crocodiles, the largest land-based creatures to survive, did so because they could hide virtually submerged under water while the fires raged overhead. Turtles, protected by their tough shells and able to last long periods without food, survived in the sea. Snakes survived in their holes: they too can survive long periods without food. A few birds, shielded from the worst of the cold by their thick feathers, used their ability to fly to avoid the fires and roam the world in search of food. Many smaller crustaceans and insects survived as well (butterflies and bees had yet to evolve), hidden away in nooks and crannies. They provided food for the smaller reptiles and amphibians – the lizards, frogs, toads and newts – and for the few little mammals that survived – the platypuses and echidnas and the diminutive, shrewlike ancestors of marsupials, afrotheres, laurasiatheres and the rest, including our forebears. Safe in our burrows, we bided our time, waiting for the worst of the disaster to pass.

Part Two

Book of Man

Chapter 6

The Southern Ape-Men

The emergence of primates

The clouds cleared to reveal our own, present Cenozoic ('new life') era, which opened with the Tertiary period (65–2.5 million years ago). All periods can be divided into subdivisions called epochs. These are most often used and are most meaningful from the Tertiary period onwards, as our evolutionary course quickens and we edge closer to our own appearance. The first epoch of the Tertiary period, then, was the Paleocene epoch (65–55 million years ago).

Warm blooded, big-brained and sociable, our mammalian advantages enabled us to evolve rapidly to fill as many evolutionary niches as possible, including many that had been occupied by the now extinct dinosaurs. Cousins of the modern platypus grew into elephant-sized uintatheriums, their heads bristling with tusks and stumpy horns, but they evolved too quickly and became extinct within 30 million years.

Deciduous trees, with broad leaves that are shed in the winter, evolved to flourish alongside the mangos and palms in Britain, and up into their branches our nimble ancestors climbed. We were now insectivorous euarchonta ('true ancestors'), similar to the later tree shrew descendants of this line. We evolved quickly into fruit-eating primatomorphs (protoprimates), such as the squirrel-like plesiadapis, whose fossilised remains are found in North America and Europe.

The continents continued their endless drifting. About 60 million years ago Laurasia split into North America and Eurasia. The divorce was particularly violent where the north-west of Scotland was ripped away from Canada, throwing up the great volcanos that became the Black Cuillins of Skye. Then, during the ensuing Eocene epoch (55–38 million years ago), India, which had broken away from fragmenting Gondwanaland, drifted north to join Asia, buckling up millions of tons of rock to form the Himalayas. The growth of this massive new mountain range caused more water than before to precipitate as rain, thus lessening the amount of carbon dioxide in the atmosphere and decreasing its greenhouse effect. This led ultimately to global cooling. Freshly evolved grasses began to spread across mountainous uplands, and newly evolved oaks, hollies and walnuts spread their leafy branches across the lowlands. Below, flowers proliferated and

Ida, imagined from her skeleton: our ancestors probably looked something like this about 47 million years ago.

the air buzzed with the sound of bees. For the first time, now, the newly evolved butterflies unfurled their bright wings and fluttered about on the margins of the forests.

Up in these trees, our clawed paws became hands with nails, our brains enlarged and our faces flattened so that our eyes could face out in unison to survey our colder, leafier world. We had become primates. We looked down, with the capacity now for surprise, as the underbrush stirred and snapped with the passing of an early, ground-dwelling herbivore and the dry leaves on the forest floor rustled with the sinuous passage of a snake.

The primate lineage split quickly into damp-nosed strepsirrhini (the 'bent-nosed' ancestors of the lemurs and lorises) and we, the dry-nosed haplorrhini ('simple-nosed'), starting with creatures such as the tiny *Teilhardina asiatica* and *Darwinius masillae*. A fossil of the latter, nicknamed 'Ida', was found in a disused quarry near Frankfurt-am-Main, Germany, and was revealed to the world in a blaze of publicity in 2009. Ida lived 47 million years ago. She had a body 11½ inches long, a tail about the same length and opposable thumbs that were useful for gripping. Ida existed soon after the split with the lemurs and was quite possibly a direct ancestor of ours as we continued to evolve into monkeys.

European roots

By now Africa, another fragmented part of Gondwanaland, had drifted north and was coming into contact with Eurasia. Its northward movement helped push up the Pyrenees and the Alps and also created the land bridge that now exists between Egypt and the Middle East. In the Oligocene epoch (38–26 million years ago), descendants or close relatives of Ida must have made their way into Egypt, where remains of the furtive, monkeylike parapithecus and aegyptopithecus have been found, with dexterous little hands and enquiring minds.

Genetics indicates that the split between the Old and New World monkeys occurred about 30 million years ago. That is an awkward circumstance for scientists because there is no obvious route by which monkeys might then have reached the Americas. Perhaps a pair of monkeys made a seaborne journey, clinging to a mat of vegetation – that, at least, is one suggestion, but the dilemma has yet to be properly resolved.

The next significant split comes at the start of the Miocene epoch (26–5.3 million years ago) when the Old World monkey lineage divided, one line leading eventually to the chattering clan of baboons, macaques, langurs and proboscis monkeys, and the other to us.

Proconsul and kenyapithecus are the names of two monkey fossils with certain apelike characteristics, which were found in Africa in the 1930s. They were once thought to be our ancestors. Now it seems more likely that they were merely close cousins of ours, whilst our direct ancestors remained in the Eurasian forests. These Eurasian forebears of ours included the ever more apelike dryopithecus ('the oak tree ape'), whose remains were first discovered by Édouard Lartet at Saint-Gaudens in the Pyrenees in 1856, as an accidental by-product of his quest for Ice Age man. Since then, other dryopithecus fossils up to 25 million years old have been found in Germany, Spain, Hungary and China. Britain's rocks from this period are mainly in the valley and estuary of the Thames and up the East Anglian coast as far as Happisburgh, Norfolk. These have not revealed any dryopithecus remains, but maybe there are some of their fossils there, waiting to be discovered.

The next branch off our line took place about 15 million years ago and resulted in the gibbons, all of whom are found now in India and Southeast Asia. Another branch off our line, about 13 million years ago, resulted in sivapithecus, who is thought to be the ancestor of orang-utans, which are found now only in Borneo and Sumatra. Although these creatures are now found in the eastern end of Asia, the forests of Asia and Europe were once alive with their chattering voices. At the western end of their range was the apelike, fruit-eating *Pierolapithecus catalaunicus*, a 13 million-year-old fossil of which was found near Barcelona, Spain, in 2004. Pierolapithecus is probably our own ancestor. With a relatively short, stiff spine we may, when necessity demanded, have been able to stand upright and walk on our hind legs.

Africa's collision with Europe was complete now. A rocky bridge extended south from Spain to Morocco and the sea water that had been trapped to the east, in what would later become the Mediterranean, gradually dried to create a vast, shimmering valley of inhospitable salt flats. It seems likely that, as the world dried and the Spanish forests died back, pierolapithecus's descendants roamed south, scampering along on all fours but sometimes standing up on our hind legs to survey the scenery, until we reached the jungles of Africa.

Sahelanthropus tchadensis (the 'Old Man of Chad') was found in Chad in central Africa in 2001. He lived about 7 million years ago and was probably our ancestor. He shared many characteristics with both us and gorillas, who branched off our ancestral line about this time. Soon afterwards, perhaps about 6–5 million years ago, another line branched off ours, which led to the chimpanzees and bonobos.

Our own line at this time was probably represented by *Orrorin tugenensis* (*orrorin* means 'original man' in the Tugen language in Kenya), called 'Millennium Man', because his remains were found in Kenya in 2000. From orrorins, we probably evolved into ardipithecuses ('base apes'), such as *Ardipithecus kadaba* (5.6 million years old) and then into the strong-ankled but still largely tree-dwelling *Ardipithecus ramidus* (4.4 million years old), whose remains were found in Ethiopia in 1994.

About 5.3 million years ago, at the start of the Pliocene epoch (5.3–2.5 million years ago), a volcano loosened the rocky ridge that separated the Atlantic from the long, low, dry valley of the Mediterranean. The Atlantic's waters burst through the barrier, creating a colossal waterfall that grew ever wider, gouging out the Straits of Gibraltar and filling up the Mediterranean. The Ancient Greeks realised later that such a breach must have occurred to create their sea, and attributed the cutting out of the straits to the greatest of their heroes – so to them the Rock of Gibraltar and the mountain behind Cueta on the African side were known as the Pillars of Hercules.

Now, apart from the thin land bridge between the Middle East and Egypt, Africa was isolated from Europe. Any pierolapithecuses or dryopithecuses left in Europe would perish as the world grew ever colder. Our destiny now lay firmly in Africa.

'Southern ape-man'

As the Ice Age set in, water became locked up in the spreading polar ice caps and the rest of the world became drier. Around the equator, the Sun beat down on Africa causing the jungles to recede and the great grassy plains of the savannahs to spread. The jungle apes – our own ardipithecus forebears and the ancestors of the chimpanzees and gorillas – all began questing out into the savannahs in their search of food, becoming ever more bipedal as they did so. But we were by far the most fiercely successful and so – runs one theory at least – the gorillas and chimps retreated back into the remaining trees of western Africa. And that is how they became what they are today – not the eternal denizens of the jungles, as they are sometimes fondly imagined, but apes who returned to the trees because our ancestors' success on the savannahs forced them to do so.

We roamed the savannahs in small family bands as hunter-gatherers, developing ever more complex social interactions and means of communication as we did so. Our upright stance may have intimidated predators, and it certainly saved some of the energy expended in using all four legs. Most importantly, it freed up our hands, enabling us to hold branches or stones and use them as weapons or tools. We had become australopithecuses – 'southern ape-men'.

The earliest australopithecus was *Australopithecus anamensis* ('lake-dweller'), who appeared 4.2 million years ago. The remains of one was found in Kenya in 1965. Anamensis was probably the direct ancestor of *Australopithecus afarensis*, who appeared by 3.6 million years ago, the date of a fossilised pair of footprints made by one walking through a damp bed of recently deposited volcanic ash, found by Mary Leakey's team in Laetoli, Tanzania, in 1978.

But the first afarensis to be found was Lucy, so-named because the Beetles song *Lucy in the Sky with Diamonds* was playing on the wireless when Don Johanson found her 3 million-year-old fossilised remains at Afar, in the Great Rift Valley of Ethiopia, in 1974. A 20-year-old woman, Lucy was 3 feet tall with a reasonably upright stance, but with an apelike jaw and very flat nostrils. She dug up roots and rhizomes, shimmied up trees to pick fruit, scavenged carcasses of animals killed by the leopards and sabre-toothed cats that doubtless terrified her, and probably caught and killed other smaller animals herself. In the early twentieth century, evidence of violence, such as baboon skulls evidently smashed by australopithecuses wielding thigh bones, did not surprise people. In the shadow of the nuclear bomb, however, scientists longed to imagine australopithecuses as peaceful creatures living in harmony with their environment, an idilic state to which we might one day return. But in the cynical early twenty-first century, Professor Robert Winston's BBC television series *Walking with Cavemen* reverted to the older view, and suggested that Lucy had been bludgeoned to death by one of her own kind.

Around us stretched the savannahs, away to the enigmatic horizon where volcanic cones puffed out clouds of ash and the distant movement of herds of horned herbivores warned us of the presence of lions. Before long, Lucy's people spawned new species. From 3.5 million years ago there appeared *Kenyanthropus platyops* and then (from about 3 million years ago) the 'robust australopithecuses', *Paranthropus aethiopicus*, *boisei* and *robustus*. These were gentle giants who lived in the savannahs in family groups, feeding off termites. But most significantly there evolved from Lucy's people the 'gracile australopithecuses', such as *Australopithecus garhi* and *Australopithecus africanus*, our ancestors.

A species is defined as a group of creatures who can breed only with each other. We have applied many different species names to the skull fragments and other fossilised bones we have found – and this in turn suggests a plethora of australopithecus species in Africa. But we do not really know if each was a separate species, or whether we are dealing with a small number of species containing a great variety of physical variations. Maybe there was sexual intercourse between widely differing sorts of australopithecuses, which produced various hybrids. But, given that we did evolve, and evolved rapidly, the general trend was probably that of like mating with like, keeping and strengthening those new traits that enabled us to survive ever more effectively. And as a result, the African savannah saw the emergence of a major new, fully bipedal ancestor in our evolutionary journey: *Homo habilis*, 'the human handyman'.

Chapter 7

Of Habilis and Hobbits

The search for the 'missing link'

During the second half of the nineteenth century, as our understanding of the world's history developed, enthusiastic amateur paleoanthropologists – those who study ancient man – were engaged in an all-out hunt for our human past. All across Europe they poked about in rock shelters and crawled into caves to see what they might find – and they were quite astonished by what they discovered. The bones of the modern humans who had lived in Europe from about 45,000 years ago, and those of long extinct creatures, started to line up in mahogany display cases alongside carefully crafted flint tools and exquisite carvings made of bone and mammoth ivory made from that time onwards.

Beyond their having been simply apelike, however, Darwin knew no better than anyone else what the immediate ancestors of these modern humans had been like. Thus the search for the 'missing link' between man and ape began in earnest. Ernst Haeckel's *The History of Creation* (1876) theorised a halfway ape-man living over half a million years ago, which he called *Pithecanthropos alalus*, 'the speechless ape'. He included rather disturbing illustrations of them, plump and hairy, with deep, sunken eyes and haunted looks, as if they realised quite how much they still had to evolve.

The natural assumption of the Europeans who discovered the remains of Ice Age men in Europe was that European humans had evolved *in situ*. Perhaps we had evolved straight out of Neanderthals, whose remains were first discovered in Germany in 1854. That belief was enforced later by Piltdown Man, the 'dawn man', whose skull was found in Dorset in 1908. But this was later exposed as a forgery, a human cranium stuck onto an ape's jaw. Such beliefs, however, were not unique to Europe: when early human remains were found in East Asia the Chinese interpreted them in exactly the same way, and asserted that humanity had evolved, of course, in China.

Prophetically, Haeckel had rejected the idea of the continuous evolution of modern Europeans from apes in Europe. Modern chimpanzees and gorillas, after all, lived in Africa, so it was there that our evolution was most likely to have taken place. That assertion was almost as upsetting to the European psyche at the time as the notion of our descent from apes at all had been in the first place. But it also inspired amateur enthusiasts in Africa to continue the quest for our human ancestry there, and in 1924 the first *Australopithecus africanus* was discovered in Kimberley, South Africa. Nicknamed 'the Tuang child', this was the first specimen recognised by Raymond Dart as 'intermediate' in the evolution of men from apes. The discovery was a major victory for the view that modern humans had evolved in Africa, but those who found the idea of African evolution distasteful argued that 'Tuang child' was nothing more than a deformed chimpanzee skull. But then Robert Broom found an almost intact africanus skull (nicknamed 'Mrs Ples'), and the argument was settled for good. It was thanks to these discoveries that scientists decided to focus their efforts on Africa, and this led in time to the discoveries of the Old Man of Chad, Lucy and all the rest.

Another vexed question was exactly how humans are related to gorillas, chimpanzees and other apes. After Darwin, late Victorian scientists divided the super-family of hominoidae (humanlike creatures) into three: the hylobatidae (gibbons), pongidae (orang-utans, gorillas, chimpanzees and bonobos), and hominidae (us). However, in 1963, Morris Goodman's pioneering studies of genetics showed that humans, chimpanzees and bonobos were much more closely related to each other than any of us were related to gorillas. It meant that if we wished to continue to use the term 'ape' to describe chimpanzees and gorillas, we had to include ourselves in that category too.

Thus, from the mid-1960s onwards, the groupings have been different – the hylobatidae (gibbons) have been placed in a family of their own, and hominoidae has been divided into two, the pongidae (orang-utans) and the hominiae, comprising gorillas, chimpanzees, bonobos and us. Since then, and through books such as Desmond Morris's *The Naked Ape* (1967), we have gradually become used to the idea of being apes.

But if humans are apes, then aren't apes also in some way human? Some scientists such as Jared Diamond have even proposed classing chimps and bonobos as *homo* species, whilst Professor Volker Sommer has advocated extending human rights to apes. Besides demonstrating evidence of their intelligence, Sommer has shown that each day chimpanzees in certain parts of Africa eat a small and nutritionally insignificant number of ants, but never termites, whereas in other parts of Africa they eat a small number of termites, but never ants. Sommer suggests that these are cultural differences, of no more evolutionary use than Hindus refusing to eat cows, or Western Europeans not wishing to eat dogs. Such behaviour exists only to enforce social cohesiveness within the group – a trait we thought of as typically human but which, if it also exists in chimpanzees, enforces their similarity to us – and of us to them.

The first handyman

But as things stand, the entirely artificial line between 'them' and 'us', between non-humans and humans, is drawn about 2.5 million years ago with the emergence of the first 'Homo' species, *Homo habilis*. To emphasise its importance, we have chosen this point to begin our present, Quaternary period (2.5 million years ago onwards). The first epoch of the Quaternary was the Pleistocene epoch (2.5 million–12,000 years ago). A very early Homo jawbone and five teeth found at Ledi-Geraru, near Afar, Ethiopia, in 2013 and announced in March 2015, however, has upset this dating, but only by a little, by being dated to about 2.8 million years ago.

These first true humans had a more upright stance than any of their ancestors, with flatter faces and bigger brains, fuelled by a protein-rich diet of meat. Increased brain size led to our imagining, planning and making sharp-edged tools of stone and bone – hence the term 'habilis', which means 'handyman' – and such activity further stimulated the brain to grow. The first habilis remains were discovered by Louis and Mary Leakey in the Olduvai Gorge, Tanzania, in 1960, so their very primitive stone-making tool culture is called Oldowan. It is the first stage in the long stretch of human history called the Lower Palaeolithic, the 'old Stone Age'.

Before long, the habilis population was joined on the savannah by two other homo species that were probably descended from them, rudolfensis (about 2.3 million years ago) and ergaster (about 1.9 million years ago). The first ergaster ('workman') was found by the Leakeys' team at Turkana, South Africa, in 1984, so he was nicknamed 'Turkana boy'. Instead of the Oldowan method of bashing rocks together to make sharp edges, we had developed a new technology of chipping rocks to make oval hand axes. These were large stones, blunt at the base for holding in the palm of the hand, but with sharp upper edges rising to a sharp point, making them powerful tools for cutting food, sharpening wooden points, puncturing hide, cutting anything and stabbing and killing animals, whether in the hunt for food or in self-defence. This technology is termed Acheulean, because the first examples of it, dating from *considerably* later, were found at Saint-Acheul in northern France. Making tools with such versatility, which would be used long after they were made, shows considerable forethought on the part of their makers.

Ergasters seem to have had far more advanced sweat glands than their ancestors, a distinct advantage on the savannahs. This obviated the need to pant, thus freeing up our mouths to make more expressive noises. This, and our ever increasing brain size, indicates an advanced ability to communicate. Remains of ergaster spines suggest we had not yet enough control of our lung muscles to be able to speak, but we were evolving in that direction. Because the area of the brain's pre-frontal cortex used for making hand axes overlaps with the area used for speech, one may have stimulated the other.

Ergaster campsites show traces of fire. We probably encountered fire due to random lightning strikes, but maybe it was at this stage that we learned to spark fires ourselves by the patient rubbing together of sticks. With fire we could cook meat, making it far easier to bite and chew. It also proved a magic talisman to scare away the dreadful predators that roamed the broad savannahs at night. It has even been suggested that gazing into flames may have ignited the first sparks of wonder that led, considerably later, to the birth of the human imagination.

In the next certain stage in our evolutionary journey, and probably evolved directly from ergasters, we became *Homo erectus*, who first appeared about 1.8 million years ago. Armed with fire, Acheulean hand axes and probably very primitive speech, their brains were now only 7 per cent smaller than ours today. As erectuses, we were so successful that we became the sole survivors out of all the earlier australopithecus and homo species. In a harsh environment, we had the evolutionary edge over them all – though the suspicion lingers that some violence on our part may have contributed to our cousins' demise.

Early erectus finds come not only from Africa but also from Dmanisi, Georgia, where skulls, bones and flake and pebble tools date from 1.8 million years ago. So primitive are the tools at Dmanisi that some scientists suggest that a handful of earlier humans (ergasters, maybe) may have migrated out of Africa, following the expanding ranges of the animals on whose remains they scavenged, and reached the Caucasus. Maybe, as Chris Stringer and others suggest, it was there in Georgia that we evolved into erectuses, with some migrating back into Africa and others colonising Europe and Asia – in which case the old nineteenth-century view of the Caucasus as the 'cradle of humanity' might not be so inaccurate after all.

Some erectus descendants roamed all the way to the other side of Asia. In 1895, Haeckel's idea of the 'missing link' between men and apes inspired Eugene Dubois to seek human fossils in the jungles of Java, and he found erectus remains there, 1.65 million years old. In 1926, archaeologists in China were intrigued by some humanlike fossil teeth being used as medicine, so they looked even further east, at Zhoukoudian, near Peking. There they found more erectus remains, initially classified as sinanthropus or 'Peking Man', closer to 800,000 years old.

Homo Floresiensis

Ultimately, however, erectuses did not flourish in the east. Most are thought to have died out several hundred thousand years ago – all, perhaps, except for the tantalising Yeti or 'Abominable Snowman' of the Himalayas, the Sasquatch or 'Big Foot' of the North American woods and the Yowie of Australian Aboriginal tradition. Mainsteam science, however, argues that sightings of such creatures are best explained as bears rearing up on their hind legs and genetic tests on 'Yeti' fur found near such sightings confirms this.

In the 1990s, Michael Morwood found some 800,000-year-old Acheulean stone tools on the Indonesian island of Flores, part of the island chain that runs from Java down to Australia, which had clearly been made by erectuses. Further exploration in 2003 produced a great surprise. In the Liang Bua cave there, Morwood and his team found several partial skeletons. Built just like erectuses, they were only 3 feet tall but their teeth and growth lines showed they were adults. They were called *Homo floresiensis* and nicknamed 'hobbits' after the diminutive, made-up humanoids in the novels of J.R.R. Tolkien.

The reduced size of these hobbits seems to have been caused by their having being confined to a small island: Flores also has fossils of diminutive elephants. The island's size had an oppositely distorting effect on smaller creatures by producing enormous rats and lizards, in which the hobbits were locked in a perpetual cycle of hunting and being hunted.

The hobbit bones from Liang Bua are a mere 18,000 years old. Hobbits probably lived on until 12,000 years ago, when a severe volcanic eruption may have wiped out the last of these erectus descendants. But the people of Flores still have tales of small, long-armed, pot-bellied, hairy people able to repeat human words parrot fashion. People called them Ebu Gogo, 'the grandmother who eats anything'. In 2005, James Vidal reported Riccus Bandar, a 60-year-old local farmer who looks after the cave where the hobbits were found, telling Morwood, 'My grandmother told me when I was about six of how, long ago, six children from the village went hunting and one of their dogs went into the cave but did not come out. They went in and saw a little man there. He was very small, standing on a rock. They were frightened and ran back. The people were very afraid.' So maybe they lived on, after all.

Chapter 8

The Neanderthals of Oldbury Hill

Archaic humans in Britain

U p to this point, we have been following down one single line of descent over the millions of years since life first emerged. But now, with the spread of *Homo erectus* throughout Asia, Africa and Europe, our family tree becomes more complex as it splits into several lines of cousins, who would later interbreed to produce the modern humans of Europe and Asia. One line was based largely in Africa, and evolved into modern humans. Another remained in Europe and evolved into the Neanderthals. As we shall see later, there is strong genetic evidence that, when modern humans first left Africa, they interbred with Neanderthals: every modern human with any European and Asiatic ancestry at all (which is to say, everyone) has lines of descent back to Neanderthals, so we can speak with every justification of the archaic humans of Europe and Asia as our ancestors.

There is a problem with what to call the archaic humans in Europe from whom Neanderthals evolved. As with the earlier stages of our human evolution, different finds of archaic humans tend to be labelled as new 'species', giving rise to a confusing plethora of names. Erectuses or their descendants, whose remains were found in 2008 in the Atapuerca hills of Spain, and dated by palaeomagnetic dating to 800,000 years ago, have been labelled *Homo antecessor* ('pioneer man'). Finds made in a quarry at Maur near Heidelberg, Germany, in 1907 were labelled *Homo heidelbergensis*, a term also later applied to archaic human finds in Africa too. Whether these heidelbergensis ancestors of ours evolved in Africa or Europe is a moot point.

At this period, northern Europe was gripped by the pulsing phases of the Ice Age. Each rise and fall in the climate was driven by what are termed 'Milankovitch cycles' in both the Earth's orbit around the Sun and also in its wobbles about its own axis. Both of these cycles bring parts of the planet periodically closer to, and then further away from, the Sun. These cosmic factors caused periodic fluctuations in the climate, which in turn caused plants and then animals to colonise, and then retreat from, northern Europe. The consequent presence or absence of food was the direct cause of the movements of our ancestors. Thus, in warmer phases of the Ice Age, archaic humans walked across the shallow valley that later became the English Channel, or over Doggerland, which now lies beneath the southern North Sea, and unknowingly reached southern England.

The earliest evidence of early man anywhere in northern Europe comes from the Cromer Beds at Happisburgh (pronounced 'Hazeborough') where, in 2010, seventy-eight pieces of simple, razor-sharp Acheulean flint tools were found. The site is on the Norfolk coast, where the sea has helped archaeologists by crumbling away the cliffs and exposing buried remains. The finds may date from 840,000 or even 950,000 years ago. The climate was probably similar to now. These people, who may have been erectus or heidelbergensis humans, may have made clothes or shelters and used fires, though no evidence for any of these has yet been found. But we know from the bones they left behind what they hunted – wild horses and deer, mainly, and they also scavenged woolly rhinoceroses and mammoths and had to contend with hyenas, bears, wolves and sabre-toothed cats.

There are many later finds there too, and at Pakefield, near Lowestoft, Suffolk, tools were found in 2005 dating to 700,000 years ago. Plant remains including water chestnuts and floating ferns, contemporary with the tools at Pakefield, suggest that the climate was temporarily warmer than it is now, with hippopotamuses wallowing in the swamps by the mouth of the great Bytham River, which drained the English Midlands.

Then the cold returned and these humans, from whom we may all be descended, were driven south. The continuous fluctuations between warm and cold with which our ancestors had to contend became more marked about 500,000 years ago. A warm spell allowed some archaic humans, probably *H. heidelbergensis* and maybe again ancestral to us, to roam north again, up onto England's South Downs and then west to Boxgrove, Sussex. An inlet of the western sea lapped below a cave in a steep chalky cliff, which later tilted back to form the gentle hillside of today. The site was rich in natural flints, which were used to fashion Acheulean tools including hand axes. The site has been described as a 'Palaeolithic Pompeii' for the quality of the finds there, preserved below layers of silt. One remarkable find of flint flakes was clearly made by someone who knelt down to fashion a hand axe, because the pile of flakes they left shows the outline of their legs. They used their tools to dismember deer, elephants, horses and rhinoceroses: they may have scavenged already dead animals, competing as they did so with lions and hyenas, but a puncture mark on a horse scapula found at Boxgrove suggests that they hunted and killed too. Human teeth show signs of scratches where stone tools were used to cut meat being held in the jaw. Marks on animal bones show they had been skinned, so probably their fur was being used as clothing in the relatively cold climate – especially important as, curiously, no evidence has been found at Boxgrove of fire.

There are plenty of other, later archaic human sites, too: at Westbury-sub-Mendip, Somerset and Waverly Wood, Warwickshire, where the ancient Bytham River used to flow through the Midlands and Doggerland towards the distant northern sea. Others camped on Stoke Newington Common in North London, where their noisy stone working anticipated the noise of modern London by half a million years.

About 450,000 ago came a very severe phase of the Ice Age. Glaciers crept down across Britain, sometimes reaching as far south as the site of London's Finchley Road Underground station – the furthest south they ever came. The old Bytham River was obliterated and the Thames was pushed south to its present course. Our ancestors were driven far south too, to sites such as the Arago Cave at Tautavel in the French Pyrenees.

Just before or, more likely, just after the height of the great glaciation about 450,000 years ago, a momentous event took place, though our ancestors were unlikely to have been around to witness it. To the north of Doggerland (and east of Scotland) was the salty North Sea. Glaciers blocked its northern outlet, but the Thames and the Rhine continued to feed water into it, so the sea level rose, flooding much of Doggerland. To the south the North Downs formed a continuous line of chalk right down into France, but against this barrier the rising water lapped with ever more urgency. Suddenly, one day, the sea burst over the crest of the downs, and a ferocious wall of water gouged its way south-west, slicing through the South Downs (which had also extended into France) and out carving a deep valley that would eventually become the English Channel (see plate 8). But it was not destined to remain a watercourse for long, for in the long periods when the cold bit deep, the waters retreated, the steppes of Doggerland re-emerged and the Channel became no more than a deep, chalky gorge containing a westward-flowing trickle from the Thames and the Rhine.

About 400,000 years ago, the climate improved and during the 'Hoxnian interglacial', as it is termed, humans returned to Britain. A wooden point, perhaps the end of a spear, was found preserved in the mud at Clacton-on-Sea, Essex, along with stone tools (but no hand axes) of a local style termed Clactonian. Other finds come from Marks Tey, Essex, and sites in Suffolk including Hoxne, Foxhall Road, Ipswich (which is rich in hand axes) and Beeches Pit near Bury St Edmunds, where campsites have been found with blackened hearths – the earliest proven use of controlled fire in Europe, and suggestive of all that goes with fire: cooked food, extended hours of activity and complex social interaction. Linked to these are the hearths found at Terra Amata, on the slopes of Mount Boron above Nice in southern France, a site of about the same age that has unmistakeable evidence of a camp with oval structures, testified by post holes and outline stones, suggestive of crude huts. So maybe people in Britain had huts at this time too.

Another important British site is Barnfield Pit in Swanscombe, on the north coast of Kent (see plate 10). A skull fragment of one of its inhabitants, 'Swanscombe Man', who was actually a woman, was found there in 1935 by Alvin Marston, an amateur weekend enthusiast, who kept searching until a second piece, which fitted into the first, was found in 1936. In 1955 a third piece, which fitted the existing two, was found by John Wymer – an extraordinary story of persistence in literally piecing together the past. Meanwhile, this ancient woman's kin sheltered beneath the overhanging rocks of Oldbury Hill near Sevenoaks, Kent (see plate 9), and hunted deer and aurochs and scavenged the carcasses of long-tusked elephants and rhinoceroses through the deciduous forests and along the babbling brooks of the Kentish countryside.

Remains from this period unearthed from the 'Pit of Bones' in Atapuerca, northern Spain, include parts of skeletons, revealing the people concerned to have had robust, muscular frames, all predominantly right-handed. They were probably akin to the Swanscombe and Oldbury people and in evolutionary terms they seem to have been *H. heidelbergensis* on their way to becoming Neanderthals. And indeed the Neanderthals' evolution was destined to take place in southern Europe, because after the Hoxnian interglacial the ice returned to Britain yet again, about 360,000 years ago, making human life here impossible once more.

The emergence of Neanderthals

The first Neanderthal remains were discovered in Belgium by Philippe-Charles Schmerling in 1829, but they were not recognised as such for a long time. The first remains that were identified at the time of discovery as being those of a very ancient type of human were the ones discovered in a quarry in the Neander Valley near Dusseldorf in 1856. 'Neanderthal' means 'Neander valley' in German: the valley had been named after the hymn-writer Joachim Neander (1650–1680) whose surname, ironically, meant 'new man'.

This discovery was one of our nineteenth-century ancestors' earliest known brushes with our ancient human origins. Yet our understanding of the Neanderthals' true place in our evolutionary history is still being honed today. Scientists agree that the Neanderthal and *Homo sapiens* lines both evolved out of the same archaic human ancestors, probably *H. heidelbergensis*. The original split was probably about 800,000 years ago, maybe in north-eastern Africa or the Middle East. But long after the initial divide took place there seems to have been occasional interbreeding between the wide-ranging bands of descendants down to about 400,000 years ago, after which the two lineages went their separate ways to evolve into Neanderthals in Eurasia and *H. sapiens* in Africa. This opens up the fascinating possibility that genes from the earliest colonisers of Britain, the tool-makers of Happisburgh, Pakefield and Boxgrove, if not Swanscombe as well, may have made their way, through a series of sexual encounters between different groups of hunter-gatherers across Europe and the Middle East, down into the ancestors of *H. sapiens* in Africa.

Though we evolved from common ancestors, Neanderthals were distinctly different to us. They had broad, protruding faces with jutting eyebrows, which developed from the age of eight onwards, designed to protect their eyes from driving sleet. They had receding cheekbones, no chin to speak of, and low craniums that jutted out behind, containing somewhat larger brains than ours. They were much stockier than *H. sapiens*, and much stronger. Surprisingly, their windpipes and mouths suggest that they had much higher-pitched voices.

Neanderthal stone tool technology is called Mousterian, after finds made by Henry Christy and Edouard Lartet in the early 1860s in the La Moustier rock shelters in the valley of the Vézère, a tributary of the Dordogne, in south-western France. Instead of chipping away at a big lump of flint to make just one tool, the Mousterian technique entailed cutting and keeping a flint core, from which smaller flints were broken off as needed using a soft bone hammer. An extraordinary degree of precision was possible, whereby the maker could decide whether to make a big, medium or small flint, which could then be shaped into whatever they wanted – a hand axe, a spearhead, or much smaller arrowheads, whenever required. Such a core could be carried a long way from where flints were found, greatly increasing the potential hunting range of the carrier. The technique was sophisticated enough to produce the sharp stone tools needed to cut and sew furs together to make warm clothes, enabling Neanderthals to survive the worst excesses of the Ice Age.

They lived in rock shelters below overhanging cliffs. The shelters at La Moustier were gouged out many millennia before by the Vézère in full flood and then left high and dry when the ice returned and the river was reduced to a stream, which probably froze each winter. Today, the lower rock shelter is within the little village of Peyzac-le-Moustier, its ground heavily excavated and surrounded by a high-barred fence, and there is another higher, older shelter below a cliff in the fields nearby.

Although the term 'Mousterian' is used for all Neanderthal technology, evidence for Neanderthals living in Le Moustier itself dates only from about 56,000–35,000 years ago. It was probably a refuge for them during a period of exceptional cold. Elsewhere, Neanderthal occupation was vastly more ancient. The Lazaret cave near Nice in south-eastern France was inhabited from 160,000 years ago and at Biache-Saint-Vaast near Lille in north-eastern France are skeletal remains and stone tools going back 175,000 years.

Finds at Le Moustier, Chapelle-aux-Saints, La Ferrassie and Le Roc de Marsal show that, at least some of the time, Neanderthals buried their dead in the foetal position in pits with tools, traces of red ochre and animal bones, which may have been meat offerings. Some burials were protected by stone slabs: at La Ferrassie in the Dordogne a 3-year-old Neanderthal child was buried in a pit with a slab decorated with cup marks. The more we find, the fewer differences there seem to have been between us and them.

Neanderthals in Britain

Finds from Le Moustier and other sites in the Vézère Valley were shown at the Paris Exhibition in 1863, and were then brought over for display in London. They electrified Benjamin Harrison (1837–1921), the village grocer of Ightham, Kent, who had found very similar tools near the rock shelters of Oldbury Hill nearby. In 1890 a dig organised there at Harrison's behest unearthed yet more Neanderthal tools.

The Neanderthal presence in Britain was determined by climate. In a rare warm spell about 330,000 years ago, early humans (who were either Neanderthals or *H. Heidelbergensis* on their way to becoming Neanderthals) hunted fallow deer in the deciduous woods of Purfleet, Essex, and left behind distinctively Mousterian stone tools. Then there is a long gap until 240,000 years ago, when people who were definitely Neanderthals returned again. Besides Oldbury Hill, Neanderthals sheltered in the caves of Creswell Crags, Derbyshire; at La Cotte de St Brelade, Jersey, where there is evidence of them hunting mammoths and woolly rhinoceroses; at Creffield Road in West Acton, London, and Baker's Hole, Ebbsfeet, Kent, where they used their Mousterian technology to produce not robust hand axes but fine flint knives. These places were part of the great Mammoth Steppe – a cold tundra that stretched away into the east, dotted with the dark smudges of woolly mammoths and the white specks of lemmings, across which seasonal migrations of the reindeer had probably led the Neanderthals north in the first place. Neanderthals even reached the caves of the Elwy Valley in Wales about 240,000 years ago – caves that Charles Darwin explored as a young student, eagerly seeking the truth about human origins. At Pontnewydd in the Elwy Valley teeth have been found – of three children and two adults, all of them taurodontic, a distinctive Neanderthal trait whereby the molars retain their roots, allowing them to remain useful even when worn right down. They mark the most northerly known presence of Neanderthals anywhere in Europe.

Although the English Channel had been created about 450,000 years ago, a wall of sediment had built up along its northern end, reducing it to being merely a dry valley. A build-up of water against this wall seems to have been breached about 225,000 years ago. A further dramatic torrent of water – the North Sea combined with the combined fury of the Thames and the Rhine – came bursting though, gouging out the yet wider channel we know today. After this, bitter cold set in, and Neanderthal life in Britain came to an end, the last ones either dying here or retreating back south into Europe.

From about 130,000 years ago, during Marine Isotope Stage 5, the Ice Age eased off and the temperature rose to produce the Eemian interglacial period. By 125,000 years ago, hippopotamuses wallowed in balmy swamps by the Thames in what is now Trafalgar Square – but there were no humans there to see them. It was not until about 70,000 years ago that the cold increased enough to lower the sea level: the North Sea dried and the great Mammoth Steppe spread across Doggerland once more. By 60,000 years ago herds of reindeer returned to Britain, and Neanderthals followed them, ending a 120,000-year human absence. At Lynford Quarry near Mundford, Norfolk, are remains of their tools and bones of woolly rhinoceroses, reindeer, wild horses and mammoths, either scavenged or hunted (a Neanderthal spear tip found in the ribs of a mammoth in Lehringen, Germany, proves that they could hunt mammoths at this period if they wished).

But while these northern Neanderthals were happily hunting on the Mammoth Steppe, the southern Neanderthals in the Middle East were experiencing a terrible shock. For their new young cousins, the *Homo sapiens*, had arrived.

Chapter 9

'Thinking Man'

The first *Homo sapiens*

All the time archaic humans were exploring Asia and Europe, their *Homo heidelbergensis* cousins were continuing to evolve in Africa. For the first 100,000 years of the Middle Palaeolithic (roughly 300,000–45,000 years ago) the flint technology we used there is termed Levallois. This was essentially the same as the Mousterian technology of the Neanderthals, flaking tools as desired off a pre-prepared flint core. It is named after finds made at Levallois-Perret on the outskirts of Paris, though modern humans in Africa were using this technique long before they reached Europe.

Before *H. sapiens* emerged, there may have been an intermediate species, *Homo helmei*, who lived in Africa after 400,000 years ago and are known from a skull found at Florisbad, South Africa. However, current thinking favours the idea that 'helmei' was simply a late *H. heidelbergensis*, or an early *H. sapiens*.

Towards 200,000 years ago, our African ancestors, under whatever species name we give them, were beset by an intensely cold phase of the Ice Age known as 'Marine Isotope Stage 6', during which so much water was frozen up in the poles that even Africa became cool and arid. Deserts spread and those people who survived at all were isolated from each other in small pockets. In one such pocket, probably in Ethiopia, this harsh environment stimulated a further evolutionary leap forward into our own species: *Homo sapiens*, 'thinking man'.

A new species in an old world

Our understanding of how we *H. sapiens* evolved from early mammals, who had developed, via reptiles, amphibians, fish and worms from single-celled ancestors, is still being modified and improved by new finds and theories. But all the main elements are in place.

Retracing the story and forming a coherent narrative, such as this, is made very difficult by the constant adjustments in dating caused by new research, and by many scientists' determination not to treat the study of the ancient past as a reconstruction of human genealogy. They go to great pains to remind us that we are neither the pinnacle of all evolution, nor the top of the ladder of creation.

Every living thing on the planet is the result of a long line of ancestors that have survived and evolved in equal measure to be here alongside us now. That is correct, but such a scientifically correct view obscures the reasons why we wanted to find all of this out in the first place and it belies our motivation for wanting to continue to learn more – because our interest in all this stems, ultimately, from our own, human quest for self-knowledge.

Our evolutionary story connects us back to all manner of apparently very different life forms, and helps us understand how much we really have in common with each of them. The greater story of human evolution is paralleled by our own, unconscious experience of development in the womb. Floating in our mother's amniotic fluid, each of us started as a single-celled egg, not dissimilar to the simple protozoa from which we are all descended. Within the first few weeks of life we grew, just as we once evolved, into microscopic, multi-celled creatures and we went through a stage when we resembled worms, complete with branchial pouches resembling gill slits. As we developed as a foetus in our mother's womb, we resembled a tiny fish complete with a tail, then an amphibian and then we passed through a stage in which we resembled an early mammal, complete with fur. It is only then that we started to become the recognisably human baby who came screaming into the world. When seen in the light of developing foetuses, we realise that the story of our evolution is one we have each experienced personally, albeit at a very young age.

Our evolutionary story forces us to reassess our place in the world. The legacy of most origin myths, including *Genesis*, was to make us think of ourselves as new arrivals in a world ready-made for our benefit. Many nineteenth- and twentieth-century scientists thought so too: the Jesuit Teilhard de Chardin, one of those who studied Peking Man, believed that 'the phenomena of Man was essentially foreordained [by God] from the beginning'. And Robert Broom, who unearthed our synapsid forebears, wrote, 'Much of evolution looks as if it was planned to result in man, and in other plants and animals to make the world a suitable place for him to dwell in.' And it is true that our own species, as defined by scientists, only appeared about 200,000 years ago, a new species in an ancient world. But 'species' is an artificial line in the sand. Our ancestors 200,000 years ago were simply the latest stage in a continuum of life stretching back to the beginning. We are not interlopers in Eden. Eden had evolved alongside us right from the start.

A great lesson learned from our evolutionary story is how much of the world as we know it now has developed *after* us. We first walked on land as labyrinthodonts long before there were flowering plants or deciduous trees. We were intelligent, burrowing cynodonts while the great limestone and chalk hills of Britain were being formed below warm seas. We were distinctly mammalian long before the first apple trees – the real precursors of the mythical Tree of Knowledge – ever flowered.

It was our human consciousness, which did not perhaps develop fully until about 40,000 years ago, that made us feel so new, like the progeny of Adam and Eve, those first, mythical humans who appeared, blinking with astonishment, in an otherwise fully formed world. And perhaps it was from that impulse of wonder that our earliest spiritual stirrings stemmed in the first place. But 200,000 years ago, that full sense of self-awareness lay far in the future.

Mossel Bay

Perhaps the earliest true *H. sapiens* remains were excavated at Kibish, Ethiopia, in 1967. They are now known to be about 195,000 years old. Other remains have been found at Herto, also in Ethiopia, about 160,000–154,000 years old.

Just as harsh environmental conditions spurred the evolution of our species, so it honed our genetic stock relentlessly. Most early branches of *H. sapiens* must have died off, hence the overall low genetic diversity of our species.

Our surviving ancestors appear to have migrated south. In August 2010, *Scientific American* reported Curtis W. Marean's discovery that Pinnacle Point Cave (PP13B) near Mossel Bay on the southern tip of South Africa had been inhabited by humans from about 164,000 onwards (see plate 11). It may have been one of the very few homes of the tiny handful of our ancestors who survived at that time. They were there when the climate warmed about 125,000 years ago (when the hippos were basking in Trafalgar Square): but it was a false dawn. There was a sudden cold, dry snap about 121,000 years ago, and then about 110,000 years ago the temperature plunged down yet again.

The Ice Age eased again and between about 105,000 and 95,000 years ago the temperature improved, though it remained colder than it is now. There was another drop in temperature about 93,000 years ago, following which the cold again began to ease. But just as things appeared to be looking up for humanity, something terrible happened. About 73,000 years ago, the volcano of Mount Toba in Sumatra erupted. Volcanic ash was blasted high into the Earth's atmosphere. The world was plunged into darkness and the cold returned with a biting vengeance. The Neanderthals only just survived in the north, and in Africa the *H. sapiens* population was driven to the verge of extinction. There were times when the entire human race probably consisted of less than a thousand couples.

African ancestors

Our earliest *H. sapiens* forebears probably looked rather like the San people or Bushmen of southern Africa, the maternal ancestors of Nelson Mandela. They had pale brown skin, which had not yet darkened into the deep black skin of their Bantu descendants, and they had the epithalmic fold over their eyes that the people of East Asia and the Americas retain, but which many others, including Europeans, have lost.

In our refuges in southern Africa, we learned to live off shellfish and starchy roots. We discovered how to fashion sophisticated stone bladelets and to bake silcrete to great temperatures so as to be able to flake it, a process requiring much forward planning and thus implying similarly sophisticated language.

Whatever our early *H. sapiens* ancestors spoke back then was the ancestor of all languages that followed. If you want a Tower of Babel – that point in time suggested by *Genesis*, before which all humans spoke a common language, and after which the languages of the world began to diverge – then here it is, in Africa, 160,000 years ago. Scientists term this basal tongue 'Proto-World' and some of its words can be guessed, for they are widespread throughout the world's diverse tongues. *Mama* and *Papa* are found in different versions all around the globe. Another widespread term is *mak*, used variously for 'child' (Tamil, *maka*; New Guinean, *mak*; Burmese, *mak* or *samak*); 'male' (Teluga *maga*); 'boy' (native American Coto, *ma-make*) or 'son' (native American Waikina *make*; Gaelic, *Mac*). In that last incarnation it is the basis of many Irish and Scottish surnames (i.e., MacDonald means 'son of Donald'). All these variants are probably derived from a word for man or boy used by our southern African ancestors, 160,000 years ago. With a little artistic licence, geneticist Steve Olson even speculated on the words our ancestors who left Africa may have spoken to each other ('Who thinks we should stay? Who thinks we should go across the water?') – *Kun mena mana? Kun mena acqwa?*

One of the most complex languages in the world now is the !Xu language of the San (where the '!' represents a clicking sound). It is not the way our ancestors spoke 160,000 years ago, but its complexity suggests that this language, uniquely, has been evolving *in situ*, undisrupted by migrations, for about that long. It has 141 sounds, including many varieties of clicks (compared to our meagre thirty-one sounds and no clicks at all): it is further evidence that all modern languages began in southern Africa.

Besides the implied use of language, there is evidence that our African ancestors had thoughts beyond the purely utilitarian. As early as 600,000 years ago they occasionally removed the flesh from the skulls of their dead, and there is a definite example of *H. sapiens* doing this at Herto, about 160,000 years ago.

Our southern Africa ancestors used red ochre to decorate themselves, and they collected bright seashells, presumably because they liked the colours. Slightly further west of Mossel Bay, along the coast towards Cape Town, is Blombos Cave, where pieces of red ochre were found covered with geometric engravings, providing clear evidence of an ever more developed pre-frontal cortex in the human brain. None of this proves fully modern human consciousness, which probably emerged later: but it does show that we, then, were well on our way to becoming what we are now.

Chapter 10

The Genetic Adam and Eve

Genetic roots

There was never one couple, 'Adam and Eve', who simply stopped being archaic humans and started being *H. sapiens*. The process of change had been going on gradually for a long time in Africa, though it had perhaps been speeded up by harsh climatic conditions. We must imagine a 'genetic bottleneck', whereby a small group, isolated by geography from the genetic input of more distant relatives, constantly interbred amongst themselves and underwent the collective, subtle change from 'them' into 'us'.

Whilst the fossil record has been of immense importance in our understanding of evolution, what we now know about the early history of our own species owes an immense amount to the new science of genetics. This allows us to draw extraordinarily detailed conclusions about the early human population by identifying genetic signatures that are common to all humanity and that (we can conclude) must have come from our early *H. sapiens* ancestors. And we can all participate directly in genetics through commercially available DNA tests, and discover our own personal links back to the earliest humans.

There were a few false starts. John Beddoe (1826–1911) went about Britain measuring head widths and noting hair and eye colour, and degrees of darkness in skin. He tried to identify certain local 'types' and work out their racial origins. He thought the darkest types, in western Ireland and south-western Britain, were descended not from survivors of the Armada, as was often speculated, but from Phoenician tin traders from Cadiz, or other incomers from Spain or Portugal. (Current thinking, conversely, suggests that dark complexions in the native British might go back to the very earliest Mesolithic inhabitants.)

The discovery of blood types by Karl Landsteiner (1868–1943) in 1901 offered more sophisticated ways of identifying races. He found that many Britons had blood type A, and many Indians had blood type B, offering the possibility (Landsteiner hoped) of distinguishing between those two peoples by that means alone. Arthur Mourant (1904–1994) wrote *The Distribution of the Human Blood Groups* in 1976, hoping to use blood types to identify the true 'cradle of humanity'. But blood types are too few and too widespread to offer anything approaching the definition required for a precise biological history of the human race. A higher-definition view was needed – and, miraculously, one was found in genetics.

Cracking the code

Aristotle, ahead of the game as ever, had realised that sperm somehow sparked life in the womb, but it was William Hervey (1578–1657), who had inherited Francis Bacon's passion for Natural Science, who peered through a newly developed microscope at the wombs of pregnant does culled from Charles I's deer parks and realised that embryos come from eggs: *ex ovo, omnia*, 'everything comes from the egg'.

Nicolas Malebranche (1638–1715) thought that female ovaries were full of infinitely small eggs that had been passed down female lines since God created Eve, whereas Nicolas Hartsoeker (1656–1725) believed that eggs entered the womb with male sperm. By Darwin's time, the selective breeding of domestic animals by the bucolic farmers of England had made it clear, if it had not been before, that both the male sperm and the female egg created embryos, which inherited characteristics from both parents. We now know that eggs and wombs develop in the foetus of female babies, and then await fertilisation by sperm later in life. (This means that, in terms of the egg from which you grew, you have existed not just for your entire lifetime, but also for your mother's entire lifetime as well.)

This understanding of how sexual reproduction works was key to the discovery of genetics by Gregor Mendel (1822–1884). Breeding and cross-fertilising generations of peas and bees in his monastery garden in Brünn, Moravia, Mendel gained a considerable understanding of the mechanism that underpinned this system of inheritance. But it was not until the early twentieth century that his work was synthesised with Darwin's law of natural selection by William Bateson (1861–1926). Bateson coined the term 'genetics' (from the Greek *genesis*, 'origin') and achieved a basic understanding of the role of genes in creating new and ever evolving life.

In 1910, Thomas Hunt Morgan established that genes were arranged on chromosomes, which were composed of protein and deoxyribonucleic acid, abbreviated to 'DNA'. In 1953 Francis Crick and James D. Watson of Cambridge University discovered the double-helix structure of DNA, and unlocked the actual working of genetic inheritance. By showing that humans and apes share most of our genes in common, and how many we both share with other creatures, from frogs to fruit flies, genetics provided the final, absolute proof that the theory of evolution was correct. It also makes us stop and think, again and again, about our own identity in relation to other species. If you look at our family trees purely in terms of the genes that determine blood groups, for example, each of us is more closely related to those gorillas and chimpanzees that share the genes for our own blood type than we are to other humans who have different blood types.

The application of genetics to population studies, and thus to the human family tree, was pioneered in the 1960s by Luigi Luca Cavalli-Sforza (b. 1922). He analysed DNA samples from people around the world and found that localised populations had distinct genetic profiles. He then tried to work out how these genetically distinct groups might be related to each other by analysing those genes that they had in common. Cavalli-Sforza's work is comparable to the leap in understanding from the *scala naturae* to Haeckel's Tree of Life. It established a definitive family tree for the human race.

In recent times, genetics has completely transformed the way we see our world and our origins. Within my lifetime the hotly debated question of whether *H. sapiens* evolved in Africa or independently in different parts of the world has been settled decisively by genetics in favour of Africa, though now the discoveries of strands of archaic human DNA in some modern humans suggests a more complex story than had been imagined before. Just in the years during which I have been gathering material for this book, new genetic discoveries have forced me to go back and rewrite whole sections of it several times. Doubtless the process of genetic discovery will continue – and all to the good, as we grow ever closer to understanding the truth about our origins.

How genetics works

Most of the genes we receive from our fathers' sperm and our mothers' eggs are delivered randomly. The gene for your dark hair or blue eyes may have come from one parent or the other, and they in turn may have received it from either their father or mother. This makes it impossible to extrapolate back up the family tree to determine from which of your many lines of ancestors such a gene may have been inherited. But two genes are exceptions to this: the Y chromosome (Y-DNA) and mitochondrial DNA (mt-DNA).

Y chromosomes are what makes a child male. They have been passing down from father to son for about 1,200 million years, when sexual reproduction began amongst our single-celled ancestors. Women do not carry Y chromosomes (or else they would be men) but their fathers, brothers and other male-line relatives do, so if you are a woman, you can have such a male relative tested on your behalf.

We all have mitochondrial DNA. It is not animal DNA at all, but a bacteria that lives within each cell of our bodies, using oxygen to generate and store energy. It has been living and reproducing within our cells ever since it first entered our single-celled eukaryotic ancestors, some 2,100 million years ago. It is passed on from mother to child in the egg: we all inherit mitochondria from our mothers, but only women pass it on to their offspring.

During the process termed myosis, which generates sperm and egg, genes are reproduced. Sometimes the process is faulty, giving rise to single nucleotide polymorphisms (SNPs) and single tandem repeats (STRs). The mutations that concern us here are the SNPs within the Y chromosome and the mitochondrial DNA. Once a mutation has arisen, it remains and is passed on to all the subsequent descendants of the person in whom it first appeared. Everyone with a specific SNP is said to belong to a haplogroup. Within one haplogroup, a fresh SNP may arise, resulting in a subgroup. Analysis of SNPs therefore allows geneticists to construct two immense, parallel family trees of life, one of Y chromosome haplogroups and one of mitochondrial DNA haplogroups. Whilst all developed animal life fits into these trees, the distinctions between haplogroups become most meaningful when applied to the two great family trees of life as produced by genetics – one of the human race as defined by mitochondrial DNA and the other as defined by the Y chromosome.

Using simple DNA tests with firms such as Family Tree DNA you can discover your SNP markers. By doing so you will contribute to our growing understanding of these genetic family trees, and you will learn your own place within them.

These two great family trees are only two out of many ways of identifying ourselves amongst the great mass of humanity, but it just so happens that they conform to the two most traditional ways of doing so. Many hunter-gatherer societies defined their family relationships in terms of female lines and this practice survived in some peoples well into historical times – the Picts in Scotland, for example, built their society around a line of hereditary queens until the 800s AD. As the Bronze Age set in, however, many tribes and city-based civilisations switched to defining themselves by the male line. Surnames started becoming hereditary in male lines at different times around the world: in the British Isles the process began about a thousand years ago.

Therefore, the two genetic family trees of humanity correspond to two social phenomena: mitochondrial DNA defines the female line, the old way of defining human society, and the Y chromosome corresponds to the male line, which is also usually the line down which surnames are inherited.

The genetic Adam and Eve

Geneticists have studied male and female line SNPs from across the world. By finding those that everyone has in common, as opposed to those that are unique to populations in certain parts of the world, and by estimating how long ago such SNPs arose, geneticists have drawn several conclusions about our earliest *H. sapiens* ancestors.

First, there was certainly a genetic bottleneck at the time when our species arose. With only a few exceptions, which we will encounter later in the story, everyone's male and female lines go back to that one little group of people who survived in Africa about 200,000 years ago.

The group probably started with a number of separate female lineages, each descended from earlier female lines of archaic human ancestors, but as time wore on the harsh climate killed off each of these lineages until only one survived. Therefore, we are all descended, through our mothers' mothers, from the same female-line ancestor. Judging by the diversity of the female haplogroups derived from this line, this woman is thought to have lived about 140,000 years ago – quite possibly in the Mossel Bay cave. She was first identified by geneticist Allan Wilson in 1986. The press (starting with *Newsweek* in January 1988), ever keen to mythologise science, dubbed this woman 'the mitochondrial Eve' (see plate 12). At the time she lived, there may have been other female-line lineages still surviving, but they were not destined to last. Eve's mitochondrial DNA would not in itself have bestowed any particular evolutionary advantage upon her, but perhaps she happened to have other advantages in other genes – or maybe her lineage's unique survival was down to pure chance.

Under Antonio Torrini's alphabetical classification, Eve's mitochondrial DNA has been classified L (and specifically LO*, which means 'L' without any sub-haplogroups). We all carry this SNP and some people in Africa still carry it without any of the subsequent mutations that identify other haplogroups. The oldest subsequent mutations that arose amongst descendants of Eve are coded L1, L2 and L3 (see chart on page 91). The former are found mostly in Africa and everyone outside Africa carries L3 and further mutations: we shall return to the story of the exodus from Africa later.

In the early *H. sapiens* group, the men probably belonged to several ancient male (Y chromosome) lineages. They interbred with Eve and her female-line descendants. Over the millennia, however, the harshness of the climate led to the male lineages gradually dying out. About 80,000 years ago (though estimates vary hugely) there lived a man who, by complete chance, became the only man whose male line was destined to survive. His existence was first reasoned in 1997 by Mike Hammer and (independently) by Peter Underhill. He has been dubbed, inevitably, the 'Genetic Adam' (see plate 12). Unlike the biblical Adam, he lived long after Eve and was almost certainly descended from her.

Descended from Eve, too, must have been Adam's partner or partners, and the partners of his sons. In the aftermath of the Mount Toba eruption, Adam's male-line descendants spread, and it so happens that nobody else's did, so in time Adam's genetic signature became unique amongst *H. sapiens*.

Y chromosomes mutate much more easily than mitochondrial DNA, so it did not take long for new SNPs to appear amongst his descendants. This is an extremely active area of research. Every day new people are being tested, new SNPs are being discovered, and theories about when and where the male-line haplogroups emerged are being adjusted. Any attempt to incorporate these findings into a narrative like this is rather like building a castle upon shifting sands, but as with other scientific findings, genetic evidence is only of any genuine value to us if it contributes to the story of who we are, so I have done my best.

Confusingly, the same letters of the alphabet have been chosen to designate both female line mt-DNA haplogroups and also male-line Y chromosome haplogroups. We must bear in mind that 'L' or 'A' in one tree means something completely different to 'L' or 'A' in the other. To denote subgroups, the system A1, A2, and then A1a, A1b, A2a, A2b, etc was devised. Because this system is confusing and sometimes changes due to modification as the science grows ever more sophisticated, SNPs are also given unique codes, such as L986 and P305 (where the initial letter has nothing to do with the alphabetical letters used to denote the haplogroups). Many writers have abandoned the A1, A2 system altogether now and simply refer to haplogroups by the initial letter, so A1, as defined by the genetic marker L986, can also be written A1 (L986). Different laboratories sometimes code the same marker differently, so L986 in one laboratory is P305 in another, hence A1 (L986/P305). Geneticists have unlocked an amazing amount of knowledge, but they have not always made it very easy for everyone to understand it.

The mention in the next paragraphs of so many haplogroups with their SNP markers looks, and is, confusing. But, as with all DNA results, they will become more meaningful once you have had a test yourself and know your own haplogroup. At that point, the story becomes very personal indeed.

Adam's immediate male-line descendants had one of two markers, A0 (L991) and A1 (L986/P305), with numerous descendants amongst the Bakola Pygmies of the Cameroons and a handful of Berbers and Ghanaians. From an early carrier of A1 (L985/P305) descended A1a (M31) and A1b (P108). From A1b (P108) descended A1b1 (L419), all with predominantly African descendants, and BT (M91/M42), which may have emerged about 60,000 years ago, probably in north-eastern Africa.

From BT (M91/M42) there branched off B (M60), which accounts for many more Africans south of the Sahara, and CT (M168), very likely in Ethiopia. This CT lineage then branched quickly into DE (M145/P205) and CF (P143). From DE, emerged haplogroups D (M174) and E (M40). Many descendants of the E haplogroup remained in Africa, becoming ancestors of many black Africans who are not A or B.

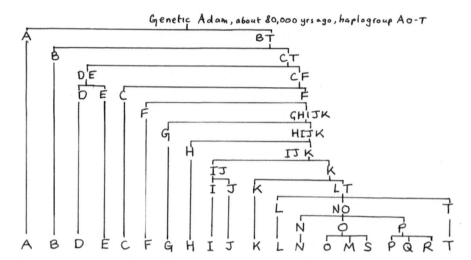

The family tree of humanity as defined by the male-line Y chromosome. It is slightly altered from the way it was a few years ago and doubtless in a few years' time it will have been modified further.

It is from the others, CF and D that most non-Africans are descended, and to whose story we shall return soon.

Sapiens vs erectus

The catastrophic aftermath of the Mount Toba eruption, 73,000 years ago, helped hone our early *H. sapiens* genetic lineages. It may also have helped us by killing off some of our competing, archaic human cousins. For there were probably still surviving *H. erectuses* in Africa. John Shea likened them to being like 'wolves with knives'. Formidably strong, a pack of erectuses armed with hand axes must have instilled terror into their *H. sapiens* cousins.

However, recent studies of archaic humans like erectus suggest that many suffered from tapeworms, and ate so much raw liver that they had an excess of vitamin A, which leads to brittle bones. That was a particularly serious problem for them because their method of hunting involved physical contact with their prey, so many bones were fractured or broken. Also, their bulky arms could not bend like ours: we can throw overarm but they could not. Our *H. sapiens* ancestors quickly developed slingshots and spears that we could throw overarm, enabling us to kill our prey – and perhaps erectuses too – from a distance. Before long, the archaic species from which we had evolved were dwindling away towards eventual extinction, whilst *H. sapiens* flourished and our genetic lineages spread right across Africa – and beyond.

Chapter 11

Out of Africa

The clouds of ash from Mount Toba sent the temperature tumbling down into the Lower Pleniglacial period, which lasted until about 60,000 years ago. Then there was then a slight warming and in northern Europe the snow gave way to cold, arid steppe land, but not for long. The next 25,000 years, from 60,000 to 35,000 years ago, saw a very unstable climate, cycling between temperatures little worse than today, and the bitterest extremes of the Ice Age – sudden bursts of intense cold known as Heinrich Events. Within a short lifetime, a Neanderthal living in Europe might see the forests he had grown up in destroyed and the sunny days of his childhood lost in a bitter blizzard of freezing snow.

It was during this period of unpredictable climate change that our *H. sapiens* ancestors made their first tentative steps out of Africa. As with the archaic humans who had trodden the same path before, they were not intrepid explorers setting off on a long journey. They just happened be in the parts of Africa closest to Asia. The ever expanding Sahara probably stopped them going south or west, the Mediterranean lay to the north, so going east was the only option. Perhaps they managed to cross the narrow 'Gates of Grief' at the bottom of the Red Sea, so as to enter the then very green and fertile Yemen, or they might otherwise have walked across the Sinai Peninsula. Either way, they reached the Middle East.

Such a migration may have happened more than once. *H. sapiens* remains have been found in the caves of Qafzeh-Skhul, Israel, dating back to perhaps 100,000 years ago – new neighbours for the Neanderthals already living there. But that is thought to have been a false start. The main migration, from whose participants all *H. sapiens* living outside Africa are descended, is thought to have taken place, very roughly, about 55,000 years ago.

This estimate is based mainly on genetics. Out of the early mitochondrial DNA female line haplogroups, only L3 and its descendant haplogroups is found in any significant quantity outside Africa, so we conclude that the early migrants probably belonged to this group. As to the Y chromosomes carried by the male migrants, they probably belonged to haplogroup CF (P143), from which almost everyone outside Africa is descended. Related to this group was D (M174), which is found in Africa and also in some numbers outside it. Maybe men carrying D left at the same time as those carrying CF, or more likely, it has been suggested, they left separately, a little later. The distribution of D outside Africa is highly suggestive of a journey, for it snakes around the Asian coast into southern India and the Andaman Islands, where it accounts for many of the darker-skinned peoples there.

The estimate of *when* the migration(s) took place is less precise. Geneticists have estimated how often new mutations occur: about once every 3,500 years for mitochondrial DNA and much more frequently for the Y chromosome, and it is on such estimates that the 55,000-year date is based. Archaeologists, climate experts, linguists and others have all played a significant part in refining such estimates, so it is hardly surprising that this date is not agreed upon universally and the trend has been to push it ever further backwards. But few now disagree that there were one or two very small but highly significant *H. sapiens* migrations out of Africa, which account for the population of the rest of the world.

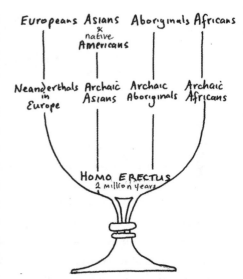

A model of the now discredited Candelabra Theory, showing how different races could have evolved separately.

'Out of Africa' vs the Candelabra Theory

Chris Stringer coined the phrase 'out of Africa' for this model of humans spreading out from a common origin in Africa about 55,000 years ago. It has also been mythologised as the 'Garden or Eden' theory – where 'Eden' is the east or south of Africa. But before genetics came of age this 'out of Africa' theory had a serious contender in the form of the Multiregional or Candelabra Theory.

The idea that modern humans evolved in Africa and then spread out to colonise the rest of the world has its problems. Psychologically, it is more comforting to be told that your ancestors had lived where you now live, than to learn that your ancestral homeland is far away, so Europeans and Asians found it difficult to adjust to the idea of having African roots. Racism played its part too: it was of course impossible for Europeans and Asians to deny any relationship to black Africans at all, but some theorists were keen to push this connection as far back into the distant past as possible.

The background to such devisive theories lies in the eighteenth century, when Linnaeus divided *H. sapiens* into five distinct sub-species. Following this, Louis Agassiz (1801–1873) envisaged five biblical Adams, one for each race, with his own, Western Adam being the one who was mentioned in *Genesis*. Then, in the

Darwinian era, Karl Vogt, in *Lectures on Man* (1864), proposed that gorillas, orang-utans and chimpanzees had evolved into Africans, Asians and Europeans respectively. That was too much, but Franz Weidenreich (1873–1948) suggested that the different archaic human populations on different continents had evolved independently into the modern humans of those regions. The idea was reaffirmed by Charles Carleton Coon (1904–1981) and again by Milford Wolphoff (b. 1942). This theory, termed the 'Candelabra Theory', suggested that the human family tree looks like a candelabra, with several very long branches connected to a base. It proposed that humanity fell into four or five races, originating in Australasia, Mongolia, the Caucasus and Africa (some theories posited two 'races' in Africa). Each race was descended from the archaic human population that had lived in those regions earlier, so were only very distantly related to each other. The Caucasians of Europe and Asia were descended from the early archaic humans (*H. Heidelbergensis* and their Neanderthal descendants) who had lived there. They could regard themselves as distinct from (and superior to) the rest.

The Candelabra Theory was equally popular in China, where the notion of a direct ancestral link back to Peking Man seemed to root the Chinese deeply in their own soil and upheld their own notion of exclusiveness and superiority. The Africans and Aboriginals would probably have been glad to distance themselves from other races by the same argument, but as they tended to be victims rather than beneficiaries of racism it behoved them better to argue for the 'brotherhood of man'.

But the theory was badly flawed, and evidence against it and in favour of 'out of Africa' has mounted up. The discovery of the 'Hobbits' of Flores was important, because it showed how, in one case at least, descendants of archaic humans had evolved into diminutive archaic humans and had *not* transformed seamlessly into the modern human population of Southeast Asia. From the 1970s onwards, also, genetics has shown how closely related all *H. sapiens* really are. The branching haplotrees of humanity as defined by the Y chromosome and mitochondrial DNA show that everyone shares the same SNPs as Africans, but all non-Africans share extra SNPs that are not found in Africa, proving that they descend from a tiny handful of migrants who came 'out of Africa' a mere 55,000 years ago.

Many white-skinned Europeans are still adjusting to this fact: as one white American correspondent of mine put it, 'Depending on what you believe, we're either descended from Africans according to science, or Middle Easterns [i.e., Noah *et al*] according to religion. Most people believe in one or the other. Yet [some white] people *still* deny having dark-skinned ancestry.'

There is in fact yet more genetic proof for the 'out of Africa' theory. That is based on very recent findings that suggest what happened when that tiny number of dark-skinned modern humans first left Africa, and encountered the Neanderthals.

Chapter 12

My Great-grandfather, the Neanderthal

Encounters with Neanderthals

The shock must have been enormous. In *The Grisly Folk* (1921), H.G. Wells envisaged our tall, intelligent *H. sapiens* ancestors drifting out of 'the lost lands of the Mediterranean valley' (for in truth he had no idea where they had come from). As they travelled north they caught 'glimpses of lurking semi-human shapes and grey forms that ran in the twilight.' These were the Neanderthals, who 'walked or shambled along with a peculiar slouch, they could not turn their heads up to the sky ... these earlier so-called men were not of our blood, not our ancestors, but a strange and vanished animal, like us, akin to us, but different from us ... perhaps bristly or hairy in some queer inhuman fashion.' 'We cannot conceive in our different minds,' Wells told his readers, 'the strange ideas that chased one another through those queerly shaped brains.'

There was probably much competition for food, and violence, yet finds around Qafzeh-Skhul, Tabun and Kebara in Israel suggest that modern humans and Neanderthals lived in caves quite close to each other, on and off, from about 50,000 to 30,000 years ago. If so, scientists wondered, had they ever interbred? Psychologically, it was a difficult question because, whilst modern Europeans were drawn to the idea that the older inhabitants of Europe were their ancestors, the Neanderthals had also acquired a reputation for crude ugliness, not least because of the writings of H.G. Wells, which made them less desirable to have as forebears. At different times the English attributed Neanderthal origins to the Irish; the French claimed that the Germans were Neanderthals in jackboots and Afrocentrists levelled similar slurs against all Europeans in general.

But as the decades have passed we have learned how well-adapted Neanderthals were to their icy environment and how their lives were not much different to their *H. sapiens* cousins. Europeans have become fascinated with the idea of having some Neanderthal blood. In the 1980s, school parties used to visit a pair of odd-looking brothers living in a cottage near Tregaron, Ceredigion, Wales, who were known as the 'Tregaron Neanderthals' and who were fondly imagined to have had Neanderthal blood in their veins.

That was a red herring, but in 1999 a boy was found carefully buried in Lagar Velho cave, Portugal. His remains were about 24,000 years old. He was wrapped in an ochre-coloured shroud and wore a shell pendant. He had *H. sapiens* bone structure, but with some distinctly Neanderthal features. Was this evidence of interbreeding? Maybe, but geneticists at the time denied that any interbreeding between humans and Neanderthals had taken place.

Neanderthal genes

Then, in 2010, Svante Pääbo and his colleagues extracted DNA from the remains of three female Neanderthals from a cave in Croatia, about 40,000 years old. They published the first draft of a Neanderthal genome in *Science* on 7 May 2010. Further, they announced that 'between 1 and 4 per cent of the genomes of people in Eurasia are derived from Neanderthals.'

In one stroke they redrew our human family tree. The African branch of the tree remained unchanged. But whilst the ancestry of humans outside Africa still goes back to the first African *H. sapiens* up the direct male and female lines, and up many other ancestral lines too, we also have a line or two going back to Neanderthals. Through the ice-driven roamings of hunter-gatherer bands across Europe, the Neanderthals of Oldbury Hill (see plate 9), Creswell Crags and Pontnewydd may have been direct ancestors of the later, *H. sapiens* population of Britain.

Pääbo's findings were intriguing. 'A striking observation is that Neanderthals are as closely related to a Chinese and Papuan individual as to a French individual. ... Thus, the gene flow between Neanderthals and modern humans that we detect most likely occurred before the divergence of Europeans, East Asians and Papuans.'

For such a pattern to have occurred, the one or more sexual encounters that caused it must have occurred soon after the human migration out of Africa, perhaps in the caves of Israel. The resulting half Neanderthal, half *H. sapiens* child or children must then have interbred with their *H. sapiens* relatives, causing their Neanderthal genes to spread into all the *H. sapiens* population outside Africa, which then proceeded to spread around the world.

In terms of genetic haplogroups, the mixed-race descendants were interbreeding with pure *H. sapiens* who probably belonged (by inference) to the male-line genetic haplogroup CF (P143), and the female line haplogroup L3. As it so happened, the Neanderthal input did not supplant either lineage. This can have happened in a number of simple ways. A male Neanderthal, say, may have produced a mixed-race son, whose partner was a *H. sapiens* female, by whom the son had only daughters, who bred with *H. sapiens* men. The descendants would therefore have had some Neanderthal genes, but not in the direct male or female lines.

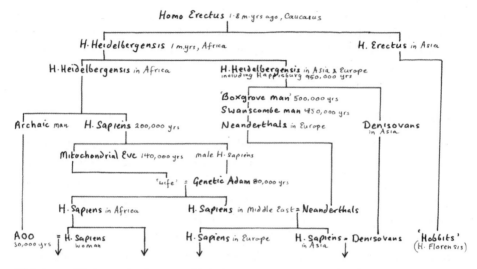

This is roughly how scientists now think the human family tree has developed over the last 2 million years. Throughout there may have been occasional interbreeding between the different lines.

The implications of Neanderthal genes

Now we know the Neanderthal genome, we can compare ourselves with them. Small differences become apparent, in the genes associated with speech and the nervous system, for instance. Knowing such small differences between us and them allows us better to define what makes us uniquely *H. sapiens*. By the same token, Neanderthal genes and skills in making warm clothes and hunting in cold climates may have helped the 'out of Africa' humans to cope better with the harsh conditions of Asia and Europe.

The discovery of interbreeding raises new questions. If Neanderthals could breed successfully with *H. sapiens*, then perhaps the very idea that we are one species and they were another is wrong. Some scientists are now wondering whether both we and the Neanderthals were simply two branches of the same much older human species. Maybe we should reclassify ourselves as advanced forms of *H. heidelbergensis* – or redraw the family tree completely and label *H. heidelbergensis* as an early type of *H. sapiens*. That is a debate yet to be settled.

Further lines of archaic descent

If modern humans interbred with Neanderthals outside Africa, might a similar phenomenon have occurred in Africa, where there may still have been a few archaic human lines hanging on alongside *H. sapiens*? In 2012 Chris Stringer found evidence of archaic human genes in the Iwo Eleru people of Nigeria, suggesting that interbreeding had taken place as recently as 35,000 years ago. But, like the Neanderthal genes in the Eurasian population, these archaic genes happened not to be in the direct male or female lines, those defined by the Y chromosome and mitochondrial DNA. In terms of these two genes, every person tested was *H. sapiens*.

But then, late in 2012, an African American man living in South Carolina had a routine commercial Y chromosome DNA test, and an extraordinary result emerged. On the basis of other (STR) markers it was known that his male-line ancestry was from the Mbo people of the Cameroons, but in terms of his SNP markers this same male line went right back an astonishing 300,000 years before it found a common ancestry with the ancestors of all other *H. sapiens*. His was a newly discovered non-*H. sapiens* haplogroup. Whilst virtually all this man's DNA was *H. sapiens*, it just so happens that his Y chromosome was from an older species. It required a new classification: the oldest *H. sapiens* haplogroup was classified A. If there was a letter in the alphabet before A they would have used it, but instead they had to call it A00 (though really it was off the alphabetical scale entirely). About 35,000 years ago, it seems, somewhere in western Africa, a *H. sapiens* woman met an archaic human male, and they had a son, who interbred with a *H. sapiens* woman. In each generation the descendants became ever more *H. sapiens* and ever less archaic, but down the male line passed that telltale archaic Y chromosome, father to son, first in Africa and then, transplanted by slavery, in America.

This was the first such story to be uncovered but now scientists know where to look and doubtless many more will emerge. Maybe one day soon a Eurasian will be tested who has a Neanderthal Y chromosome. And what an exciting day that will be.

Colonising the world

The genetic profile of the world is immensely complex, so extrapolating back to work out what the genetic profiles of the early colonisers of Asia, Europe and beyond may have been is fraught with difficulty, not least because the scientists studying the individual haplogroups are constantly refining their ideas. But let us attempt a general outline.

Soon after they first reached the Middle East and interbred with Neanderthals, the main 'out of Africa' male line, bearing the male-line genetic marker CF (P143), seems to have split into haplogroup C (M130) and haplogroup F (M89). These were not so much physical splits in population groups as genetic markers that arose within the small human population milling about the region. Within one band there were probably men with each marker, quite unaware of the genetic distinction between them. But as bands spread out, it might make sense for one man with his sons to go one way and another man with his sons to go another, so when a new genetic maker arose in one of those lineages, it might ultimately spread out to become the distinctive male line genetic marker of the new population of a whole region of the world.

Aside from the probably separate migration into southern India and the Andaman Islands by people belonging to haplogroup D, the main colonists of Asia belonged to groups C and F and their derivative subgroups.

With so much water locked up as ice in the vastly enlarged polar regions, Ice Age sea levels were much lower than today. Having reached south-eastern Asia, modern humans could make most of the journey to Australia on dry land. There was only 60 miles of sea to cross. Perhaps a makeshift log boat was being used for fishing and it was swept away south by a storm. The genes of the early colonists probably included one or more man carrying the male sub-haplogroup C (M347) (an offshoot of the main haplogroup C (M130)), and females carrying mitochondrial haplogroups M and Q.

A problem of dating seemed to arise here, for an ochre-covered skeleton found at Lake Mungo, New South Wales, was once thought to date from about 68,000 years ago. In that case it had to be from an earlier human migration that had ultimately come to grief. But now the consensus is for a date of about 42,000 years ago, which fits well with the story of the human dispersal around the globe after 55,000 years ago.

The term 'Aboriginal' for the native peoples of Australia is, of course, a misnomer, for it indicates a people who have always lived in the same place (it was used originally by the Romans for the Latin people, who were believed to have been autochthones, born from the Italian soil). The Australian Aboriginals may have been none too pleased when geneticists informed them that they were immigrants. But in fact, as Bruce Chatwin wrote presciently in *The Songlines* (1987), their own traditions seemed to recall the very event of their arrival, for many songlines (paths recorded in traditional songs) 'appear to enter the country from the north or the north-west – from across the Timor Sea or the Torres Straight – and from there weave their way southwards across the continent. One has the impression that they represent the routes of the first Australians – and that they came from *somewhere else.*'

Meanwhile, the rest of Asia was colonised by other roaming bands of hunter-gatherers. In terms of male-line genes, these were mainly subgroups of C (M130), and haplogroups descended from F (M89). Whilst F (M89) is now rather rare in its original form and found mainly in India, it was the ancestor of G (M201), which probably emerged in the Caucasus about 46,000 years ago; and of H (M69), which may have appeared about 42,000 years ago and is particularly common now in India; and of IJK (L15), which had probably emerged in south-western Asia (perhaps Iran) about 44,000 years ago. From IJK there quickly emerged two new subgroups, IJ (M429), maybe in Iran about 40,000 years ago, and K (M9), perhaps in the same region.

From K there soon appeared three new branches: L (M20), mainly found in Iran and India; T (M184), mainly found in western Asia; and NO (M214), which emerged about 35,000 years ago, somewhere near the Aral Sea (on the border of modern Kazakhstan and Uzbekistan). The NO lineage split into three: P (P295); N (M251), common in northern Asia and O (M175) mainly in eastern Asia (from which emerged later groups M (P256) and S (M230), commonest in Papua New Guinea). P (P295) emerged in central Asia and from it came the last two of the major male-line haplogroups, Q (M242) and R (M207), destined to become the commonest in Europe.

Amongst the genes that are now very common in Asia is the genetic marker C (M217). This is thought also to have been the genetic sub-haplogroup to which Genghis Khan (d. AD 1227) and his Mongol horde belonged. They spread this marker throughout Asia through their pillaging, extinguishing many other male lineages with their swords at the same time.

Papua New Guinea was colonised from Indonesia, considerably later than mainland Asia. Haplogroups M, S, C (M338) and C (P55) were amongst the male-line markers of the intrepid mariners who did so, and the main female line groups were E and Q. It was only in about 1500 BC that descendants of some of these colonisers developed the double-hulled boats that would take them further, to the Solomon Islands and Fiji, reaching Hawaii by about AD 500 and New Zealand by about AD 1000.

The Denisovans

The humans of various genetic lineages who penetrated into south-eastern Asia had a surprise when they encountered another branch of the human family tree, the Denisovans.

The Denisovans were descendants of *H. Heidelbergensis*, and had diverged from the lineage that led to the Neanderthals about 640,000 years ago. We do not know the extent of their range because so far their remains – a girl's finger bone, a toe bone and two molars, about 50,000 years old – have been found only in the Denisova cave in the Altai Mountains on the border between Russia and Mongolia, about 200 miles north of Calcutta.

When they were found in 2008, the remains were assumed to be Neanderthal. But because of the very constant, cold climate in the cave the girl's genes had survived. When Svante Pääbo sequenced her genome in 2010, he reported to *Nature* (vol. 468, issue 7327) that it was so distinct from Neanderthals as to be effectively a new species or, at least, a distinct new branch of our human family tree. The genes reveal too that the Denisovan girl had brown hair, brown skin and brown eyes.

Once the Denisovan genome was known, traces of it have been found throughout the modern human population of Southeast Asia and the Aboriginal Australians. People in these regions have up to 3 per cent Denisovan genes. As they (like Europeans) also have up to 4 per cent Neanderthal genes, it means that some people from these regions have up to 8 per cent non-*H. sapiens* genes.

The Denisova cave had been used at different times by Denisovans and modern humans. There had clearly been interbreeding in the early days of the *H. sapiens* colonisation of eastern Asia – quite possibly in the Denisova cave itself. Perhaps, geneticists are now speculating, Denisovan genes helped incoming modern humans to cope with some of the many diseases to be found in south-eastern Asia.

In 2013, a small dose of Denisovan DNA was found in the 400,000-year-old bones of Atapuerca in Spain, suggesting that at least some Denisovans had migrated west, too – unless they had appeared in the west and migrated east. But, unlike in Asia, this dose has not been passed into the subsequent population of Europe.

The Americas

Meanwhile, some hunter-gatherer bands wandered north-east, benefitting from the low sea levels that had created a land bridge where the Bering Straits are now. They entered the Americas, reaching the Delmarva Peninsula in Maryland by about 26,000 years ago, using the rock shelter at Meadowcroft, Pennsylvania, about 12,500 years ago, and then penetrating south. (It was once thought that people had reached Brazil by 32,000 years ago, but the dating that led to that conclusion has apparently been discredited.)

America may have been settled by several groups. The first group spread the Amerind group of languages and the second, later group spread the Na-Dene group of languages. The predominant male-line genetic haplogroups of these settlers were C (M217) and Q (M242). The main female haplogroups associated with this original peopling of America were A (which is particularly common amongst Eskimos), B, D and C (and here let us remember again that letters of the alphabet were used, very confusingly, to code both male and female haplogroups, and denote different groups in the two trees).

For the most part, the peopling of the world, like our ancestors' departure from Africa, was the result of the wanderings of bands of hunter-gatherers who made their individual journeys in pursuit of food and shelter. That these journeys – when combined over generations – resulted in long-scale migrations was unknown to them. If they thought about their movements at all they probably assumed their ancestors had always been roaming around broadly the same area that was their world. Had they been shown their ancestors' journeys on a world map, and learned for how long they had been travelling, they would probably have felt sick with shock.

Slowly, Asia, Australia and the Americas were colonised. But there was one more region to be conquered, in which the most extraordinary developments would take place, and in which we now lay our scene: Europe.

Part Three

Book of Ice

Chapter 13

Our Crô-Magnon Family Tree

The Aurignacian phase (45,000 to 28,000 years ago)

Our ancestors roamed the icy steppes of Asia, hunting reindeer, fending off wolves and hyenas in order to scavenge the carcasses of larger creatures. Always on the horizon, dark against the white, snow-filled skies, was the lumbering presence of mammoths.

On the steppes they honed their technological skills, from the construction of skin-covered, mammoth bone shelters, to the manufacture of bone-carved burins and fine-pointed needles used to make well-fitting fur clothes, which would also be necessary for their descendants to survive the freezing conditions of Ice Age Europe. How much of these abilities they developed for themselves, and how much they learned from Neanderthals and Denisovans, we do not know.

As they strode towards the setting sun they unknowingly entered eastern Europe and the period we term the Upper Palaeolithic (45,000–11,500 years ago). It happened about 45,000 years ago, though estimates vary by several thousands of years. Once in Europe, science calls our ancestors 'Early European Modern Humans'. But the Victorian term was 'Crô-Magnon', and this retains a potent sense of the ancient, the mysterious, perhaps even the frightening, and evokes a world that seems profoundly alien, yet to which we are intimately connected.

The culture of these first modern human occupants of Europe is termed Aurignacian, after the Aurignac cave in Haute-Garonne on the northern edge of the Pyrenees, first explored by Édouard Lartet in 1860. The culture lasted from about 45,000 to 28,000 years ago, though some argue that Aurignacian culture dates back to when the ancestors of the Europeans were still roaming the Asian steppes.

In some ways they were newcomers, Asians of African descent, but through the interbreeding of their out-of-Africa ancestors with Neanderthals in the Middle East, and perhaps through the earlier interbreeding of the Eurasian and Africa *H. Erectus* and *H. Heidelbergensis* populations, they probably had lines of ancestry going back to the earlier peoples of Europe – they who had lived at Swanscombe, Boxgrove, Pakefield and Happisburgh up to a million years earlier. And further back in their evolutionary story, their ancestors had been the furry, tree-dwelling protomonkeys like Ida who had lived in the European forests, 47 million years ago. So in some senses, they were not newcomers at all, but descendants of Europe's earlier inhabitants, returning back home.

Whose ancestors are they?

From this point onwards, this book will focus ever more closely on Britain and the story of its inhabitants. For much of the Ice Age, however, Britain was uninhabitable, so the ancestors of its later inhabitants lived further south in the refuges of central Europe and central France – and it is there that their story lies.

Here the gap between what most of us know about our ancestry, and the true nature of that ancestry, becomes relevant. In 1999, the statistical work of Joseph T. Chang, a statistician at the University of Yale, resulted in an influential paper called *Recent Common Ancestors of All Present-Day Individuals*. Through a complex series of equations, Chang concluded that everyone alive in AD 1200 who has *any* known descendants alive today must in fact be ancestors of *everyone* now living, through one ancestral line or another.

His paper caused quite a stir. Maybe he was correct statistically, but could the blood of an Australian Aboriginal in AD 1200 really have reached western Ireland by today, or the blood of a Hebridean Viking in AD 1200 have made its way to the Congo? It only takes a little population movement to make the answer 'yes', but it still seems rather unlikely in all cases. Therefore, subsequent conservative estimates have pushed the date back from 1200, but only as far as AD 300.

Therefore, whilst the rest of this book focuses on Britain, there can be no doubt, on the basis of Chang's statistics as well as common sense that, from the Arctic to Africa and India to South America, and regardless of where the bulk of their genes come from, *everyone* alive now has at least a small proportion of genes from the Upper Palaeolithic inhabitants of Ice Age Europe.

Discovering the Ice Age

The exploration of our ancestral past in Ice Age Europe started, effectively, with the discovery of Neanderthal bones in Germany in 1856. Since then it has continued unabated and new finds are being made yearly. The story of this exploration runs parallel to the broader story of the discovery of our evolution from the dawn of life to the first appearance of modern man. In many ways it is a microcosm of that greater story, focused more closely on our own, immediate forebears.

Although the Ice Age held Europe in its grip for so long, it was not widely known about until the mid-nineteenth century. It was first deduced through eighteenth-century studies of glaciation in the Alps, made by the likes of the German dramatist

Goethe (1749–1832) and the Scandinavian geologist Jens Esmark (1763–1839). Instead of imagining the Earth as having cooled gradually since its formation, Esmark realised that temperatures had fluctuated enormously and included ages of immense cold. His theory was championed by Louis Agassiz, whose 1840 *Study on Glaciers*, backed up by extensive fieldwork undertaken with William Buckland in Scotland, provided firm proof that there had been several Ice Ages.

Once it was understood that Europe had had an Ice Age at all, nineteenth-century enthusiasts started exploring the rock shelters and caves that our ancestors may have used to survive, and developed archaeological techniques for finding, studying and categorising the human remains they discovered there. In the process they discovered Neanderthals and learned about Ice Age animals too, including mammoths.

The first great explorer was Édouard Lartet, a French lawyer who discovered dryopithecus remains in the Pyrenees in 1856. Hearing of discoveries of strange old bones in the caves in the Dordogne region, he teamed up with Henry Christy, a friend of Darwin's supporter Sir Charles Lyell. Funded by Lyell, Lartet and Christy began exploring there in earnest, hoping to find remains of early man. In the first few years of poking about in rock shelters and caves they found numerous flint tools, charcoal from fires, and bones of long-extinct Ice Age animals buried as much as 12 feet deep below the accumulated debris of the ages.

This was tracing ancestors in its most exciting form. In 1859, the geologist Joseph Prestwich presented a paper at the Royal Society in London arguing that the link between extinct Ice Age animals and human tools 'appears to be established beyond all reasonable doubt … in a period of antiquity remote beyond any of which we have hitherto found traces, this portion of the globe was peopled by man.'

At La Madeleine in the Vézère Valley (see plate 19), meanwhile, Lartet and Christy dug up a mammoth tusk engraved with a picture of a mammoth – solid proof that clever, intelligent humans had lived in France alongside such great Ice Age animals. They exhibited their finds at the Paris Exhibition in 1867 and it was then that the term 'prehistoric' first entered the popular vocabulary and imagination.

Crô-Magnon

Despite all these discoveries, the bones of the early people themselves remained elusive. Lartet found some in Aurignac Cave in 1860 but could not prove their age. The first traces that were confidently identified as being of Ice Age modern humans were discovered in 1868 in the rock shelter of Crô-Magnon (see plate 14).

Crô-Magnon means 'big cave' in the local dialect. It is a rock shelter that stretches back about 6 feet deep into the foot of a limestone cliff. It is in the Vézère Valley, a tributary of the mighty Dordogne, in a region full of valleys gouged deep into the limestone hills, whose sides are peppered with rock shelters and caves. These valleys retain an air of calm safety, a sense of being defined places in contrast to the endless hills beyond. There is a definite feeling of home about them. As they were home to our European ancestors for over 25,000 years, that feeling is not perhaps a misplaced one.

When the railway came to the area in 1868, a station was built by the Vézère to service the little town of Les Eyzies-de-Tayac-Sireuil. On the opposite side of the tracks a hotel was being built to accommodate the visitors whom it was hoped the railway would attract. The hotel had its back to the limestone cliffs and was next to the rock shelter that the local farmer used for storage. It was in the process of digging the hotel's foundations that workmen unearthed the first bones. Édouard's son, Louis Lartet, came quickly to the scene and excavated the bodies of four men, a woman and a baby. Some of the skulls were damaged, suggesting violent deaths. The depth of debris that had accumulated over their graves was, he wrote, 'evidence of great age'. They are now dated to about 27,000 years ago.

The hotel is still there and is proudly named the Hôtel Crô-Magnon, a lovely, creeper-covered building, whose landings are full of display cabinets containing the Upper Palaeolithic remains found there. The hotel makes the perfect base for exploring the area, especially if you ask for the room whose bathroom window looks down to the rock shelter itself.

Discovering cave art

As more and more finds accumulated, our nineteenth-century ancestors grew used to the idea of Ice Age ancestors who could carve pictures of animals onto pieces of tusk and bone. But the great discovery of art on cave walls had to wait until Don Marcelino de Sautuola, enthused by the ongoing discoveries of Christy and Lartet in the Vézère Valley, decided to explore a cave on his own land at Altamira, not far from Santander in northern Spain. When he started exploring in 1875 he found bones of bison and horses, some of which had clearly been split open so that the nutritious marrow could be eaten. When he returned to discover more in 1879, he took with him his 5-year-old daughter Maria. While Don Marcelino and his men dug down, Maria ran around looking *up*, and 'suddenly made out forms and figures on the roof'. 'I pointed these out to my father,' she said, 'but he just laughed.' But then he held up his lamp and stopped laughing. Above them on the cave roof swarmed a herd of bison, horses, deer, the very creatures whose bones lay below, but now seemingly alive in the flickering light of the oil lamps.

The Spanish were fascinated: the king himself came to see the discovery. But the scientific world was unprepared for the shock. There was still a firm belief in the constant, upward progression of civilisation, so despite the portable engravings that had been found, the idea of such magnificent art being produced so long before Classical Greece seemed absurd. The experts of the time pronounced the drawings to be nothing more than graffiti made by local boys and some even accused Don Marcelino of having faked them.

But now prehistorians knew to look up as well as down and further cave pictures were not slow in being discovered. An amateur archaeologist, François Daleau (1845–1927), discovered engravings of animals at Pair-non-Pair in Marcamps, not far from Bordeaux, in 1883, for example. So savage had been the attacks on Don Marcelino, however, that the discoverers either kept quiet, or assumed that the images they had found must be more recent. In 1895, however, a schoolboy called Gaston Berthoumeyrou found some pictures in the cave of La Mouthe, just south of Les Eyzies. When a local archaeologist, the Abbé Émile Rivière, investigated he found a stone tallow lamp engraved with an ibex, palpably ancient, and realised that some of the drawings were partially covered by deposits of chalk and stalagmites that must have taken thousands of years to accumulate. There could be no doubt of their great antiquity.

Thereafter the floodgates were opened and the story of our human family tree was enriched immeasurably by the discovery of many caves whose ceilings and walls were decorated with some of the finest art our species has ever produced.

The problem of dating

By 1900 most people now understood that, with mammoths and other large prey in fairly constant supply, Ice Age life, though extremely tough, had not been a relentless drudge. Despite the hardships they faced, our Upper Palaeolithic ancestors had a sophisticated culture expressed through great art, which provides us with a true bridge across the millennia. 'However distant these ancient people may be from us in time,' the French scholar Émile Cartailhac (1845–1921) wrote of the cave art at Font-de-Gaume, 'these undreamed-of paintings ... are tremendous in every respect, and surpass all ethnographical parallels. We are drawn to them and feel closely related by sharing the same devotion to art and beauty. We should not blush to call them our ancestors.'

Some doubt remained, however. Some anti-Darwinists claimed cave art as evidence *against* an upward progression from monkeys to humans, arguing that the paintings were the work of Adam, before his expulsion from Eden. To this day, other anti-evolutionists dismiss cave art as a grand hoax. In the 1950s the Surrealist artist and writer André Breton denounced the mammoth pictures in Pech Merle as fakes and the owners sued him. A court case ensued in Cahors during which the pictures were subject to rigorous scrutiny, from trunk to tail. The court found in favour of the mammoths and Breton was forced to pay damages.

François Daleau at Pair-non-Pair was one of the pioneers of scientific archaeology – digging carefully down through the layers and observing in them changes in the types of tools and the sorts of animal bones being found. Dating sites by such methods was of course extremely problematic and necessarily imprecise, but in 1949 William F. Libby discovered the radiocarbon dating technique. By studying the decay of the radioactive isotope carbon-14, which is found in organic material such as wood and leather, scientists can date remains with remarkable accuracy to up to about 60,000 years ago. This has enabled us to build up an ever more accurate chronology of our ancestral past and to confirm that Ice Age art goes back to about 45,000 years ago.

An Ice Age family tree

A vast amount of what we know comes from the area around Les Eyzies, and the village is an interesting barometer of how we now feel about our Upper Palaeolithic ancestors. Up on the cliff above the museum stands a limestone statue (made in 1931) of one of the Neanderthals who had made the valley their home, and in whose footsteps every visitor there follows. The National Prehistoric Museum's foyer includes a chart showing the evolution of Hominids, ascending by steps to ourselves. It is not quite a family tree, but it is almost so, and is reminiscent of the *stemmata* (prototype family trees) found in the hallways of patrician Roman households that proclaimed, in effect, 'welcome, visitor: this is who we are'.

The museum hosts an immensely useful chronological display of finds dating back from Mousterian times, enabling us to see how life and culture in the Vézère Valley, and by extension right across Europe, changed as the millennia rolled on. Again, this is not presented as a family tree, yet that is really what it is, and on a very grand scale, for it is illustrated copiously with tools made by our real ancestors, across a great span of our ancestral history.

In place of names of our ancestors' names, which we can never hope to discover, we have divided up the Upper Palaeolithic into cultures and given them names and time spans (in a manner reminiscent of the Mesopotamians, who made up and named their pre-Diluvian kings, so as to fill in a great span of time before the present for which they had no other points of reference). We took the names from the French sites where remains were first found, hence the four

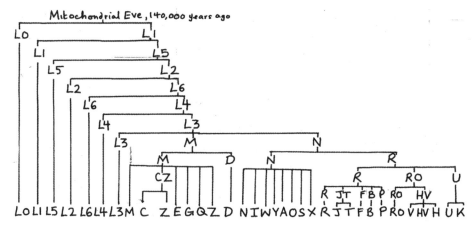

The family tree of humanity as defined by mitochondrial DNA, which goes back mother to mother.

main successive cultural phases of Europe's Upper Palaeolithic – Aurignacian, Gravettian, Solutrean and Magdalenian. These terms help give some form to our Ice Age family tree. And now, we also have genetics.

Genetic haplogroups in Ice Age Europe

In terms of the great genetic family tree of humanity as defined by female-line mitochondrial DNA, the early people who roamed into Europe may have included people belonging to haplogroup N, which was descended from the original 'out of Africa' female-line haplogroup L3, and N's descendant group R. From these developed the seven female-line haplogroups that now account for 95 per cent of all European female-line lineages, X, U, K, H, V, J and T. These are the female haplogroups that Professor Sykes popularised as his *Seven Daughters of Eve*, making up stories and names for each – Xenia, Ursula and so on.

None of these haplogroups are exclusive to Europe. A small number of women carrying the female haplogroup X (which may have emerged in western Asia about 30,000 years ago) also took part in the early drift into America. U (which appeared about 55,000 years ago) may represent an early spread of successful hunter-gatherers, some of whom even reached and merged back into the population of northern Africa. From U came the descendant female-line haplogroup K, maybe as early as 40,000 years ago, spreading from western Asia into Europe. Group HV emerged in the Near East about 30,000 years ago, and later divided into groups H (about 25,000 years ago, perhaps in the Caucasus) and V (about 10,000 years ago). J and T are descendant groups of R. J may actually have emerged in Europe, about 45,000 years ago and T appeared about 25,000 years ago, perhaps in the Middle East.

The widespread nature of these groups in Europe today has been affected hugely by subsequent population movements, but sometimes mitochondrial DNA is extracted from very ancient human remains and tells us something definite about the genes that were in Europe at specific times in the past. Bones from 24,000-year-old bodies found in southern Italy, for example, had mitochondrial DNA that appears to be either R0 (a descendant type of R) or its derivative haplogroup HV.

Whatever their mitochondrial DNA was, the early inhabitants of Europe probably developed a common feature of being fair-skinned. The dark skin pigment melamine blocks sunlight and is very useful in hot, sunny regions. But in cold, northern climes it prevents the absorption of sufficient sunlight to produce vitamin D. Low levels of vitamin D can lead to rickets, and women who have suffered from this are unlikely to give birth successfully. As a result, the fairer a woman's skin, the better her chances of reproducing in Ice Age Europe, so natural selection would quickly have favoured the fairer skinned, and bred out the darker-skinned. (This is not a factor that seriously affects dark-skinned people in modern Europe because vitamin D is plentiful in modern diets.)

It is hard to be too specific about the male-line Y chromosomes in the Aurignacian population of Europe, because so much has changed since. The earliest colonisers may have carried the markers for male-line haplogroups G (M201), I (M170), J (M304), K (M9), N (M251) and R (M173). But the early colonisers may have included some more 'Asian' genetic lineages that later happened to become rare or extinct in Europe, whilst some of the groups suggested here may in fact have come in later. Through DNA testing these rather abstract codes become personal as each of us discovers to which of the Y chromosome haplogroups our male lines and other ancestral lines belong. By such means, many of us can discover how we fit, personally, into the epic story of humanity's struggle to survive in Ice Age Europe.

Chapter 14

How to Visualise a Flying Rhinoceros

Aurignacian Europe

After a relatively mild interlude, which may have encouraged the westward migration of our ancestors into Europe in the first place, the last phase of the Ice Age took its icy grip, starting with a severely cold 'Heinrich Event' (as geologists call such cold snaps) 43,000 years ago. A few thousand years after this the temperature rose back to only a few degrees below what it is now, before suddenly plunging down again.

Because we came west from Asia, the earliest evidence of human occupation in Europe is found in the east, at Bacho Kiro in Bulgaria, Moravia in the Czech Republic and then the Swabian Alb in south-western Germany, where finds date back to about 43,000 years ago. Our ancestors lived in tents made of hides stretched over branches or mammoth tusks, which they found, used as needed and left behind in established campsites for future use. These camps were mostly in the forests or on the tundra, depending on how cold the climate was at the time, but valleys exerted an irresistible lure for our ancestors, especially those containing caves and rock shelters. Especially in harsher climatic times, we could pitch our tents below the overhangs of rock shelters or in the mouths of caves for as much shelter as possible. We did not live *in* caves, though, for their deep interiors were even colder than outside and smoke from fires would have asphyxiated everyone. At times we may have stopped wandering all our lives after the reindeer, and became only semi-nomadic, perhaps sticking to a set territory about which we moved seasonally, fishing, gathering fruits and nuts and making our great hunts.

Aurignacian culture is defined by what was left behind. They fashioned tools Levallois-style, striking blade shapes off a prepared flint core, but whereas their ancestors had used bone hammers for making flint tools, the Aurignacians made unprecedented use of antler, bone and ivory to fashion items that were useful in their own right: spear points, chisels, wedges, spatulas, curved beak-shaped awls, drills, needles and harpoons. They used these mainly for hunting, making warm fur clothes and preparing skins for shelters. They also they made pendants, bracelets, beads – and statuettes.

For a long time, the earliest sites and stone tools left by modern humans in Europe seemed to predate the earliest remains of the humans who had created them by several thousand years. However, two *H. sapiens* teeth found in the Grotta del Cavallo in southern Italy have been dated to about 45,000–43,000 years old. They are currently the oldest modern human remains known in Europe.

The last Neanderthals

Castel Merle is a small valley hemmed in by low cliffs, opening out as its stream flows down into the broad valley of the Vézère (see plate 18). Below the cliffs are a series of shelters and caves used throughout the Upper Palaeolithic and which indeed were still being used by local farmers into and beyond the Middle Ages. It is now one of the very few sites in the area being excavated, and the little band of archaeologists, when seen and heard from a distance, can be remarkably evocative of the earlier human occupants of this ancient ancestral home of ours.

The westward movement of modern humans into Europe brought our ancestors back into contact with our Neanderthal cousins. The fluctuating temperature threw the migration of herds into disarray and as they followed the wandering animals, the Aurignacians and Neanderthals ended up on the same plains and in the same valleys where the rock shelters were. The rock shelters of Castel Merle in the Vézère Valley had been used by Neanderthals long before Aurignacians appeared, after which there is evidence of both being there. Perhaps they alternated, or maybe humans and Neanderthals lived peacefully in different shelters at Castel Merle at the same time – but we cannot be sure.

It was here in the 'bleak land on the edge of the snows and glaciers' that H.G. Wells's *The Grisly Folk* described the interaction between the two turning nasty. The Neanderthals stole a child, the men gave chase and the enemy fought back: 'Perhaps the big Neandertaler male, his mane and beard bristling horribly, came down the gully with a thunderous roar, with a great rock in either hand.' Thereafter, the two species were at war. 'Many and obstinate were the duels and battles these two sorts of men fought for this world in that bleak age of the windy steppes, thirty or forty thousand years ago. The two races were intolerable to each other. They both wanted the caves and the banks by the rivers where the big flints were got. They fought over the dead mammoths that had been bogged in the marshes, and over the reindeer stags that had been killed in the rutting season. When a human tribe found signs of the grisly folk near their cave and squatting place, they had perforce to track them down and kill them; their own safety and the safety of their little ones was only to be secured by that killing.' Eventually, the genocide was complete.

'We are lineally identical,' wrote Wells, 'with those sun-brown painted [*H. sapiens*] beings who ran and fought and helped one another, the blood in our veins glowed in those fights and chilled in those fears of the forgotten past. For it was forgotten. Except perhaps for some vague terrors in our dreaming life... .'

Wells's writing is very much of its time, and his imagination was fuelled by cracked human bones found in a cave at Krapina, Croatia. They were taken as evidence of a fierce, inter-species battle. Now, however, it seems that the bones resulted from ritual cannibalism – of a sort that would have revolted Wells – being practised amongst our very own *H. sapiens* ancestors.

But whatever the truth, the Neanderthals did die out. The last evidence of Neanderthals at Le Moustier is from 32,000 years ago and the last Neanderthals of all lived out their final days on the rock of Gibraltar, 24,000 years ago. And then they were gone.

Their demise may have been due to bloody conflict with modern humans, such as Wells had imagined, but the old idea of our ancestors simply killing off an inferior race has been tempered by a subtler theory. Neanderthals were very strong, big-brained and clever, but they required about twice as much food as their new rivals, relying on close-up contact with their prey, killing with stout, large-bladed stabbing-spears. Aurignacians could survive on far less. They made sharp spear tips out of antlers – something Neanderthals seem never to have thought of doing – and could throw spears overarm, enabling them to kill animals from a greater, safer distance. If Neanderthals tried to adopt such methods, they would not have succeeded for, like their archaic human ancestors, their shoulders were not so flexible. Thus, in extremely harsh climatic conditions, simple competition for food, as opposed to outright violence, may have been what doomed them.

'The Transition'

But before the end, there was some interaction. Having followed their distinctive Mousterian culture for millennia, Neanderthals in France seem to have been stimulated by the presence of Aurignacians into the development of a new, Châtelperronian culture (45,000–35,000 years ago). Neanderthals began to make simple geometric patterns, such as those found engraved on sandstone at Cosnac, France. They used perforated teeth and shells as pendants, and made leaf-point flint blades (as opposed to hand axes), perhaps for hunting mammoths. Good collections were found at Beedings, West Sussex, and Glaston, Rutland, both high points from which to survey the surrounding hunting grounds. They were, surely, trying to be like Aurignacians – unless, as Chris Stringer suggests, the makers themselves were recent Neanderthal-*H. sapiens* hybrids. Similarly, some stylised ochre drawings of what appear to be seals, found in the Nerja caves near Malaga, Spain, were carbon dated to between 43,500–42,300 years ago. Because the evidence is for Neanderthal occupation there at the time, it has suggested that this was Neanderthal art. That seems unlikely: but it may again have been the work of a Neanderthal-*H. sapiens* hybrid.

But if we affected the Neanderthals, maybe they changed us too. Before modern humans appeared in Europe, there was no art and thus not very much evidence of spiritual thought. Yet once we reached Europe, all that seems to have changed. Was it contact with the European Neanderthals that had stimulated or inspired Aurignacian art, just as much as we had engendered Châteperronian culture in them?

Nobody seems sure. But it does seem clear that, throughout our human evolution, the pre-frontal cortexes in our brains had been developing apace. Now, suddenly, a quite extraordinary transition happened, for which the evidence is the appearance of art. Before, we had buried our dead, and scratched geometric shapes on pieces of bone, and both are remarkable indications of an advanced, thinking brain. But for the first time, in Aurignacian Europe, our ancestors suddenly started painting pictures of animals and making sculptures of stylised humans. That indicates a profound leap forward in the nature of our brains – the last stage in our development from single-celled organisms into what we are today. All the evidence is that this transition occurred in Aurignacian Europe, about 40,000 years ago.

In *The Prehistory of the Mind* (1996), Steven Mithen proposed that, prior to this transition, our ancestors had a generalised intelligence and also, separately, mental modules dealing with social intelligence, technical intelligence, linguistic intelligence, and intelligence about the natural world. Each existed on its own, but at the transition, the barriers between these different compartments collapsed. Suddenly, fully conceptual thought became possible. The agency for this collapse may have been our advanced ability to speak. One might never imagine a flying rhinoceros, but if you have words for 'rhinoceros' and 'flying', it is only a matter of time before they will be combined to trigger the concept of a rhinoceros flying. Whilst most animals dream, none of them (and probably not even the Neanderthals) could articulate what had been dreamed – but we could. Now there was literally no end to what our imaginations might create.

Following this, David Lewis-Williams wrote in *The Mind in the Cave*, 'People could [now] think of, say, social relations in terms of natural history intelligence – thus totemism was born: people could speak of human groups as if they were animal species. Similarly, anthropomorphism (the ascription of human characteristics to animals) was achieved by traffic from social intelligence through to the compartment of natural history': animals could be imagined as people.

Lewis-Williams believed that this 'great leap forward' in the way we thought was stimulated by the presence of Neanderthals: by assessing the differences between us and them, we inadvertently increased those differences and precipitated an evolution in the workings of our brains.

It is a problematic theory, though, because it posits that this mental sea change happened in Europe, long after the human race had dispersed. Did the same thing happen, later and for other reasons, amongst humans in other parts of the world? But if it did so, what were those other reasons? Or did the descendants of Europeans with this advanced mental ability spread slowly around the world, disseminating their advanced mental genes? That seems more likely, but it remains a theory about something that will probably remain unknowable.

A completely different school of thought, the 'continuity hypothesis', is the preferred view of Stephen Oppenheimer and many others. They argue that there had been no 'great leap forward': full, human consciousness had been developing slowly and steadily as part of an ongoing process of human evolution that was occurring all over the world, stimulated mainly by the increase in the human population and the resulting cultural exchange between different groups of modern humans.

Still, it is clear that art, that most visible manifestation of advanced human thought, first exploded into the world through the minds of our Aurignacian ancestors in Europe about 40,000 years ago.

Chapter 15

The People of the Lion Man

The Swabian Alb

The lion man from Hohlenstein-Stadel.

The Swabian Alb is a region of low limestone mountains in Baden–Württemberg, Germany, north of the Alps and on the north side of the broad valley of the Danube. In 1939 an exploration of the Hohlenstein-Stadel cave there revealed what remains one of the most extraordinary pieces of Ice Age art: the Lion Man.

Standing about a foot high, he has a lion's head and a human body. Nobody is sure whether the body is really male or female. Insofar as its fragments have been reassembled it lacks either penis or breasts: as it was carved painstakingly from a mammoth tusk, the sculptor may simply not have been able to include such subtleties, or maybe they broke off. Its age is uncertain: anywhere between 32,000 and – the latest view – 40,000 years old. If so, the Lion Man stands at the gateway of the human imagination.

About 30 miles away in the same mountains is the Hohle Fels cave, near Schelklingen. Here was found a 1½-inch tall version of the Lion Man and also the Venus of Hohle Fels. Found in 2008 and made about 40,000–35,000 years ago, she is made of mammoth ivory, just under an inch high. She is fully human but, unlike the Lion Man's fairly realistic proportions, she is immensely stylised, a great big fat woman with incredibly broad, child-bearing hips, a very pronounced vulva, huge breasts and stubby hands. She is deeply scarred with lines that seem to emphasise her roundness. A tiny nodule serves for her head and doubled as a ring, so that she could be hung around one of our ancestors' necks. She is not a pornographic image, scientists assert: rather, the parts emphasised are the most important for birthing and raising children. As such she is almost universally accepted as a totem of childbirth.

There are other carvings too from these and the neighbouring caves of Geissenklösterle and Vogelherd, such as 'the worshipper', a tiny figure with arms upraised as if in worship; a lion's head; a bison; and a tiny mammoth with zigzag patterns on its back. And in the Hohle Fels and Geissenklösterle caves they also found fragments of flutes made from mammoth ivory, and one made from a vulture's wing bone, one dating back 42,000 years. The tunes sung then might be lost, or perhaps they are still sung, albeit with different words, as nursery rhymes and other familiar, ageless ditties. And if songs can be passed on, unknowingly, for countless generations since Ice Age times, what other intangibles may we have inherited from the caves of the Swabian Alb? They say, for example, that fear of spiders is a behaviour learned from our parents, so it may have been passed down untold numbers of generations, perhaps since the Ice Age. And for how long have we been teaching our children to say 'touch wood' for luck? In many such unexpected ways our ancestors' world may still be with us now.

Aurignacians in Britain

Slowly the Aurignacians spread north and west. In warmer periods people made their way across Doggerland, probably following herds of reindeer. They reached as far as Kent's Cavern at Brixham, on the south coast of Devon. A human maxilla – part of the upper jaw – was found there in 1927. In November 2011, Tom Higham, Tim Compton, Chris Stringer and others announced in *Nature* that its bone collagen was definitely *H. sapiens*, and it dated to about 44,000–41,000 years ago. It is currently the oldest known fragment of a *H. sapiens* in the north of Europe (and one of the oldest in Europe at all) and must have belonged to one of the earliest colonists of these northern lands.

When another severe Heinrich Event occurred about 35,000 years ago, glaciers ground down over much of Britain, as far as the Thames Valley. The whole of Britain and northern Europe became entirely uninhabitable and the hunter-gatherer bands were forced down south to join their cousins in the chill comforts of central and southern Europe.

When the cold relented just enough to encourage animals to start returning to the north, humans followed them. About 34,000 years ago (by the latest dating) they reached Goat's Hole Cave on Wales's Gower Peninsula. One of their number died there: aged about twenty-seven, 5 feet and 8 inches high and weighing about 11 stone, his body was ritually decapitated, perhaps so his companions could eat his brains and thus allow his memories to live on in them. Then he was laid to rest, covered with red ochre and dressed with a pendant of perforated periwinkles and a bracelet of mammoth ivory, and a mammoth skull was placed carefully at the head of his grave. He was rediscovered in 1823 by William Buckland. Assuming such sophistication could not possibly be so ancient, Buckland thought he had found a Roman lady, whom he dubbed 'the Red Lady of Paviland', who had been buried among much older bones of animals who had died in the Great Flood.

But he was wrong: this was a burial of great sophistication practised by our Ice Age ancestors.

The Vézère Valley

Not long after the burial at Paviland, the cold bit deep again. Those parts of Britain not covered by glaciers became freezing, arid deserts and again we retreated south. One of our chief places of refuge was the Vézère Valley in France's Dordogne region, whose limestone landscape, pockmarked with caves and rock shelters, is not at all dissimilar to the Swabian Alb, from which its earliest *H. sapiens* inhabitants had probably come. Besides the Le Moustier and Crô-Magnon rock shelters already described, the Vézère Valley is home to many other famous shelters and caves such as La Madeleine and Lascaux. But occupation of these came later. The earliest sites to be occupied by modern humans during the Aurignacian were the Abri de Pataud ('Petaud's cave') in Les Eyzies and the group of rock shelters at Castel Merle, 6 miles away north-east, upstream.

Travelling around the area today to visit its shelters and caves makes one realise that France's Upper Palaeolithic remains are not just scattered about randomly, and that 'cave men' did not find caves liberally strewn about the place for their convenience. On the contrary; many of the caves and rock shelters exist in two very tight clusters, one in the Dordogne region (mainly the Vézère Valley and its tributary valleys) and the other 240 miles to the south in the Pyrenees, including the great Grotte de Niaux near Tarascon sur Ariège, and extending through the mountains and along the north coast of Spain towards Altamira.

In the Abri Castanet at Castle Merle were found stone blocks that may have been rings for securing ropes or tent skins. One was engraved with a vulva, perhaps being penetrated by a penis. And below the Aurignacian debris was a bit of the cave wall that had broken off and fallen down. On it was painted a bison – the oldest known piece of parietal (cave wall) art in the world.

Following the Vézère south-west, our ancestors came to the mighty Dordogne. Travelling east along its banks they reached Pécharmant near Bergerac, where there were rich deposits of flints, which they took back to the Vézère Valley. Further east along the Dordogne, near Bordeaux, they came to a collection of rock shelters and caves in the low limestone valley of another of the Dordogne's tributaries, the River Moron, including Pair-non-Pair. Amongst the finds there was something that seems to link the cave directly to the Swabian Alb – a vulture-bone flute. Engravings of ibexes, which are highly unlikely to have lived in the flat countryside around, suggest that the artists also had travelled a long distance to be there.

At Pair-non-Pair, a small opening led to a chamber where, into the ceiling, a hole had been bored, which the inhabitants probably used to hang up skins to stop the cold (and perhaps animals) from coming in. The way they lived there was most unusual: near the opening was a high chamber, whose tapering walls were engraved with creatures, and further back inside was a second and final big chamber in which people had lived. Normally, people lived near the opening and made their paintings and engravings further in.

The engravings at Pair-non-Pair were probably coloured with ochre, for balls of it, and bones of wild cattle used as palettes, were both found in the debris. The engravings were all of prey animals: deer, ibexes, horses, bison, aurochs (wild cattle) and mammoths, one seemingly rather young. None of the horns or antlers are very big, and the mammoths lack any prominent tusks. None of these peculiarities, of course, can be fully explained.

There are several pairs of animals facing each other, perhaps illustrating some sort of story. A giant stag (termed a megaloceros) is shown bellowing, as he would have done in the autumn rut. Two horses, drawn one above the other, are shown craning their necks back to look behind them. The artist used a natural crevice in the cave wall for the upper edge of one of these horse's necks, so that when a flame (or a modern torch) is held below it, the darkness of the crevice transforms into a horse's flowing mane, blown about by the cold winds of the tundra beyond the cave mouth.

A handful of Aurignacian line engravings were found in the Aldène cave at Casseras (in Herault, just north of the eastern Pyrenees), including the heads of a bear and a rhinoceros. In Chauvet cave in the Ardèche in south-eastern France are charcoal drawings dating back some 32,000 years depicting, particularly, rhinoceroses, bison and bears (the cave cannot be visited, but an exact replica is being made nearby). Their style is extremely similar to some of the carvings found in the Swabian Alb and even to some found in the Coliboaia cave in the western Carpathian Mountains of Transylvania. As with Pair-non-Pair, this suggests that there was movement between these different places – and that there existed, in that sense, a common Aurignacian culture across Europe.

Finding caves

The archaeological evidence suggests people came back to rock shelters and caves time and again over thousands of years. The art they left on the walls suggests that these places were not just utilitarian shelters, but were important socially or spiritually too, perhaps as seasonal meeting places for interrelated bands, families and 'tribes'.

The caves are not too hard to find now, thanks to guidebooks, maps and signposts, but they are otherwise well hidden. How people ever found them in the Upper Palaeolithic stretches the imagination, though at Pavlov in Moravia engravings on a mammoth tusk look very much like a map showing mountains, the course of a river and campsites marked by rings, all of which correspond well to the locality where it was actually found. It may be the world's first map, or at least an effective *aide memoire*, but it is unique.

Elsewhere, maybe families returned to painted caves deliberately often, so as to imprint their whereabouts in their own and their children's memories. Perhaps elaborate instructions were encoded in songs or stories – possibly stories for which some of the cave art itself acted as *aides memoire*. Or maybe we had not yet lost the innate homing sense of other animals, like the swallows and martins that migrate from Africa to the Vézère each summer and return to the exact crag on which they were born, without intellectualising the process at all. Despite this, one suspects that some painted caves may have fallen into obscurity and lain undiscovered for thousands of years before people found them again.

The rediscovery of these caves in the last 150 years, and the constant stream of visitors who have been coming ever since, can be seen as a modern phenomenon. But perhaps it is just a continuum of our ancestral attachment to these places, which has lasted, on and off, for some 35,000 years.

Chapter 16

The Reindeer Hunters of Creswell Crags

The Gravettian phase (28,000–22,000 years ago)

The Aurignacian ended with a sudden dramatic drop in temperature about 29,000 years ago, followed by an abrupt rise, though not quite back to Aurignacian levels, and nowhere near as warm as it is today. It was succeeded by the Gravettian culture. The Gravettians are unlikely to have been a different people to the Aurignacians. They were simply their descendants, who started making slightly different tools, enabling scientists to give them a new label, to help punctuate this long phase of European history. They made fine burins for carving wood or bone; flint blades that were finer and longer than before, and characteristic pointed blades with a triangular cross-section. This culture is named after the rock shelter of La Gravette in Bayac, in the tiny Couze Valley, which feeds into the Dordogne a few miles downstream from its confluence with the Vézère. Many finds were made here between the 1930s and 1950s by Ferdinand Lacorre. Since then, earlier examples have been found in Crimea, dating back about 32,000 years, but this style did not reach western Europe until about 28,000 years ago.

About 27,000 years ago five people were buried in the rock shelter of Crô-Magnon (see plate 14), their ornaments including a fine ivory pendant and perforated shells, which had probably formed a necklace. It was these people who were later exhumed by Louis Lartet. Just to the east of the Vézère Valley is another smaller region of limestone caves clustered around tributaries of the Dordogne. These caves include Cougnac, where a megaloceros was depicted on the cave wall in ochre, and Pech Merle ('blackbird hill'), where a famous pair of horses was drawn about 24,000 years ago, with big backs and bellies, tiny legs and ridiculously small heads, one of which utilised the natural shape of the rock.

In the relatively mild spell with which the Gravettian began, the steppes and tundra of central Europe teamed with game. In parts of south-western Russia not far north of the Black Sea there was such an abundance of food that temporary camps became semi-permanent villages with circular huts. At Kostienki are four large pits, 11 by 6 feet in size, which had skin roofs supported by mammoth tusks and bone. Nearby at Adeevo were seven more, amongst the remains of which was found a small clay model of a mammoth. From these settlements hunters set out as the need arose to hunt bison, horses, reindeer and the other creatures that passed by in herds. They seem not to have risked hunting mammoths, probably preferring to scavenge bones and ivory from those already killed by lions or dead due to natural causes.

Meanwhile, northern hunters following the reindeer herds penetrated as far north as the limestone gorge of Creswell Crags, Derbyshire, where they found shelter in the same caves the Neanderthals had used long before. Some of their tanged points – spear points with a tail that could be fitted into a spear shaft – were found in Pin Hole Cave there, dating from about 28,000 years ago.

Judging by their art, the Gravettians had a complex society, sophisticated stone tools and a high appreciation of beauty. The practice of following reindeer could have turned quickly to herding – maybe it did – and if the climate had improved sufficiently and remained stable they may eventually have discovered agriculture and metalworking, resulting ultimately in a society no less sophisticated than that which Caesar discovered when he invaded northern Gaul in 58 BC. But any such developments that may have lain in the future were halted by that old enemy of mankind – climate change. Starting about 25,000 years ago, the onset of the Last Glacial Maximum led to two severely cold Heinrich Events in quick succession, the first being about 23,000 years ago. Grassy steppes grew arid with cold and the forests withered under icy blasts from the north. The glaciers pushed south, extinguishing the camp fires at Creswell Crags and the remnants of those ephemeral human generations who had lived in Britain retreated south. They joined their southern cousins in an ever shrinking string of refuges, particularly those of the Vézère Valley, in the world between the ice sheets and the steely cold waters of the drying Mediterranean. But whilst European humanity was at risk at times from extinction, the remixing of people led to a flourishing culture in which stone-blade technology improved and art flourished.

Of fish and horses

Not surprisingly, Italy, Portugal and Spain were favoured places to live. They had climates akin to northern Scotland now – harsh, but nowhere near as bad as further north. At the cave of La Piletta near Ronda in southern Spain, we are shown around by the owner, Señor Bullón, a genial old man who uses an old oil lamp to show off the Gravettian rock art there with the air of a modest aristocrat giving a guided tour of his ancestral mansion. As we follow him deep into the winding tunnels, we see dark charcoal smudges arranged in parallel lines – marking time, perhaps, or enumerating something else that was important to their makers. Here and there are graceful outlines of wild horses: one pregnant horse is decorated with ochre spots. There are also cattle and deer and a mountain goat with horns curving away behind it fluidly. In one vast chamber, far from the entrance, we cross an almost level floor to inspect the far wall, on which had been drawn an enormous fish. They did not cover the walls with paintings: the wall next to the fish is completely blank. The paintings obviously had their place and purpose. What these were we can but guess. But the way our ancestors prepared their colours has been decoded. Red paint was made from ochre or ground hematite and black pigment from manganese dioxide, both mixed with fat or water. Often, drawings were made using pine or juniper charcoal and then painted over.

In the mountains of north-eastern Portugal, about 250 miles north-west of La Piletta, is the Vale do Côa. Until recently, all known Upper Palaeolithic rock art was within rock shelters and caves, and was thought to have been inspired by the experience of being inside them. But here, things were different. It was a different experience, too, when we visited on Midsummer's Eve 2006, lurching down the rutted track in a jeep from the archaeology base at the tiny village of Peñascosa. Breathtaking views of the steep valley bounced around the open windows as the guide explained how the first discoveries of rock shelters, containing some fairly conventional paintings, were made in 1989, while the area was being mapped prior to the construction of a hydroelectric dam.

The dam project went ahead anyway but in 1992, as bulldozers ate hungrily into the rock faces, archaeologists working in the valley of Canada do Inferno noticed something quite extraordinary. The area was scattered with great schist stone slabs, which stuck up out of the hillsides, presenting clear, flat surfaces. People had responded to the unspoken invitation of these flat rocks for centuries, decorating them with engravings of such things as trains, bridges and crucifixes. But many pictures, it was now realised, were far older. The archaeologists had chanced upon an open-air gallery of Gravettian art.

It took an international campaign and a fortuitous change of government to halt the dam project in 1995. The area became the Parque Arqueológico Vale do Côa in 1996, and in 1998 it was declared a World Heritage Site.

After twenty minutes' bumpy journey, we arrived at our chosen site, a valley adjacent to Canada do Inferno, named Peñascosa after the nearby village. By engraving images on the rocks, our Crô-Magnon ancestors had fixed the Vale do Côa inextricably in their own time. Aside from the jeep, the archaeologists' hut and a Roman wall (which seemed ludicrously modern) there was little to jar the sense of being back in Gravettian times.

At first, it was difficult to see any *arte rupestre*, as the Portuguese term their rock art. Our guide had to point out the first few engravings, but as our eyes became used to them it became easier to spot more and we realised the hillsides were alive with images of wild horses, wild goats and the great, wild cattle called aurochs.

Besides the schist slabs, nature had also strewn the valley with lumps of sharp quartz, perfect tools for scratching images. People also brought flints from the nearest deposits, over 100 miles away, as extra engraving tools. Some images were pecked out by hammering a sharp, pointed tool into the rock whilst others were created by elegant and unbroken lines. In some cases the pictures follow natural cracks and contours in the rocks, as if the artists were drawing out what Nature had put there already. One goat is engraved so as to allow natural cracks to form its sweeping horns. A depiction of a fish appears on first sight to be half lost: its front half can be seen, complete with fins and even striations suggesting scales, but where its rear half would be, the rock is missing. But is this in fact a leaping salmon, with the broken edge of the rock representing the foaming surface of the river?

If the engravings were ever painted, rain has long since washed away all traces. But once the valley's sides may have been alive with animals painted in reds and browns and perhaps adorned with wreaths of leaves and flowers as well, just as the locals still adorn their Catholic statues on holy days.

One striking engraving in the valley depicts a man with a large penis, apparently ejaculating. But the most arresting image is that of two horses. Originally, only the upper part of the rock was exposed, showing a couple of rather indifferent looking ponies. But when archaeologists cleared away the soil from the base, they exposed two horses in the act of copulation, the mare below, the male rearing up over her. Instead of just one head and neck, the stallion has three, drawn to create an unmistakable sense of motion. If this was indeed an attempt to create a vivid sense of movement then it predates the techniques of twentieth-century animated films by 20,000 years or more – and it works.

Gravettian goddesses?

Besides drawing on the Vale do Côa's fixed slabs, people also scratched images on smaller pieces of schist to take away with them – sixteen pieces have been found lying about in the valley, examples of mobile art intended perhaps as souvenirs or talismans for people travelling off on hunting expeditions. But in terms of portable art, the Gravettian period's most iconic productions are Venus figurines. Evolving out of the Aurignacian prototypes, they appear in Gravettian times in a greater variety of materials, carved in ivory or stone or fashioned from baked clay. A prevalent style abides: prominent vulvas, big fat breasts, hips and bellies, some obviously pregnant. If a head is shown at all, it is invariably small and faceless.

Most famous is the Venus of Willendorf, Austria, carved from limestone and coloured with red ochre. She has a life-sized head, but it is egg-shaped and covered all over with a pattern like braded or beaded hair. From Dolní Věstonice near

Pavlov, Moravia, comes a quite different figurine made of clay, baked dark shiny brown. But again the focus is all on the immense hips and pendulous breasts: her round head has no more than an abstract slit across it to suggest a face.

There are many more examples from the refuges of central Europe. Far fewer have been found in the west, but those that have, such as those found at Grimaldi and Savignano in Italy, are stunning. Styles vary here too: the Venuses of Sireuil and Tursac, both in the Dordogne, are of amber-coloured calcite and are extremely stylised: the latter could be mistaken for something else unless you already understood the convention. The mammoth ivory Dame de Brassempouy, on the other hand, is startlingly realistic. Only the head survives (in the National Museum of Antiquities in Saint-Germain-en-Laye) – a girl, clearly, with long neck, nose, eyebrows and braided hair, but no eyes or mouth as if (as everyone suspects) the depiction of a fully realistic woman was taboo.

At Lespugue in Haute-Garonne was found a quite bizarre Venus. She is long and thin, with no arms. Her head is miniscule and featureless, scarcely noticeable as one stares at her extraordinary midriff, in which cluster a series of egg shapes stylising her breasts, buttocks, thighs, stomach and vulva.

In the Abri de Pataud in Les Eyzies was found a stone carved with a reasonably slender Venus with big breasts. More intriguing are the Venuses found in the Abri de Laussel, which is 5 miles to the east of Les Eyzies, on the wooded northern side of the Beune stream, which runs into the Vézère. Here in 1911, carved in bas relief on a huge limestone boulder (and now detached and on prominent display in the Musée d' Aquitaine, Bordeaux), was found the Venus de Laussel (see plate 13). At 1½ feet tall, she is typically broad-hipped and pendulously breasted. Her abdomen bulges out on the curving surface towards the viewer, and over it is clasped her left hand. In her right hand she holds a horn, which her faceless head is turning to observe. It is thought to be a bison's horn and appears to have been adapted for drinking. The horn has been scored deliberately with thirteen lines, perhaps, it has been theorised, representing the thirteen days of the waxing moon or the thirteen lunar months of the year. The whole thing was painted with red ochre, and if this represented blood then it may have been linked to the female menstrual cycle. Some believe her horn also resembles the crescent moon and that she is a Gravettian precursor of mother goddesses with their moon emblems from Neolithic and Bronze Age times, but we must always be cautious in imposing such specific interpretations on images so ancient.

Four other reliefs of human figures were found at Laussel too, of which the clearest was the Venus de Berlin, which was taken to Berlin and destroyed there by Second World War bombing: a model is in the Musée d'Aquitaine. It shows another fat woman, again faceless, and holding in her extended arm a 'C' shaped object, wider at one end than the other, presumably a crude version of the

Laussel Venus's horn. Interestingly, if Laussel was indeed the home of a 'Venus' cult, there is also an engraving of a slim human figure shown in profile, minus the head, known as 'La Chasseur' (the huntsman) but now thought in fact to be a pre-pubescent girl – a young precursor, perhaps, of the bulbous matriarch.

The Laussel Venuses are extremely unusual in that they were engraved on rock and then painted. Elsewhere, the Gravettian Venuses were portable objects, so probably performed a function quite different to cave art. They were probably talismans for fertility and childbirth and are found so often because every family band probably had one, to be clasped to the womb after intercourse to engender conception, and to be clutched as a comforting, guiding force during labour. They were probably passed down from mother to daughter as embodiments of the notion of a generic female ancestor. Maybe such an ancestress was becoming, by extension, a female spirit – we cannot yet say a goddess – who was believed to have animated the Universe. But we do not know. The most we can say of them is that they were goddesses-in-waiting.

The Solutrean phase (22,000–18,500 years ago)

As the bitterly cold Last Glacial Maxim continued, vast areas of Europe were uninhabitable and the northernmost population was squeezed ever tighter into just a few refuges, particularly Solutré-Pouilly, near Chalons-sur-Saône, an extraordinary limestone escarpment that rears up like a sphinx high above the Saône Valley in central-eastern France, not far from the Alps.

Finds made here give their name to a new culture, the Solutrean. It is an artificial phase like any other, whose relatively brief duration – a mere 3,500 years – was defined by a unique style of stone tool-making not seen before or since. That is assuming, of course, that all tools made in Solutrean style do actually belong to this period, and have not just been assigned to this phase because their style corresponds to it. In fact, Solutrean-style tools did continue to be made, in France at least, until about 17,000 years ago – thus overlapping inconveniently with the next, Magdalenian, phase. The French call tools made in this anomalous style 'Badegoulian', because of finds made at Badegoule, just north-west of Les Eyzies in the Vézère Valley.

The confining of much of Europe's sparse human population into a few refuges seems to have led to the honing of flint-working skills, resulting in fine leaf-shaped spearheads, elegantly fashioned on both sides, used mainly for hunting wild horses. But some points were made smooth by heating and were so brittle they could only have had an aesthetic purpose.

The Solutreans were the first people to make eyes in their needles, through which sinew-thread could be threaded, making it vastly easier to sew warm clothes than before. They also developed the *atlatl* or spear-thrower, made from bone or antler, designed to give a thrown spear extra thrust. From this phase too come the earliest traces of ropes and probably fishing nets (the imprint of a piece of rope was found at Lascaux) and maybe weaving was invented too – there is obviously a problem in archaeology because such ephemeral things as cloth are unlikely to have survived, so may actually have existed much earlier.

Whilst these innovations were arising in Europe, America was being colonised from north-eastern Asia. Human remains found on the Delmarva Peninsula in Maryland have been carbon dated to between 26,000 and 19,000 BC. Later on, 'Clovis' stone tools started being used in America. They only date from about 13,000 years ago onwards, and probably arose independently, but they are so similar to Solutrean ones in Europe that some believe that Solutreans actually reached America, travelling perhaps in hide boats along the southern edge of the (then huge) polar ice cap. That theory has yet to be proved but it is an intriguing one for everyone, on both sides of the Atlantic.

Chapter 17

Leading the High Life at La Madeleine

The Magdalenian phase (18,500–11,000 years ago)

From the primeval seas to apes and then to *Homo sapiens*, our ancestors had increased in ability, but the world had yet to see anything so magnificent as what was to follow now, under the culture of the Magdalenians.

This last great sweep of Upper Palaeolithic culture is generally subdivided into the Lower Magdalenian (18,500–16,500 years ago); Middle Magdalenian (to 13,500 years ago) and Upper Magdalenian (to 11,000 years ago). It started with a reasonably warm phase, but a prolonged Heinrich Event from 17,000 to 14,500 years ago saw another colder burst so bitter that even the mammoths were driven off the northern steppes to take shelter in the Vézère Valley.

Magdalenian culture is named after La Madeleine cave (see plate 19), just up the Vézère Valley from Les Eyzies. It was one of the first Palaeolithic sites to be explored thoroughly, by Édouard Lartet in 1863, and it was here that he found the famous engraving of a mammoth on a fragment of mammoth tusk, incontrovertible evidence that our Ice Age ancestors truly were skilled artists. La Madeleine is one of a series of caves leading off a ledge near the top of a cliff. The routes out from the ledge into the woods behind the caves were easily blocked by thorn bushes to keep out wolves and hyenas. Like the similar nearby sites of Roque St-Christophe and the Grotte du Sorcier, it was as secure as a stone-built castle or a modern high-rise apartment. Today it commands views of the beautiful, weed-tressed Vézère and the meadows beyond but it is easy to imagine the great herds of reindeer on the tundra grassland that our ancestors used to watch from this vantage point. If ever a site appeared to have been fashioned for human habitation by benevolent deities, this is it.

Life at La Madeleine was as splendid as the location. Judging by what they left behind, our ancestors here wore fine skin clothes adorned with shells, and were surrounded by beautifully carved weapons and artifacts fashioned from stone, bones, antlers, teeth and ivory. Their riches probably matched those of a Magdalenian woman, aged about twenty-five, who was found in 1934 at St Germain-de-la-Rivière, to the west of La Madeleine, not far from Pair-non-Pair. She was buried in the foetal position below a dolmen of two limestone blocks supported by four limestone pillars. Her fine attire included shell beads and a necklace of seventy red deer canines, which were rare commodities in those times and must have taken many years to collect.

Who was she? A Magdalenian queen? Archaeologists balk at such terms, but she was clearly not a nobody. Had she perhaps been revered as a living embodiment of the Venus figurines that had been carved so lovingly by her Gravettian ancestors?

Magdalenian tools

The Magdalenians abandoned the elongated leaf-shaped flint tools of their Solutrean forebears and returned to the more traditional shapes of Gravettian times, but they made these much finer and smaller than before, a trend that seems to have accelerated as the end of the Upper Palaeolithic approached. But Lartet and Christy termed the Lower Magdalenian 'the Reindeer Age' because up to four-fifths of all bones found at Magdalenian sites were of reindeer (the other fifth included red deer, horses, bison and a few mammoths, probably scavenged rather than hunted). Reindeer bones were the raw material for vast numbers of tools, including fine, eyed needles and newly invented harpoons, first with single barbs, then two. Once such a weapon had pierced an animal's pelt it could never be shaken free. All the hunters had to do was follow the wounded creature until it collapsed from exhaustion. The Magdalenians improved on the spear-throwers invented by their Solutrean forebears, decorating them beautifully to look like thin mammoths or ibexes. Three found in the Dordogne area are so similar that they must have been the work of the same person.

The Magdalenians probably had dogs or, at least, domesticated wolves. The connection between man and hound may go back much further, but the genetic divergence between dog and wolf lies here, now, about 15,000 years ago.

Caves of bison and horses

The Vézère Valley's best known cave is Lascaux, whose plethora of lively paintings of animals dates from between 18,500 BC and 15,000 BC. But since it was first discovered by local schoolboys in 1940, air from outside, mixed with human breath, caused the growth of a white fungus that threatened the pictures, so the original is now closed and we can only visit an exact replica nearby. Along the Beune Valley, which meets the Vézère near Les Eyzies, however, are a string of caves brimming with Magdalenian art that can still be seen and admired in its original state. Combarelles, full of engraved animals about 14,000–12,000 years old, was discovered in 1901 by the Les Eyzies schoolmaster Denis Peyrony. There are bears depicted here, and we found ourselves face-to-face with a great lioness, engraved in elegant curved lines that convey dramatically the lethal muscularity of her body, whilst natural calcite on the rock forms her steaming breath. Seeing predators like this is unusual. On a bone pendant in Les Eyzies someone engraved a wolverine, but the creatures that competed with us for food seldom inspired such artistic reverence as our prey. There are many horses depicted in Combarelles, all seeming to face back towards the entrance, perhaps indicting the way out. Some are drawn one on top of another; others are mixed in amongst mammoths and reindeer.

Four days after he discovered Combarelles, Peyrony climbed a rocky outcrop nearby and found the entrance to Font de Gaume (see plates 15, 16 & 17). Inside he was greeted by paintings from 17,000–13,000 years ago. Males are painted brown and females are painted red. Horses predominate – 116 of them, compared to nineteen bears, thirteen mammoths, a snake, a wolf and thirty-seven bison, some scratched over older mammoths. Recalling the much older engravings at Pair-non-Pair, some animals are shown meeting: a male bison touches heads with a composite bison-mammoth; a magnificent reindeer with huge, sweeping antlers lowers its head as if to nuzzle a female reindeer kneeling in submission before him. Maybe these meetings illustrate now-forgotten stories told here by our Magdalenian ancestors. Most memorable was a row of bison, depicted so vividly that we almost heard the deep rumble of their hooves as they stampeded past.

We had a similarly memorable encounter with bison in the Grotte de Niaux, 150 miles south in the Pyrenees. The people lived down below in rock shelters (fashioning tools out of flint cores brought from Pécharmant, which is not far from the Vézère Valley). The cave was reserved for other-worldly life, its outer chambers decorated with rows of black and red dots, dashes and signs, and a unique outline drawing of a weasel. Here were found two sets of footprints, left in clay by two Magdalenian children. Further in, we reach the Salon Noir, a roughly circular cathedral-like chamber, 65 feet wide, which rises up into pitch blackness. We stand a while in the thick, unnerving darkness before the guide switches on a muted lamp and moves its light gently over the horses and ibex on the cave wall. There is a bison. Only one foreleg is painted: when the lamp is held to one side, a fissure in the rock casts a shadow, which suddenly becomes the second foreleg. A rocky lump above, lit in the same way, becomes the bison's powerful shoulder. Overall, the bison appears as our ancestors saw it in real life, a massive, powerful creature, turning in mid-stampede, about to face its assailants. And it is not alone: over there is a whole group of them, stampeding about. Arrows are flying, some mid-air, their sharp heads painted black and others already penetrating the animals, their tips painted red – bloody arrowheads that had struck their mark.

Some caves are dominated by horses. Further up the Beune Valley, and not far from Laussel, is the Abri de Cap Blanc. The back of the shelter comprises two panels on which images of eight large horses were carved about 14,000 years ago.

The main panel shows two small groups of horses meeting: the focus is on one left of centre, who is pregnant. The whole work is suggestive of a single artist who was left-handed, and a woman was found buried here whose strong left wrist bone suggested left-handedness. Was this a female sculptor, buried in front of her masterpiece? Her remains, sadly, reside now in a museum in Chicago. There is no evidence of domestic occupation here, so everything suggests a fertility shrine to a (presumably female) horse deity. As Christine Desdemaines-Hugon wrote, 'How peaceful the animals look, gentle in expression and attitude, their bodies fitting comfortably within the shelter, which becomes a world in itself. With, perhaps, the promise of life incarnated at the centre.' It prompts us to think of the many horses depicted earlier in Upper Palaeolithic art (and a possible horse cult at Duruthy near Biarritz, where depictions of horses were accompanied by horse skulls), and of the much later Bronze Age depiction of the White Horse at Uffington, Oxfordshire (formerly Berkshire). In the Iron Age, the horse goddess had a name – Epona. Was it she who was venerated at Cap Blanc, an equine deity revered as a guide and perhaps even as the female-line ancestor of the sculptor and her people?

The mammoth caves

Horses dominate the Beune Valley, but away to the east in the limestone hills of the Ardèche, Chauvet Cave is dominated by forty woolly rhinoceroses. And in the cave of Pech Merle, not far east of the Vézère Valley, the animal present in greatest numbers is the mammoth – twenty-one of them compared to only twelve bison; seven horses; six aurochs and six deer. Eleven of the mammoths are in the 'black frieze' in a chamber known as 'the chapel of the mammoths', a densely worked area of images superimposed upon one another, all seemingly centred upon a horse.

The presence of mammoths here may have been inspired by a natural rock formation covered with accreted calcium that looms above us on the way in, like a mammoth turned to stone. So mammoths were in our ancestors' minds as they explored: we can actually see the footprints of a Magdalenian boy who trod that path, preserved in the soft mud to this day. In the walls, too, are

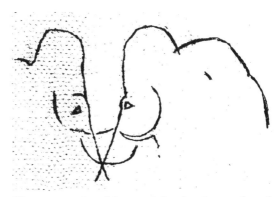

The centre-point of the panel showing the meeting of mammoths in Rouffignac cave.

what seem like natural faces, half animal, half human. Imagine – our ancestors encountered half-man, half-animal images in the rocks 10,000 years before the myth of Theseus, who penetrated the Cretan labyrinth to encounter that other, great horned beast, the Minotaur.

Mammoths rule too in the hills 9 miles north of Les Eyzies. Here, on a quiet hillside above the Binche (which also feeds into the Vézère) is Rouffignac Cave (also called the Crô de Granville or the Miremont Grotto). Here are twenty-eight bison, twelve ibexes, seventeen horses, ten woolly rhinoceroses, a bear and six creatures like headless snakes – and 157 mammoths, dating from the very last, intensely cold flourish of the Ice Age about 12,500 years ago. To create and see them our Magdalenian ancestors had to crawl along in cold darkness for hours on end, but now the floors have been lowered and a miniature railway conveys us back in time. The walls are soft and have been deeply scoured by the claws of cave bears, waking from their hibernation in the spring: it was only after these had been hunted to extinction that our forebears dared venture in themselves. Occasionally, we spot mammoths, created by adding new lines to the bears' older scratchings. One very old mammoth, known as 'the Patriarch', is characterful and cartoon-like, created by human fingers scouring lines in the malleable rock.

At the far end of one branch of the cave system, and into harder rock, we reach the Grand Plafond, whose ceiling is covered with black manganese drawings of mammoths, sometimes paired with bison. A young mammoth is depicted with tiny tusks and an operculum or anal flap, which is visible because its fur has not grown too long. The flap was to stop its anus freezing, and is a feature known from real mammoth corpses found frozen in Siberia, proving that the Magdalenian artists knew their subjects in intimate detail.

We come next to Rouffignac's Henri Breuil Gallery. One panel showing three woolly rhinoceroses is thrilling enough, but on the next wall below a layer of flints is a panel 29 feet long, on which two lines of mammoths are meeting. They are drawn in black manganese on the pale surface of the rock, with humped backs, high foreheads, the downward sweep of their trunks and the upward curve of their tusks. Below is a layer of coarse-grained calcite, which has risen up since the drawings were made and obscured the mammoths' legs, so they appear now to be walking through the morning mist. The rear mammoth of each group hangs back, just as modern African elephants do, to keep watch on the family from behind. At the centre of the panel the limestone bows outwards and on this the artist chose to make the two leading mammoths meet. Their trunks touch and their eyes gaze solemnly at each other. There is no hint of conflict. There must be a story here, maybe an origin myth. The Mongols' *Secret History* tells how Genghis Khan's earliest human ancestor, Khorilatai, was born from the meeting of a male wolf and a fallow deer near the source of the Onan River in Mongolia.

Did the people of Rouffignac tell of a similar meeting between these mammoths, and a similar birth of ancestors?

Tectiforms and hands

The Vézère and Beune caves are peppered with tectiforms, symbols with a base line supporting what looks like a sun umbrella, drawn in cross section. They have been interpreted as tents or huts but may have been symbols for a place of habitation or, in a broader sense, for the people who inhabited such a place. Bernifal cave, which was found near a tributary of the Beune by Peyrony in 1902, contains a mammoth's head with a tectiform drawn at an angle on it. Maybe this meant 'the camp/people of the mammoth'. Rouffignac, that great palace of the mammoths, has thirteen tectiforms that may have conveyed a similar meaning.

Another group of images that may convey coded information about their makers are hands. They appear in the caves of Font de Gaume, Chauvet and Cosquer near Marseilles: El Castillo cave, not far from Altamira, is full of them, and in Bernifal, two left hands were engraved not far in from the entrance. Such

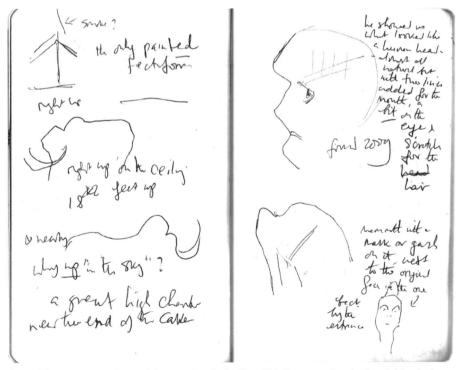

A tectiform, mammoths and human heads in Bernifal Cave, as sketched quickly during a torchlit visit there.

images are made either by hands pressed into soft clay; or smeared with paint and pressed onto the cave wall; or by drawing around a hand or pressing a clean hand onto the cave wall and then blowing powder mixed with saliva around it to create a negative impression.

Hands are a common motif in rock art all over the world. Some of the best collections are in the Gua Tewet and Kalimantan caves in Borneo, about 14,000–12,000 years old. Outlined in ochre, they are arranged to form branching trees. Jean-Michel Chazine suggested they were family trees, with each hand representing an individual or family group. Sometimes these Bornean hands are linked to each other or to drawings of people and animals by dotted lines, perhaps illustrating origin myths, but it is impossible to be sure. Whether the Magdalenians in France placed similar significance in their less joined-up hand depictions we can but speculate.

Heads and women

We are intrigued by our Magdalenian ancestors' depictions of animals, tectiforms and hands, but more fascinating, and even less decodable, are their pictures of themselves. Had they portrayed themselves with their same grace and style they gave to their horses and mammoths, we might have images of our ancestors to rival those produced by Classical Greece. But for the most part, the ancient taboo against the realistic depiction of human bodies and faces, which caused the Aurignacian and Gravettian 'Venuses' to be so severely stylised, persisted into Magdalenian times.

In Rouffignac are two cartoon-like human heads (nicknamed 'Adam and Eve') and a figure that is recognisably human, between two bison: these and a fourth depiction are all placed in highly inaccessible locations – hidden perhaps from profane gaze. In Cougnac is a group of human heads nicknamed 'the ghosts'. Bernifal has a human head, too, looking left, mainly composed of natural rock but with some lines added to make features

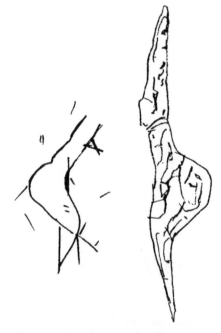

Two examples of the way late Magdalenians depicted women, from Courbet Cave in the French Pyrenees, France and Nebra, just west of Leipzig, Germany.

including the mouth. Also in Bernifal, just to the right of a floating mammoth, is a little human head with dots for nostrils and eyes and curving, quizzical eyebrows, of which Christine Desdemaines-Hugon wrote, 'that searching look seems to echo our own ... . We are in direct contact with our ancestors here, there's no doubt about that, and all of a sudden we would like to have the answers, all the answers.'

The Magdalenians' depictions of women are often slim, in sharp contrast to the obese Venuses of earlier times. But they were still incomplete, often lacking heads or even upper bodies at all. A slender torso, legs and emphasised pubis found carved on ivory at Laugerie Basse near Les Eyzies in 1864 was the first of its kind ever discovered in France, but at the rock shelter of Roc-aux-Sorciers at Angles-sur-l'Anglin, Poitiers, about 150 miles north of the Vézère Valley, is a panel showing three slender, styled women, shown from armpit to ankles, with emphasis on their vaginas. Desdemaines-Hugon thought they might represent a woman before, during and after giving birth. They seem to anticipate the Triple Diana of Iron Age Italy, who was maiden, child-bearer and old crone all in one. And of the female figures drawn on a slate found at Teufelsbrücke near Weimar, Germany, Rudolph Feustal wrote that they might be 'ancestral mothers, animal mothers, guardians of the hearth or protectors of the family', but of course we cannot know any such things for sure. Towards the end, depictions became so stylised as to show only the downward curve of the back and the outward bulge of the rump. The viewer was expected to know that such an abstract form depicted, or meant, a woman. As with tectiforms, the image was on its way to becoming a hieroglyph – but it was a false dawn and – maddeningly – the Magdalenians stopped far short of inventing writing.

Sorcerers

The Grotte de Sorcier is a cave above the village of Saint-Cirq, a few miles down the Vézère west of Les

My notebook sketch of the 'sorcerer' at Saint-Cirq. (See also plate 20.)

Eyzies where the valley broadens out, but is still edged with high hills peppered with cliffs and shelters. The small cave leading back from the rock shelter was first excavated in 1858 but only in 1952 did anyone notice that the ceiling was engraved. A bison faces the entrance and further in is an ibex; the lower half of a woman; a horse whose legs form two triangles that may also be human vaginas; what appears to be a monkey's head, and he whom Abbé André Glory termed 'the sorcerer', and who is now termed, less emotively, an 'ithyphallic personage'. Dating from about 17,000 years ago, this 'sorcerer' seems to float, pot-bellied, with a big round head half turned towards the viewer and a big, dangling penis. For all this, he lacks the realism of many of the cave's animal depictions.

A similar character lurks 6 miles east in the Grotte Sous-Grand-Lac, Meyrals, whilst in Cougnac is 'le Sorcier fleche', with a body very similar to the Saint-Cirq sorcerer, but pierced with three or four long arrows. Near him is 'le Sorcier a l'arc musical', a headless human figure, heavily stylised, with three arrows piercing his back. Both were drawn in black lines about 15,000 years ago, onto much bigger red drawings of a mammoth and a megaloceros (or giant deer), which could be 10,000 years older. Nearby at Pech Merle and obviously related to these is a similar human figure, also impaled by arrows.

Mostly, Magdalenian depictions of men are incomplete, or extremely simplistic, or else they are therianthropes, half man, half animal – unless they are supposed to show men wearing animal masks. Down in the Pyrenees, in the cave of Les Trois Frères, a 'sorcerer', about 14,000 years old, is outlined in black. He stands in profile, legs bent, with enormous, dangling genitals, a horse's tail and forearms bent like a kangaroo's. His head is turned so that his eyes stare out at us. On his head he has the ears and antlers of a reindeer. Also in the cave, and older by 6,000 years, is a whirling scene of animals, mainly horses and bison, centred on another man in profile. He has a bison's head, facing left, and his back is curved like a bison's as well. There are two similar part-human depictions nearby at the Grotte du Portel, whilst at Gabillou, not far north of Lascaux, are two more men who are part bison, about 18,000–15,000 years old. Lascaux itself contains a man with a birdlike head and an erect penis, lying or floating in front of a bison, which, though facing him, is turning to look the other way. Next to him is a bird on a stick and a broken line. This curious scene is about 18,000–15,000 years old and surely illustrated a story. At Combarelles near Les Eyzies are more than fifty human figures, either incomplete or therianthropic. One that we saw had a realistically muscular thigh and lower leg, but scarcely any head to speak of. The most memorable is the 'mammoth man', a very simply drawn figure, probably male, with the head and sweeping trunk and tusks of a mammoth.

Calling them all 'sorcerers' suggests they were shamans, communing with animal spirits or the spirits of animal ancestors, and this interpretation may

1. Mount Helikon, Greece, home of Hesiod, who wrote about the world's birth out of the primal chasm in his great genealogical work, the *Theogony*.

2. Sir Francis Bacon, a pioneer of the Natural Science that revealed so much about our true origins.

3. Carl Linnaeus, whose invention of taxonomy paved the way for our rediscovery of our ancient family tree of life.

4. A fossil trilobite, *Cnemidopyge nuda*, from Llandrindod Wells, Radnor, Wales – a distant cousin of ours, whose kind dominated the ocean floor for millions of years. *Dwergenpaartje / Wikimedia Commons*

5. Concrete models of labyrinthodonts made by Richard Owen (1804–1892) for the 1854 Great Exhibition, lurking on the lake shore in Crystal Palace Park, London. Modern views of what labyrinthodonts looked like make them more elongated, less squat. Few people walking past on their way to gaze at Owen's models of the more glamorous dinosaurs (which he first named and popularised through these statues) realise that our ancestors were labyrinthodonts for several tens of millions of years.

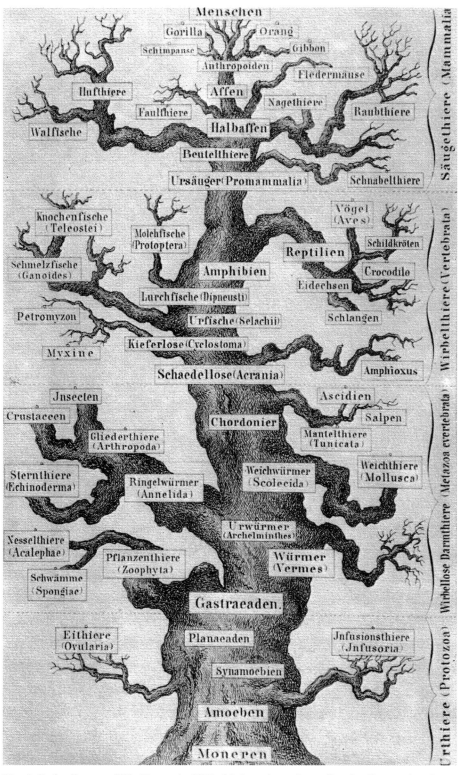

6. Haeckel's family tree of life. Drawn in 1874, this is perhaps the earliest family tree that shows we humans ('Menschen') as part of the broader family of life on Earth.

7. Arthur's Seat looms like a giant mammoth over the houses of Edinburgh. It is an extinct volcano, pushed up towards the end of the immensely long, slow fusion of England and Scotland, in a time when our ancestors were amphibians.

8. The Seven Sisters, part of the White Cliffs of Dover, overlooking the English Channel. The chalk was laid down during the Jurassic period and the channel itself was carved out in two sudden events, about 450,000 and 225,000 years ago.

9. Rock shelters on Oldbury Hill near Borough Green, Kent. This is what remains after extensive quarrying in the nineteenth century, but the place is still immensely evocative of our Neanderthal ancestors who once lived there.

10. A mighty modern sculpture of a Lower Palaeolithic hand axe marks the entrance to the Swanscombe Heritage Park at Swanscombe, Kent, where 400,000-year-old human remains were found, and which is laid out with informative sign boards to inspire and educate visitors by evoking our ancestral past.

11. Pinnacle Point Cave, Mossel Bay, South Africa – one of the grandest ancestral homes of our early *Homo sapiens* ancestors. *Copyright and courtesy of Out & About Travel, who organise visits there*

12. When the media sought to make sense of the new discoveries being made by genetics, it turned back to the familiar story of Adam and Eve and coined the terms 'Genetic Adam' and 'Mitochondrial Eve' for our earliest male and female genetic ancestors. The pair illustrated here are on the font of St James's, Westminster, the church built by Henry Jermyn in the 1680s.

13. The Venus de Laussel, some 25,000 years old, in the Musee d'Aquitaine, France.

14. The author returning to an ancestral home of us all, the Crô-Magnon rock shelter in the Vézère Valley, France.

15. Font de Gaume in the valley of the Beune, a tributary of the Vézère, a scene typical of the area with limestone cliffs, peppered with caves, sheltering secluded valleys.

16. Our Crô-Magnon ancestors creating their Ice Age art at Font de Gaume, as imagined by Charles R. Knight in 1920. Whether they really worked in teams or alone, we do not know. *FunkMonk / Wikimedia Commons*

17. Part of the original sketches of the cave art at Font de Gaume, as produced by Denis Peyrony and his colleagues in 1910. *Wellcome Images M0004858 / Wikimedia Commons*

18. Castel Merle in the Vézère Valley, where our modern human ancestors and Neanderthals alternated – or maybe even lived side by side and interbred.

19. The caves of La Madeleine, one of our grandest ancestral homes during the Upper Palaeolithic, perched up on a cliff with fine views across the broad Vézère Valley beyond.

20. An imaginative reconstruction of an Ice Age shaman outside the Grotte de Sorcier at Saint-Cirq in the Vézère Valley – a vivid evocation of our ancestral past there.

21. The Kercado Neolithic passage grave, Brittany, about 6,800 years old – a portal to the world of the dead.

22. Cheddar Gorge, Somerset, home of ancient ancestors of ours at the end of the Ice Age.

23. Reconstructed round huts and defences at Choirokitia in Cyprus, an early Neolithic farming community.

24. Les Pierre Plats passage grave on the Breton coast. Inside are fine carvings of 'shield idols', which are thought to be stylised female spirits – like Persephone in Greek myth, perhaps, presiding over this underworld of the dead.

25. The Coldrum Neolithic long barrow near Trottiscliffe, Kent. When the bones of one of the bodies it contained were removed in the nineteenth century, the vicar complained he had 'lost his oldest parishioner'.

26. The great horned 'altar' of the Tomnavery Neolithic stone circle in Aberdeenshire. The 'altar' faces the mountain of Lochnagar in the distance.

27. Adam's Grave on the southern edge of the Marlborough Downs, Wiltshire. The biblical Adam is not buried here, but the name reflects a local belief that this Neolithic long barrow contained a very ancient ancestor of ours – which it probably did.

28. An imaginative wax reconstruction of Ötzi the Iceman, in the South Tyrol Museum of Archaeology, Bolzano, Italy. Ötzi was one of the pioneers of metalworking in Europe and carried the male-line genetic marker G (L91). *Thilo Parg / Wikimedia Commons*

29. The grave circle at Mycenae, Greece, built about 1450 BC: a graphic link between the epitome of Bronze Age culture and its far more ancient Megalithic roots.

30. The ramparts of Maiden Castle, Dorset, one of the most imposing of Britain's many Iron Age hill forts, dating from about 550-300 BC. Just south of Dorchester, it commands the land between here and the sea.

31. Uffington Castle, a fine Iron Age hill fort up above the Vale of the White Horse, Oxfordshire.

32. Noah's Ark defies the flood waters, as illustrated on the font of St James's, Westminster. According to the Bible, all modern humans are descended from Noah and his sons.

33. In this oil sketch, Rubens imagined Cadmus, founder of the Greek city of Thebes, watching a fierce race of warriors sprout up as a result of his having sown the teeth of a slain dragon on his ploughland. This Greek myth was one of many explaining the origins of particular races and peoples. *Rijksmuseum, Amsterdam/Wikimedia Commons*

34. In a field in Beckhampton, near Avebury, Wiltshire, stand two stone giants from the Neolithic period, known in more recent times as Adam (seen here in the distance) and Eve (in the foreground). They were named because they reminded people of an ancient couple – a couple so ancient, in fact, as to represent the earliest ancestral parents of us all.

35. Mount Ararat in modern Turkey, where Noah's Ark was said to have settled, and from which Noah's descendants – our ancestors – were believed to have spread out to recolonize the world.

36. Silbury Hill, Wiltshire – a Neolithic mound built perhaps to illustrate a very ancient myth about the origins of the world.

37. St Michael's Mount, Cornwall. Cornish legend recalls that the giant Cormoran and his wife Cormelian lived nearby on Trencrom Hill, and spent their time collecting rocks and chucking them about. A rock that slipped out of Cormelian's apron fell into the sea and became the mount.

38. The Devil's Dyke, Sussex, now attributed in folklore to the Devil, but perhaps imagined by our earlier ancestors as the work of the world-shaping mammoths or serpents.

The bison-headed 'sorcerer' of Les Trois Frères. The lines coming down from his mouth could be a flute, or emanations of his spirit.

be correct. The idea that these were men in animal masks seems initially unlikely because the merging of human and animal seems too real. But many modern shamans in surviving tribal cultures still believe their trances can cause them actually to become animals. Maybe these paintings are records of similar shamanic experiences. If so, we wonder whether the animals depicted on cave walls are not supposed to be animals at all, but shamans transformed fully into beasts. But that interpretation may be too literal: perhaps it is more relevant to recall that many tribal societies still believe that humans and animals are inhabited by the same spirits, which can take whatever form they wish.

Either way, we can see that the origins of minotaurs, werewolves, satyrs, fauns and many other mythological creatures who are half human, half animal –not to mention jackal-headed Anubis and ibis-headed Thoth of ancient Egypt – might be very deeply rooted indeed in our Upper Palaeolithic past.

Chapter 18

Voices from the Caves

La Marche

The taboo against depicting humans realistically is one of the few things about Upper Palaeolithic art about which we can be certain. In many ways, their fears remain with us. Even in the liberated West, many people feel affronted if photographed or filmed without permission. Aboriginals will neither depict people, nor speak the names of the dead, for to do so traps the dead person's spirit in this world and prevents them from returning to the timeless Dreamtime. Perhaps such feelings have come down from our Upper Palaeolithic ancestors.

Perhaps, too, our ancestors feared the consequence of defining themselves too clearly. Our minds were advanced enough to recognise beauty in the creatures we were killing and dismembering. We had begun perhaps to feel like interlopers in Eden, fallen from grace (and perhaps, by fixing beautiful images of animals on cave walls, we hoped to atone for our destructive actions – and by giving a sort of permanence to the animals we had killed, maybe we hoped also to perpetuate the human spirit of ourselves as the images' creators as well). We may have felt, too, like children in a world moulded by the mighty spirits of great animals like the mammoths, which were so much bigger, stronger and apparently wiser than us. As yet mankind had made little impact on the landscape itself, so our ancestors did not have the hubris to attribute the world's creation to gods in human form. But it was dawning on us that we were different, and our conscious minds were already tugging us away from our animal roots, and towards a strange new, human-centered world. That fear of growing up, perhaps, is what we really shied away from when we refused to depict ourselves with any degree of realism.

On an antler found in La Vache cave below the Grotte de Niaux (and now in the national archaeological museum at Saint-German-en-Laye) is a scene that must have taken place daily in the Upper Palaeolithic, but which is shown so rarely in art – a hunt. In the foreground stands a mighty aurochs, a powerful bull with crescent-moon horns. Set back from him, so made smaller by correct perspective, stand three hunters, heads bent forward in concentration. Though they are little more than stick men, the scene looks realistic. But what if Magdalenian artists had defied the taboo and depicted our ancestors close up, as realistically as the animals they drew?

Astonishingly, this did occasionally happen. At the Riparo di Vado all'Arancio, Grosseto, Italy, is a limestone plaque on which is a 14,000-year-old drawing of an old man's head and shoulders. Shown in profile, he has a bushy beard and is apparently wearing a cap. In similar style is the left-facing head of a gaunt old woman found at Roc-aux-Sorciers near Poitiers. Her eyebrow and deep-set eye are natural shapes in the rock but her long, pointed nose, smiling mouth, sharp chin and two lines suggesting long hair have been engraved deliberately.

But if you really want to see what our Magdalenian ancestors looked like in real life you can go about 20 miles south of Roc-aux-Sorciers to La Sabeline museum in Lussac-les-Châteaux. Here are some of the engravings found in the nearby Grotte de La Marche and the somewhat less exciting Grotte de Fadets (other engravings from La Marche are in Saint-Germain-en-Laye; the Musée de l'Homme in Paris and the Musée Sainte-Croix in Poitiers). Since 1937, some 3,000 stone slabs have been found at La Marche, covered with engravings of animals including mammoths and lions and also about 115 images of people. They are from roughly 16,000–15,000 years ago. They are not better known largely because of arguments over their authenticity, but the Abbé Henri Breuil (1877–1961), the greatest authority on Palaeolithic art, thought they were genuine and recent studies all point to the same conclusion.

Some are head-and-shoulder portraits, but fifty-one have complete bodies. Thanks to poor health and hunting accidents, the Magdalenian population was always predominantly young, but there are a few characterful old men with beards. Some people have long hair though a few are bald and some wear caps, a couple of which have ear flaps. One cheerful young man with a long nose has scars running down his cheeks, as if he has been in a ritual initiation. Others are drawn very roughly with snout-like faces, looking more like monkeys than humans. Some of them are having sex and there is a puzzling drawing of two older, bearded men in close proximity to each other, with large penises, perhaps enjoying a sort of dance – but goodness knows what these grizzled ancestors of ours are really up to.

Few of the pictures are clear to see. The slabs have rough surfaces and the engraver had to work hard to scratch their lines. Almost all have been obscured: in some cases another image was drawn over the first one, and then further lines were added, so sometimes one can only just pick out the faces and bodies – but they are there.

What was going on? Was this the same artist who made the Roc-aux-Sorciers face mentioned above? He or she was fascinated with human forms and faces and had a real talent for capturing them. But doing so was taboo, so the artist obscured their own work, presumably voluntarily (through guilt, at having inadvertently captured people's souls?). That seems most likely, because if others had disapproved of the work they would simply have smashed the slabs to pieces.

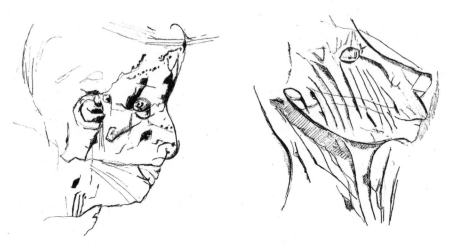

Two of the many ancestral portraits at La Marche, minus many of the extra lines made deliberately to obscure these works of art.

But such an explanation cannot be the full story, as many of the animal pictures from these caves have been deliberately obscured in the same way: as with so much of Magdalenian art, we simply do not know the full story.

Unless some exceptional disaster befell the Magdalenians of La Marche, they must be the ancestors of us all, many, many times over. La Marche is an exceptional gallery of our ancestral portraits from 15,000 years ago.

The search for meaning

Like all art, the work of our Upper Palaeolithic ancestors from Aurignacian to Magdalenian times invites us to imagine and seek meaning. For those of us seeking our ancient ancestors it offers the tantalising prospect of understanding and getting to know our Upper Palaeolithic forebears to a degree that is impossible with the countless generations who went before them.

But what does it all mean? Salamon Reinach (1858–1932) knew that the Arunta Aboriginals painted pictures of animals they hunted so that the real ones would multiply, and he attributed similar motives to the Upper Palaeolithic painters. But the archaeological link between the animals depicted, and remains found near such paintings, is weak. Lascaux is full of reindeer remains, but only one reindeer is depicted on the walls. At Niaux, bison and ponies are depicted in most numbers, yet the people there ate mainly ptarmigan, ibex, reindeer, fish and shellfish brought a long way from the sea. Maybe the animals being depicted were sacred and therefore not hunted – but in that case, why bother to pray for their numbers to increase?

Dale Guthrie of Alaska University argued that much cave art was testosterone-fuelled graffiti left behind by teenage boys. There is certainly a link between art and testosterone, because at Tuc d'Audoubert in the French Pyrenees is a sculpture of two bison copulating, and around it are footprints of dancing adolescents, perhaps engaged in a puberty rite. But the concentrated effort expended on the sculpture itself suggests a purpose more sober. Collecting the raw materials to make paints required a huge effort and communication over long distances to acquire the right minerals. It took a long time to grind pigments and make brushes and other equipment, suggesting that under some circumstances artists may even have been exempt from practical, daily work. To enter the caves required pre-prepared torches and oil lamps (some of which have been found still *in situ*) and in some cases complex wooden scaffolding must have been constructed to reach inaccessible ceilings. This was a serious, purposeful activity.

In the mid-twentieth century, Max Raphael (1889–1952) and Annette Laming-Emperaire (1917–1977) thought cave art might reflect social organisation. Clans might come together in their own sacred caves, where panels of animal pictures illustrated their origin myths. There are some great painted chambers like those at Lascaux and Niaux into which people could have gathered fairly easily and which may have been decorated for public display. But a great many more cave paintings are hidden deep down in places that, before modern excavation, required a long, scrambling squeeze down very narrow passages in pitch darkness – with faith in goodness knows what to bring you back safely to the fresh air again afterwards. Such places were scarcely appropriate for communal assembly. On the other hand, though, perhaps the fact that such sanctuaries simply existed and were only visited by a select few was enough to give them a cohesive power in society.

Shamanic visions

David Lewis-Williams and many French scholars think the key to the mystery lies in shamanism. We may think that, rather like the clouds that Hamlet pointed out to Polonius, which they thought looked like certain animals, shapes on cave walls may have suggested images of animals, which the early image makers simply improved. But Lewis-Williams pointed out that we think in terms of flat images only because we are used to seeing them. Show a photograph to a primitive tribesman who has never seen a flat image before and he will not recognise it as a picture at all. That presents the problem of how the first flat images could possibly have come into existence, before the human mind was used to processing such things. Lewis-Williams's theory is that it all began with drug use.

Shamanism is the oldest known form of human spirituality and probably goes back to Upper Palaeolithic times. Cave paintings of 'sorcerers' virtually prove it. Shamans practise techniques similar to those inherited by mystics in later religions: all sought enlightenment on a higher plane of being. 'Deep mental absorption,' wrote Steve Jones in *The Serpent's Promise* (2013), 'can persuade the brain that an inner thought has an outer source.' Such 'enlightenment' can be achieved by long periods of meditation or prayer in cold, dark, solitary conditions, usually accompanied by fasting – practices common in medieval monasteries and which probably started in Upper Palaeolithic caves. Such conditions can be shown by scientific experimentation to stimulate the production of melatonin in the pineal gland at the base of the brain. From this come visions.

The slow, deep breathing of Eastern mystics and the long periods of repetitive dancing practised by some Native Americans have the similar effect of depriving the brain of oxygen. With this come the associated physical symptoms of tingling limbs and trances (and, ultimately, physical collapse). Similar effects are created by shamans and mystics through narcotic drugs, such as psilocybin, the drug found in 'magic mushrooms'. Siberian shamans drink the urine of reindeer that have eaten fly agaric mushrooms, another rich source of psilocybin. Robert Graves suggested that the 'ambrosia' drunk in ancient Greece contained this same drug too.

All such practices can be replicated in laboratories and have similar profoundly 'spiritual' effects on people. These include hallucinations and entopic phenomena, visions seen within the eye, as if on a flat surface. These start, as Lewis–Williams writes in *The Mind in the Cave*, with 'dots, grids, zigzags, nested catenary curves, and meandering lines', adding that 'because these percepts are "wired" into the human nervous system, all people, no matter what their cultural background, have the potential to experience them.' All such features exist in cave art, and are found in many later Neolithic sites as well. When I was in my twenties, someone once slipped such a drug into my drink without my realising it. I experienced a sudden loss of all vision, after which I saw only a flat whiteness, with the alarming image of a flat black disc like a sun rising up from below. So to that extremely limited extent I have had a 'shamanic' experience and can relate a little to what Lewis–Williams writes.

As the trance grows deeper, the brain tends to start interpreting such imagery in terms of familiar or cultural icons. I interpreted the disc I saw as a rising sun and have thought of it like that ever since: only while editing these paragraphs did I realise that I had *not* seen a rising sun, but simply a black disc. It is at this stage, then, that a meditating Christian monk might interpret his entopic phenomena as an angel, or an Upper Palaeolithic shaman might think he was viewing an animal spirit.

Following this stage comes the sensation of falling into a vortex. Then the hallucination grows more intense and the person believes they have become their vision: shaman becomes animal. Such experiences are reported by religious and shamanistic practitioners, and drug users, all over the world and have been replicated perfectly under laboratory conditions.

In terms of Upper Palaeolithic art this seems to explain more than most theories. Visions could be sought in the depths of caves, where sensory deprivation was combined with fasting and probably ingestion of hallucinogenic seeds or mushrooms. When flat visions came in the early stages of the experience, they were interpreted in terms of what was most familiar – animals, and later these flat images were painted onto the walls of the caves in which they had been experienced. In all likelihood people believed these flat images had passed through the rock walls from a timeless world beyond. The rock wall of the cave was a membrane between two worlds. Painting was merely a means, they may have believed, of fixing images that had been there all along.

The images of 'sorcerers' pierced by arrows that appeared towards the end of the Magdalenian might represented the intense pricking, piercing sensations experienced by shamans during hallucinations. The caves may have been interpreted as the vortex down which the vision seekers thought they were tumbling. They thus became ever more sacred places where evidence of earlier visions was painted and to which successive generations could return for their own other-worldly experiences. Once myths had developed, novice shamans would be taught these and would naturally interpret their visions as episodes from these stories, making them seem ever more real. In the final stage, shamans seemed to become the animals of their visions. This may account for the many half-man, half-beast depictions that have been found from the Magdalenian, and going right back to the Lion Man of Hohlenstein near the very start of the Aurignacian.

Perhaps the appearance of the later Magdalenian sorcerers, which were drawn onto older animal pictures, has a more profound implication. Maybe here we have the evolution of human thought, deliberately challenging the ancient taboo against human depiction. Up to then, the depiction of animals implied that spiritual and earthly power lay outside the human sphere. But now, towards the end of the Magdalenian, was that assumption being challenged by people who thought they could do better? Was there here an early assertion on the part of these bipedal descendants of apes, these great-great-grandchildren of cynodonts and coelacanths, that mankind was different from and superior to beasts?

In broader terms, cave art helped us come to terms with being fully conscious, fully human. It is the outward, lasting expression of the less tangible social ethics, social organisation and religious beliefs that evolved during the Upper Palaeolithic to enable our newly aware ancestors to deal with the harsh realities of life. We cannot go back and discover whether and how Magdalenian society stratified itself, but from Magdalenian art we have at least the sense that a complex social organisation, with room for the likes of artists, existed.

It all comes from our having evolved advanced brains. Upon such foundations are piled endless layers of accreted beliefs. Here in the caves lie the origins of our social order, our myths, our gods, our religions. Cave art is a window onto the birth of our fascination with where we are going, and with where we came from. Our quest for our ancient ancestors started here.

The caves remain

Caves were visited periodically by our ancestors over tens of thousands of years. Long after we stopped painting in them, they remained sacred to many cultures, including the Bronze Age Minoans, who worshiped Zeus in his cave on Cretan Ida. 'On the religious plane', wrote Samivel in *The Glory of Greece*, the Minoans 'always remained "cave men", for the memory of those primordial caverns, matrices of the race, was still to haunt them when in later days they built their mighty palaces' with their sacred grottos, 'beehive' vaults and labyrinthine floor plans reminiscent of the twists and turns of caves. 'Cave men' at heart, too, were the ancient Greeks, many of whose oldest cults, such as those of Pan on the Acropolis and Demeter at Eleusis, were based around caves. Even after Jesus emerged from his cave at Gethsemane, Christian monks and hermits sought spiritual solace by returning to caves – and some of them received visions perhaps not dissimilar to those experienced by our Ice Age ancestors, albeit interpreted quite differently.

Maybe this latest, Victorian rediscovery of the painted caves is only one of many. Visitors squeeze into them now in as great a number as the authorities will allow. By visiting caves such as those in the Vézère Valley we grow closer to our ancestors by familiarity with the landscapes they inhabited, which seem to comfort and cradle us as well. We see the prints and outlines of our ancestors' hands on the cave walls and their preserved footprints on the muddy cave floors. We gaze – albeit uncomprehendingly – into our ancestors' souls through the human and animal images that they chose, so carefully, daringly and painstakingly, to depict. One thing is certain – our relationship with these ancestral caves is far from over.

Part Four

Book of Grain

Chapter 19

The False Spring

Creswell Crags

Towards the end of the Magdalenian, about 15,000 years ago – about 13,000 BC – the ice began at last to melt. Our ancestors saw grass sprouting up where in their childhood glaciers had ground forward in a seemingly unstoppable path. The new-sprung meadows teemed with bison, horses and reindeer. By 11,500 BC the climate was as warm as it is now and forests clothed the landscape.

As before, the opportunity arose to go north. First the mammoths waded through the fast-flowing river that coursed down the English Channel, then herds of reindeer and red deer followed them, their branch-like antlers moving like a stunted forest above the foaming water. The sight of them grazing happily on the South Downs was too much temptation for the Crô-Magnon hunters,

What appear to be a stag and a bear, drawn from photographs taken while in Church Hole, Creswell Crags.

descendants, no doubt, of the people of La Marche and the Vézère Valley, watching them from the south bank, who girded their loins and followed them. And so too did the wolves and lynxes, enemies for the new inhabitants of Britain.

Generations later, descendants of those first human colonists came to Kendrick's Cave at Great Orme on the North Welsh coast, where they left a horse's chinbone, covered with a dense pattern of zigzag lines, about 11,000 BC. They found their way back to the shelters of old too, including Creswell Crags, on the modern border of Derbyshire and Nottinghamshire.

That they did so seems remarkable, not least because (without modern roads and signposts) you would not even know Creswell's gorge was there until you stumbled upon it in the woods. Probably, they had found it by following the river. Once you are in the gorge, though, it has the same enclosed, homely feel as the Vézère Valley. Edged with limestone cliffs, topped with woods and with caves at their base, it was a hidden paradise, even before the Duke of Portland had the valley floor dug out to create the modern lake.

Since humans had last been to Creswell the ice had been at work. The new arrivals found that some of the cave roofs had shattered in the cold and tumbled down to fill once habitable spaces with rubble. Finds from the remaining caves, which sheltered the newcomers, include long bone needles carved out of antlers, and 'backed' blades (where the back of the blade was deliberately blunted to allow it to be pressed down with a finger and used as a knife). The culture that produced these was Upper Magdalenian, of course, but when the artefacts were found here by Dorothy Garrod and Leslie Armstrong in the 1920s, they termed them, proudly, 'Creswellian'. And as the descendants of the Magdalenians of the Vézère Valley that they surely were, the new occupants brought with them a love of art. In 1876, Sir William Boyd Dawkins found a rib bone in Robin Hood Cave carved with the head and back of a horse with a very prominent mane. The horse seems to be in a stockade, whose long straight lines may double as some sort of counting system. The lower part of the horse and its legs are drawn on the back of the rib and once it may all have been coloured with ochre. It is in the British Museum and a good replica can be seen in Creswell Crags' museum. Poor Dawkins was accused of faking this treasure, but most authorities now believe it to be genuine and, having seen the horses depicted in the Vale do Côa in Portugal (which were unknown to Dawkins) I agree: indeed, it's hard to believe that the artist who engraved this piece had not seen them too. Maybe it was a treasured ancestral possession, brought up from the south by the returning incomers.

In Creswell Crags' Pin Hole Cave was a piece of bone carefully carved with crosshatched lines. This and the horse suggested there might be parietal art there too. The Victorian excavators had lowered the cave floors considerably, making it hard to examine the cave ceilings in detail, so it was not until 2003–4 that a group of specialists began scouring the walls and ceilings for images. No paintings were discovered but they found images scratched on the rock by burins and flint tools, many adding to natural shapes and cracks in the limestone. There are triangle shapes in Church Hole and Robin Hood Cave, similar to many found in France, which probably represent vaginas. There is a male figure possibly with an erect penis, whose face is somehow beaked – half man, half bird, perhaps.

There is more, hard to see at first until the guide points them out and the eye becomes accustomed to picking out shapes: a stag, also startlingly similar to ones in the Vale do Côa; a bear's head, mainly formed from natural rock but enhanced with a few lines and a rather human-looking eye; a bison's (or perhaps an aurochs') head; a horse's head, very feint; the neck and head (plus eye) of an ibis, deeply incised, which you have to crane your head back to see. Other carvings are ambiguous, perhaps representing birds or (more likely) nude women in part of the cave which may have been a birthing chamber. Later, examining my photographs, I thought I saw another bear's head too.

Whatever else these images may have been, these were statements by the early Britons that they had come so far, achieved so much and would not go quietly into oblivion without leaving their mark.

The Cheddar Gorge mammoth

Towards the very end of the Upper Magdalenian, while our ancestors were still rediscovering the ancient rock shelters of Britain, a band of hunters returned to the Mendips in Somerset and did what we can still do today. They travelled over the high, dull plateau, shivering in the cold wind, until they found a valley sloping down towards the west. As you walk down, the sides loom up quickly, boulder-strewn, as wild now as they were then and cliffs of high, grey karst limestone enclose you. If you feel suddenly trapped and vulnerable to anyone who might happen to be standing at the top holding a rock, then so might a mammoth, and the idea came to the early people here that this would be an ideal place to trap animals.

Further down, at the base of the 450-foot deep Cheddar Gorge (see plate 22), the roaring waters had already

The mammoth of Gough's Cave, Cheddar Gorge.

carved out deep caves, full of natural stalagmites to fill our ancestors' minds with wonder. The early hunters used the cave mouths as shelters. The gorge became a base camp from which they conducted their hunts and to which they returned after seasonal forays out onto the lowlands below – lands later to become the Somerset marshes, stretching out to the Severn Estuary, but which were then drier, broader lands reaching away to the far more distant, colder ocean. They had flints from Wiltshire with them, and Baltic amber. One animal rib found here shows a criss-cross pattern, rubbed with ochre, and on the other side is a set of lines, maybe used for counting.

Human bones were defleshed, perhaps for ritual purposes, but as some of the bones also bear human tooth marks we know our ancestors had eaten each other, and discarded the bones irreverently amongst those of animals. But a skull found here was not only defleshed but also shaped carefully to turn it into a cap, or cup. This practice was also discovered at La Placard in Charente, whilst at Isturitz in the Pyrenees some skull caps were even engraved with images of animals, suggesting a reverent, ritual purpose.

Their mindset was Magdalenian, and in Gough's Cave within the gorge they sought out natural shapes that, to them, suggested the greater spiritual presence of animals (or, perhaps, animal ancestors). Recently, one trace of their work was found – the back, head, tusks and trunk of a mammoth from about 11,000 BC. The tusks are natural curving lines in the limestone and the eye is a natural hole too. Only the back and head have been engraved. It is no bigger than an outstretched hand. It comes out poorly in photographs but is easier to see when you are face to face with it. The outline is drawn in exactly the same style as the mammoth depictions in the Vézère Valley. It represents one of the last flourishes of Upper Palaeolithic art, here in a cave in a gorge in Somerset.

Gough's Cave is easy to visit, and next to it is the eccentric Marquess of Bath's superb Ice Age museum, full of models of Magdalenians and the animals they encountered, including a memorably terrifying stuffed hyena.

Younger Dryas

The spring was a brief one. About 10,800 BC, the Loch Lomond Stadial or Younger Dryas (named after an alpine flower, *Dryas octopetala*) plunged the temperature back down again. Within a century, the stultifyingly cold desiccation of the Ice Age had returned and the days of plenty were a distant dream. Wolves roamed through the snowfields below the ice-caked trunks of dead trees and the wind joined them in their howling. The last humans fled back south and Britain was deserted once more.

Chapter 20

The Stag Dancers of Star Carr

The Azilian

At last, about 9,500 BC, the climate warmed again. By hunting so many grazing animals, we may inadvertently have allowed forests to spread across the tundra. The dark foliage then trapped more sunlight, which caused the world to start to warm. So we may have contributed to global warming, even then. Certainly, the Ice Age has not returned since. Whether this is truly the first *post*-glacial stage, or just a long *inter*-glacial one, we simply don't know. But given the history of the climate, if glaciers did return to grind away the motorways and car parks and superstores with which we have covered our land, it ought not to surprise us.

Whatever the future holds, the change in the climate seems so momentous to we whose civilisation has thrived as a result, that we have used it to mark the end both of the Pleistocene geological epoch and of the Upper Palaeolithic age of human culture. It marks the dawn of the present, Holocene, epoch. In geological terms we are still in the first stage of the Holocene, and we have termed this chronostratigraphic sub-division 'the Flandrian stage'. In terms of cultures, the Holocene opened with the Mesolithic, or 'Middle Stone Age', whose first cultural subdivision is called the Azilian in France (after the Mas d'Azil cave in the Pyrenees) and the Tjongerian or Ahrensburg elsewhere in northern Europe (but there is some local disagreement over both the terminology and the precise dating of these sub-phases).

As the climate warmed, reindeer started journeying ever further north and hunters followed them, leaving the southern refuges in the Vézère Valley and returning again to Britain, this time for good. They found Britain covered with lush new forests of hardy conifers, which were joined before long by birch and ash with a scrubby underbrush of hazel trees. The Mesolithic spring had come, and along the forest edges golden curtains of hazel catkins basked in the Sun's returning warmth.

Whilst the weather may have been better, life seems actually to have grown harder for our ancestors. The grand old days of hunting great, meat-rich animals across the tundra was gone now. Instead, we and our dogs scrabbled for ever smaller prey in ever denser woodlands. We still made flint tools, and indeed these continued to develop into ever finer points, called microliths because they are so small. But when we made bone harpoons we had no time to decorate them with carved animals, as we had in the past. In Aveline's Hole in Burrington Combe in the Mendips, and Long Hole in nearby Cheddar Gorge itself, the Mesolithic people scratched a few crosses: discovered in 2005, they are not dissimilar to some found in France. And then, with a few dots and lines painted on pebbles found at Mas d'Azil, Upper Palaeolithic art came to an ignominious end. Our ancestors had no choice but to lay down their engraving tools and stomp away through the boggy woodland, desperately searching for something to eat.

The horned one

Art may have disappeared but the old animal cults of the Upper Palaeolithic lingered on, because animal spirits were invoked with ever more urgency to guide the hunt. In 1947 an amateur archaeologist, John Moore, started digging at Star Carr, near Pickering, Yorkshire. He discovered a Mesolithic campsite dating from the 8,000s BC, on the edge of what was then a lake – a liminal place where practical life merged with religion. There is evidence that aspen and willow trunks had been split – the first surviving evidence of European carpentry – and laid down to create a walkway by the edge of the bog. Nearby is evidence of round huts, probably made of bent hazel poles covered with brushwood or hides. Many barbed arrow and spear points have been found too, made from red deer antlers.

Twenty-one 'antler frontlets' have been found at Star Carr too. They were made from the antlered skulls of stags. Two holes were bored into each skull cap, presumably so that we could tie them onto our heads and wear them as headdresses. One is in the Ashmolean Museum in Oxford. Perhaps these were used as a disguise while hunting, but it is hard to escape the conclusion that ritual was involved, perhaps harking back to the shamanistic dances seemingly portrayed in the half-man, half-stag cave paintings at Les Trois Frères and elsewhere, back in the Magdalenian.

A possible descendant of such shamanistic dances is the Horn Dance performed by Morris dancers to this day, 110 miles south-east of Star Carr, at Abbots Bromley, Staffordshire. When this same, horned shaman emerges into the half-light of Celtic mythology, he is a horned deity called

One of the Star Carr stags' skulls, pierced with holes so they could be worn as headdresses, in the Ashmolean Museum, Oxford.

Cernunnos. In Ireland, the *Cattle Raid of Cooley*, recorded by Dark Age monks from the pre-Christian *seanchaidhe*s or story-telling genealogists, makes a passing reference to the Partraighi, 'the people of the stag', an Irish tribe who may also have retained a similar, spiritual connection to these magnificent animals right down into the Iron Age.

Cheddar Man

The best known Mesolithic Briton must be Cheddar Man, whose remains were buried in Gough's Cave in Cheddar Gorge about 7150 BC. In his pioneering work on Britain's population genetics, Brian Sykes analysed Cheddar Man's mitochondrial DNA, and learned that it belonged to the female sub-haplogroup U5. Tests on local schoolchildren produced no match, but their teacher, Adrian Targett, belonged to exactly the same subgroup, as did Cuthbert, the butler of the gorge's owner, Lord Bath. They might be descended in the direct female line from Cheddar Man's mother, or are more likely descended from a remote cousin of hers. But either way, Sykes's work was a landmark in proving a genuine genetic link between the earliest post-Ice Age inhabitants of Britain, and us. There have been many incomers since, but some of our genes go back, for sure, to Britain's Mesolithic inhabitants.

The making of the British Isles

As the ice melted, sea levels rose and waves broke ever further inland. About 8000 BC the land route between Ireland and Britain was broken and the few thousand people living in the far west unwittingly became the core population of modern Ireland.

During the Younger Dryas, Doggerland, with its herds of mammoth and bison, had extended from Yorkshire to Denmark. As the ice melted, this was reduced to a land bridge stretching from Norfolk to Holland. By 7,000 BC, in a phase warmer and moister than today, people hunting across this narrowing strip of land realised it was becoming treacherously boggy. It finally broke during a sudden, cold snap about 6,200 BC. A recent theory suggests not a slow breach of this last land bridge, but a sudden event caused by the 'Storegga Slide', when a 180-mile long stretch of the Norwegian coastline suddenly collapsed into the sea. A great wall of water surged across the North Sea and burst with terrible force over the land bridge. We became an island: in Classical Greek terms, we had been sundered from the world and now lay beyond the encircling arms of Ocean. Tales of the loss of the land bridge probably haunted our forebears for many centuries afterwards. (Edmund Spenser writes about such an event in his

Faerie Queene (1590/96), but that is a later theorising about a similar event, not a genuine folk memory handed down faithfully, as some may wish to believe, over some 8,000 years).

The population of the new island of Britain is estimated to have been about 5,000 strong. Every one of those people who left living descendants must be an ancestor of all living Britons now, many thousands of times over. Among the most evocative survivals from this time are several sets of footprints, dating to about 6000 BC, preserved on the muddy shoreline of the Severn Estuary at Goldcliff, Monmouthshire. They allow us to follow, literally, in our ancestors' footsteps.

As the woods closed in, life favoured shorter people. We lost some of the heroic stature of our Upper Palaeolithic ancestors, pursuing ever smaller game, or relying ever more, as at Goldcliff, on shellfish. Writing in the first century AD, Tacitus describes a Baltic tribe, the Fenni, who preserved a way of life probably not dissimilar to that in Mesolithic Britain: 'astonishingly savage and disgustingly poor … they have no proper weapons, no horses, no homes. They eat wild herbs, dress in skins, and sleep on the ground. Their only hope of getting better fare lies in their arrows, which, for lack of iron, they tip with bone … the only way they have of protecting their infants against wild beasts or bad weather is to hide them under a makeshift covering of interlaced branches.' Yet, adds Tacitus with a typically moral Roman twist, they possessed so little that they were unafraid of loss, and were 'so well content that they do not even need to pray for anything'.

The last of the mammoths

When did the last mammoth die in Britain? The most recent remains found in Britain were unearthed by Dr Adrian Lister at Condover, Shropshire, in 2009 and date from about 12,000 BC, but maybe there are later ones yet to be discovered, who had returned during the Younger Dryas.

As the Mesolithic climate became ever warmer and moister across Eurasia, the mammoths floundered in insect-infested swamps and pushed with ever more difficulty through the spreading deciduous woods of hazel, birch and alder that sprang up across the tundra. But they lingered on a long time in Siberia and the last of them, greatly diminished in stature, died on Wrangel Island off the north-eastern coast of Siberia about 1650 BC, while the Thirteen Dynasty sat on the throne of Egypt.

Their remains and those of their elephantine ancestors spurred fresh stories wherever they were unearthed. Mammoth skulls have inconspicuous eye sockets but right in the centre they have a single, big hole for the trunk. Adrienne Mayor showed how such skulls could easily be misinterpreted by our ancestors as those of one-eyed monsters. The perception that the associated bones were those of large human-like creatures could have led to them being reassembled in that way – hence the Classical myths of the gigantic cyclopses, who had a single eye in the centre of their monstrous heads.

Frozen corpses of mammoths are still being found in Siberia. The Siberians who found such wonders in the past thought they were giant molelike creatures who lived below the earth and occasionally burrowed upwards, where they died of cold. They called them *mammants*, a word brought to the west by Dutch explorers in the sixteenth century (and first used as a term for something enormous by the American statesman Thomas Jefferson). One mammoth, discovered in 1977, was only eight months old. Nicknamed 'Dima', he was radiocarbon dated to about 40,000 years ago, the period when our Crô-Magnon ancestors were first settling in Europe. Another was Lyuba, a female mammoth calf found in 2007 on the Yamal Peninsula, and carbon dated accurately to 41,800 years ago. She was so well preserved (by both the cold and lactic acid bacteria) that traces of her mother's milk remained in her intestines. We saw her when she was exhibited at the Natural History Museum in 2014 and could see her anal flap, traces of reddish fur on her stomach, and her ribs showing through her withered, leathery skin, which was pockmarked with holes from fungus that had attacked her after she had thawed out, making her skin look like the cratered surface of the Moon. It was an extraordinary experience to be looking so closely at a genuine woolly mammoth.

Replacing the mammoths in England came that other venerable giant, the English oak. It first spread its gnarled branches across our British hills about 6,000 BC, a newcomer to a land already well trodden by human feet. For almost 2,000 years it ruled supreme. But then came the sound of stone axes biting wood. Farming arrived, brought across the white-crested waves by a new people, who would change the face of Britain forever. But who were these sophisticated newcomers, and where did they come from?

Chapter 21

From the City of Plastered Skulls

The Natufians

W e each derive our ancestry from many different lines of ancestors. Whilst some of our forebears were hunting and gathering in Mesolithic Britain, other forebears of ours, also descended from survivors of the Ice Age, were living in the Middle East. Back in the Younger Dryas, that last, short phase of the Ice Age about 10,800–9,500 BC, so much water was locked up in ice around the Poles that the climate became dry across the world. With game in short supply, the tightly packed hunter-gatherer bands in the Middle East relied ever more on fruits, large-grained grasses and pistachio nuts (we are not accustomed to associating the rise of civilisation with pistachios, but this is what archaeology tells us).

Initially, we camped in places where such goodies grew naturally, but soon we started deliberately to encourage them by clearing away less useful plants. We then took natural selection into our own hands by selecting and sowing seeds of the particular plants that yielded the most, starting the development of large-seeded grasses into grain-bearing crops. Once we were tending crops, we had to stay in one place, so instead of following herds of animals we started herding them using dogs and restricting their movements by building stockades. The earliest evidence for such early farming comes from the Wadi Al Natuf, Palestine, hence the term 'Natufian culture'. From the seeds sowed there, literally, grew the Neolithic, the 'New Stone Age', the age of agriculture.

It all seems very impressive, but we were not the first species to behave in this way. Since the Cretaceous, insects such as termites, ants and bees had been withdrawing from Nature into environments they could control themselves. Termites cultivate their own fungus crops, ants guard aphids and feed on their sugary secretions, and by pollinating nectar-rich plants, bees effectively farm and increase the populations of the plants on which they rely for food. Ultimately, though, we have taken the exercise further than they – and with what ultimate consequences we do not yet know. Without farming, the world today would probably not sustain a human population above 600,000 souls. Thanks to farming, our numbers have increased rapidly, to 250 million by AD 1, and 500 million by 1750, when industrialisation enabled the further massive explosion in our numbers to the staggering seven billion of today.

Çatal Hüyük

Neolithic culture spread by grown-up children cultivating land near their parents' fields, or by families setting off across unsuitable terrains in search of new, fertile lands. It stimulated new social organisations, from tribes and cities to kingdoms and empires. Jericho in Palestine is perhaps the world's oldest settlement still inhabited today, with its roots planted firmly in Natufian culture. Its first walls were built about the 7000s BC, probably to protect the settlement against floods that had been caused, it turns out, by the clearing away of the valley's vegetation to create fields.

Another very ancient settlement was Çatal Hüyük in Anatolia (Turkey). Founded about 7500 BC, it grew rapidly into a 32-acre town of linked single-storey mud-brick houses. The houses were entered via holes in the roof using ladders. Inside, the walls were painted with lively hunting scenes – Ice Age art, revived in a Neolithic town. They had Venus figurines too, carved from bone or stone, as obese and big-breasted as ever they had been in Aurignacian times.

About 7,200 BC, the Natufians of 'Ain Ghazal, in Wadi Zarqa near Amman, Jordan, decorated skulls with lime plaster, placing shells in the eye sockets. One from the latter site is in the Ashmolean Museum, Oxford. Another is in the British Museum, as are three primitively sculptured clay figures, with slit mouths and nostrils and eerie eyes, inset with black stones, which gaze out balefully on the world. Once, they probably had artificial hair and painted skin colour too. It seems as if, with the onset of farming, the age-old taboo against depicting people was disintegrating and ways of thinking about the past, and our relationship to it, had started to change too.

Choirokitia

Nobody knows for sure whether farming started once, with the Natufians in the Middle East, and then spread all over the world, or whether it arose spontaneously in several places, at different times. So the question of whether farmers spread all the way to China, or farming appeared there spontaneously, is a moot point. The Chinese insist they discovered it for themselves. There are theories about farming spreading to South America, and you can read exciting but rather far-fetched theories of civilisation there being seeded by Egyptians and suchlike, though it is far more probable that it developed there spontaneously too. But it seems highly likely that farmers did spread east from the Middle East into Pakistan and India, south to Egypt and the Sudan, and out across the Mediterranean to Cyprus.

In the hills set back from the south coast of Cyprus, between Larnaka and Limassos, is one of the very earliest farming settlements outside the Middle East:

Choirokitia (see plate 23). It was founded about 7000 BC by immigrants from Anatolian, who brought with them domesticated sheep, goats, pigs, barley and two sorts of wheat (called 'einkorn' and 'emmer'). To harvest their crops they used flint sickles fitted into bone or wooden handles and fastened with animal glue.

They built their village on a raised area surrounded by a high wall, on the hillside stretching down towards the fertile Maroni Valley. The valley snakes its way to the coast around a low hill that shields much of the settlement from the prying eyes of passing sea travellers. Already, the age of innocence, if there had ever been one, had passed. That is suggested too by the walls, which were made at great effort. Going in and out of the village involved tortuous, labyrinthine stairways that snaked up to and between the windowless houses. It was all designed to confuse and intimidate the stranger.

The village's houses were small and round, with flat roofs of wooden beams covered with reeds. The walls were of stone and mud brick, plastered with mud and probably painted. Nearby at Kalavasos-Tenta, a similar hut contained a painting of two people, one with raised arms: a similar figure was found depicted on a stone bowl at Choirokitia itself. Everywhere, as at Çatal Hüyük, were stone figurines. But unlike many Neolithic sites, Choirokitia's were predominantly male, with prominent penises.

They buried their dead beneath their own huts, sealed over by dried mud floors. Women were sometimes buried with shell and bead ornaments, just as their ancestors had been in the Upper Palaeolithic. Some had deliberately broken stone vases with them, but not always. Some men were buried with a heavy stone on top of them – to stop their spirits coming back to haunt the living, perhaps.

The Choirokitians probably sat in their little houses at night, telling stories of the epic journey that had brought their ancestors across the sea from Anatolia. One possible insight into their mindsets is that, from their village, you can see in the distance a conical hill, Mount Stavorouni, which in later, Classical times was called Mount Olympos, after the mythological home of the gods in Macedonia. Perhaps the Choirokitians had chosen the site so that they could see this hill. Maybe they worshipped deities who lived on its peak. Maybe they believed this was the first mound of earth that the deities had ever raised up out of the primeval sea, and from which the rest of the world had grown.

Megalithic Brittany

The Choirokitians tried to live in splendid isolation, yet in fact they were part of an inexorable movement of Neolithic farmers west. By the 6,000s BC, domesticated goats grazed near fields of swaying barley below the rock of the Acropolis, and mud huts stood where one day the city of Athens would flourish. As farmers travelled further west, emphasis often fell first on animal husbandry: migrating farmers, perhaps with the help of local hunter-gatherers who had learned their ways, combined hunting with penning, rearing and slaughtering herbivorous animals. The cultivation of fields for crops followed more slowly in its wake.

Farming spread in two directions. One branch went west along the Mediterranean coastline, then north up the Atlantic seaboard. The other went along the Danube from its mouth at the Black Sea, up into the Alps and then north along the Rhine (which rises very near the Danube's source). Working up the Rhine, farming spread to the North Sea and then west along the French coastline. These two branches of Neolithic farmers seem to have met on the bony peninsula of *Ar-mór*, 'the land of the sea', which we now call Brittany, in the late 4000s BC. This meeting of anciently related cultures stimulated an astonishing outburst of monument building in the area around the seaport of Carnac (Morbihan).

The building of structures out of big stones, termed 'megaliths', gave its name to the Neolithic cultural phase known as the Megalithic. It was not an entirely new phenomenon. The Magdalenians at Saint-Germain-la-Rivière had built a small dolmen out of stones to bury a dead woman. Once farming took hold in Anatolia, the people of Nevali Cori and Göbekli Tepe arranged great stones in circles as early as the 8,000s BC. Thereafter, farmers sometimes manipulated naturally occurring stones to build graves, or erected them as single markers or in groups.

In one way this behaviour was practical. If a stone lies in the middle of your field you will naturally think of moving it out of the way of the plough. Because farming marks landscapes in a way that hunting never did, the impulse to stand stones up to indicate some form of possession of the land might follow on naturally. But there always seems to have been a spiritual dimension to such activities too. Once a stone has been erected and used ceremonially, it could become the cultural focus of a local community.

The spiritual aspect of standing stones may date back to the worship of deities in the form first of trees, then of erected tree trunks, and finally in more permanent, upright stones. Or maybe some standing stones marked places where lightening – doubtless believed to have been thrown by a deity – had struck the Earth. Perhaps such stones were memorials to the dead (a practice that continues with gravestones), or maybe they represented actual ancestors transformed into stone (just as we still erect stone statues of our great and good). Whatever their intention, such stones surely acted, like all Neolithic monuments, as places of assembly.

By about the 6000s BC the Neolithic farmers who had reached Portugal started building monuments for themselves. The oldest site is believed to be the Cromeleque dos Almendres at Nossa Senhora de Guadalupe near Évora, barely 30 miles from the Atlantic. It comprises a huge, double circle of standing boulders, to which was added later a larger double oval, on a site occupied from about 6,000 to 3,000 BC. Its builders were probably direct ancestors of the earliest monument builders in Brittany. The spread of farming north up the Atlantic seaboard leads to Galicia in the north-western corner of Spain, an area liberally peppered with individual standing stones called menhirs, and graves, called dolmens, made of large natural stones. Many of these are within a few miles of the sea. Most of those we can see now post-date the earliest in Brittany, suggesting a cultural backwash down the coast. Good examples include the Lapa de Gargantáns near Santa Lucia de Moraña, 10 miles from the Atlantic, a granite menhir with a squarish base, tapering upwards with curved sides bearing several zigzag carvings and cup marks, dating from about 3500 to 2000 BC. Not far away, the Dolmen de Axeitos, also called A Pedra do Mouro, is a communal Neolithic grave from about 4000 to 3600 BC: sitting near the end of the Ribeira peninsula, it is barely 2 miles from the sea on three sides. Further north and slightly further inland, it is possible to visit no less than six dolmens on a well-signposted driving route around Vimianzo, most said to date from about 4000 BC. The variety of styles is interesting: some consist of a dark burial chamber lined with upright slabs supporting a huge capstone, whilst others such as the Pedra Arca Piosa had two capstones, one over the burial chamber and the other covering an entrance passage, also lined with slabs of stone. The stone chambers were made first, then filled with earth and the capstone would be dragged up, before the chamber below was cleared out again. Over the whole structure, earth was piled up, to create a long mound or barrow. Locations vary: the Pedra Arca Piosa was up on a hilltop, gazing out towards a nipple-shaped mountain, so was perhaps linked to a developing belief in a mother goddess, but others, such as the Pedra da Lebra, were on low-lying ground: its only significant view was up to the hill of the Pedra Arca Piosa.

Galicia's megalithic sites are impressive, but the scale of monument building in Brittany, where the two branches of farming culture met, is unprecedented anywhere in the world. Its heroic scale baffled the builders' own distant descendants, who attributed the work to giants or even, until the critical approach of the eighteen and nineteenth centuries took hold, to the Romans. But it is now known to have been the work of Neolithic farmers, beginning about 4800 BC and lasting until 2500 BC.

The Breton monuments comprise variants on two main themes: standing stones and passage graves. Some standing stones were individual menhirs, some of extraordinary height, such as the *menhir brisé* at Er Grah, which once towered 67 feet into the air. Other standing stones, some the height of a man, were grouped in horseshoe shapes (called cromlechs) or squares (termed quadrilaterals). Others, at Kermaro and Kerzerho, for instance, stood in incredibly long parallel rows that marched across the low-lying landscape like invading armies. In the woods at Kercado, not far from Carnac, is the world's oldest passage grave, built about 4800 BC (see plate 21). Like some later examples, Kercado's upright stones were decorated with double axe symbols. Elsewhere in the area, at Mané Lud for instance, you can see carvings of animal horns. On the beach at Locmariaquer is the passage grave of Les Pierres Plates, some of whose uprights have been carved with multi-breasted cartouches that archaeologists term 'shield idols' (see plate 24). These are thought be styled, engraved, flat versions of the Upper Palaeolithic Venuses, still present and haunting the imaginations of our Neolithic ancestors.

The front of Kercado was indented inwards and lined with dry stone walling, to create a semi-enclosed forecourt. This pattern was followed by many later barrows. Archaeologists believe this forecourt was where dead bodies were de-fleshed, either by hand, or by birds (and maybe they believed that the spirits of the dead, so released, could soar away into the sky). The bones would then be added to the barrow's contents, not, it seems, as individual skeletons, but as part of a communal collection of bones.

These places of communal burial really do suggest an ancestral cult. The world began and the deities awoke our ancestors. The ancestors' mortal remains lie mixed together in the barrow and their spirits inhabit the air around us. We are descended from the ancestors and when we die our bones and spirits will join theirs. That is probably how we viewed our world, back in Neolithic Brittany.

Chapter 22

The Heroes from the Sea

First farmers in Britain

Straining at our oars in precarious, wood-framed, hide-skinned boats akin to coracles, our terrified animals tied up firmly in the keel, we first intrepid farmers battled our way through the foam-crested waves to reach Britain in about 4300 BC.

In his *History of the Kings of Britain*, Geoffrey of Monmouth imagined Brutus of Troy leading his intrepid band of Trojan followers to land at Totnes on the south coast of Devon. Spreading out from there, these first human colonists 'began to till the Ground and build Houses, so that in a little Time the Country look'd like a Place that had been long inhabited.' That was pure myth, but it belies a sort of truth, for some of the earliest incomers from the south probably did land along the Devonshire coast, for it is directly opposite Brittany. They then made their way up onto Dartmoor, which was then far warmer and less acidic than it is now. The Spinster's Rock dolmen near Drewsteignton ('druid's stone town') on the northern edge of Dartmoor dates from a little later, about 3500 BC. But, with its three massive uprights supporting a stone like the cap of a giant mushroom, it is extremely similar to many dolmens found in the Carnac region of Brittany.

Meanwhile, other farmers were crossing from Calais to Dover, drawn by the alluring sight of the White Cliffs, which had been carved out of the chalk of the South Downs by the booming sea below. So these early migrants came from both the routes – up the Atlantic seaboard, and up the Rhine – along which farming had been spread by their intrepid ancestors, both originating in the Middle East.

Three thousand years earlier, their forebears had farmed at the Wadi Al Natuf, Çatal Hüyük, Choirokitia and maybe, coincidentally, around Troy itself. Now, they farmed on the fertile hills of Britain and Ireland, covering the landscape with ditched enclosures, long barrows and standing stones, which endure to this day as stirringly evocative reminders of those ancient, pioneering ancestors of ours.

Long barrows

Apart from the granite uplands of the South West, the highest points in southern and central England, and some further north as well, are mainly the plateaus and downlands of chalk and limestone. They were created from the shells of marine crustaceans between about 250 million (in the case of the Pennines) and 60 million (for the South Downs) years ago, a huge span of time during which our ancestors had remained consistently small and furry. But now we had evolved into Neolithic farmers and these chalk and limestone uplands became our favoured homes. Here we built ditched enclosures, vantage points of relative safety from which we looked down at the treacherous, boggy woodlands, infested with wolves, boars and aurochs, which filled the valleys and low-lying areas. We established ridgeways along the calciferous hilltops from Somerset through Wiltshire and as far east along the South Downs as Beachy Head in Sussex and along the North Downs to what would one day become Canterbury. We now can still walk in our ancestors' footsteps, for they remain public footpaths – the Ridgeway, the Pilgrim's Way and so on.

Neolithic settlements seem unremarkable compared with the later Iron Age hill forts, many of which were built over them, but they can be impressive in their own way. On the southern edge of the Marlborough Downs above the Vale of Pewsey, for example, you can climb up to the earthen rings around Knap Hill and admire the view west along the scarp of the downs to the hilltop crowned by Adam's Grave (see plate 27), a Neolithic long barrow that contained some fine leaf-shaped flint arrowheads and a small community of skeletons, most probably the people of Knap Hill. Their skulls had been smashed open, presumably after they had died, so that their brains could be eaten, thus allowing them to live on inside their descendants. This same barrow was also called Wodensbury, but whether named after the Saxon god Woden (Odin), or Adam, people have long recognised a close connection between such long barrows as this, and our own ancestry, however it has been mythologised.

What started in Brittany spread all across Britain. But on British soil, the horseshoe-shaped cromlechs of the Carnac region became stone circles, an early example of the quixoticness that our island seems to exert on his inhabitants. Some of the earliest circles, oddly, are in the north, such as Castlerigg (c. 3200 BC) and Sunkenkirk (c. 3000 BC) in the Lake District. Our long barrows varied in shape, too. Some continued the rather rounded Bretton style of Kercado. Those at Coldrum (on the North Downs near Trottiscliffe in Kent, see plate 25), and Belas Knap and Hetty Pegler's Tump in the Cotswolds all have the same plump squatness as their continental counterparts. But there are also longer, narrower ones, such as the West Kennet long barrow near Avebury, Wiltshire, just north of Adam's Grave, and Kit's Coty above the Medway in Kent, whose great mound used to stretch right along the top of the hill on which its surviving stones still stand.

We can, and should, spend a great deal of time at long barrows. Often, we can walk around and (if safe) upon them, and in the case of some that have been restored, such as West Kennet and Belas Knap, we can even go into the burial chambers within. These are tangible monuments to our Neolithic ancestors, intended to exist in harmony with the natural world – the world from which their builders had emerged. They were never placed insensitively, in the willy-nilly way people now locate car parks and superstores. Instead, they were conceived as organic additions to the hills and vales around them. Some, like Coldrum, Julieberry's Grave, near Canterbury, Kent, and the Cairnholy chambered cairns in Kirkcudbrightshire, rise above natural slopes. Others echo the view behind them, like Windover Long Mound, above the Long Man of Wilmington in the South Downs, whose rising form exactly mirrors the curves of Firle Beacon on the horizon.

Of course it is easy to read too much into these surviving monuments but one interesting theory was developed in the 1930s by Alexander Keiller and his young assistant Stuart Piggott while investigating Avebury: that tall, thin stones might represent the male (penis) and wide stones, many of which are roughly diamond shaped, could represent the female (vulvas, or wide, child-bearing hips). Often, such differently shaped stones were paired up, perhaps representing male and female together. The stones of the West Kennet long barrow certainly fall into these two types, and there are many other examples nearby both at Avebury and just to the west in the Longstone Cove in a field at Beckhampton (see plate 34), where you can see two stones, one phallic, the other diamond shaped, which the locals called Adam and Eve. But where you go from there is unclear – were they believed to represent, or actually to be, petrified ancestral human parents, or perhaps a couple of ancestral gods?

Maybe the diamond-shaped stones are spiritual descendants of those depictions of the fat, broad-hipped Venus figurines of earlier times. Linked to her, too, may be the perceived feminine aspects of the long barrows themselves. In *The Modern Antiquarian*, Julian Cope boldly likens the Kercado-style barrows, such as Belas Knap, to 'the truncated form of a squatting woman', where 'the vagina is represented by the huge megalithic doorway'. Hunter's Burgh on Wilmington Hill in the South Downs does indeed seem to rise up out of the bulging downland hillside like a swelling womb that also burrows down into the body of the Earth. It creates an extraordinary sense of connectedness between the cavernous Earth below, the here and now of the green hillside, and the eternity of the sky above. Some Neolithic monuments seem to have been built to respect certain hills that (with a little stretch of the imagination) can be seen to resemble reclining women or female deities. The Easter Aquhorthies stone circle in Aberdeenshire, for example, sits on an exposed hillside gazing out towards Mither Tap, whose peak can be seen as a breast, rising up from the lower hills that are a woman's recumbent body.

But in the Orkneys we encounter this female force on surer ground, in the form of three stone-carved figurines, found at Notland, dating from 3000 BC. The first was found in 2008 and nicknamed the 'Westeray Wife'. It is a very simple echo of the old Venus figurines, with just a round head and fingernail-shaped body, two small round breasts and a crude, scratched face. But we know her well by now, and recognise her without difficulty.

Marking time

If the way our Upper Palaeolithic ancestors thought about time and their relationship to it was ever simple, then that simplicity started to become less so as the Neolithic developed. A simple idea of the past merging quickly into an eternal continuum, perhaps akin to the Dreamtime of Aboriginal mythology, probably sufficed for nomadic hunter-gatherers. But the Neolithic lifestyle forced people to think about greater expanses of time than ever before. The longer a farming community remained settled, then the older its buildings and monuments became and the greater the number of bones and skulls piled up in its burial places. All were constant reminders of the swift passage of time and the inevitability of death.

An awareness of time provokes a need to mark it. This was both a psychological necessity and a practical need for farming communities dependent on the seasons. Some stone alignments and the positioning of some barrows were surely intended to help people observe the movements of the heavenly bodies for this purpose. Rodney Castleden argued convincingly that various Neolithic monuments on the hills around Lewes, Sussex, including the Cliffe Hill long barrow, were positioned to mark key sunrises during the year when viewed from the artificially created Neolithic 'Castle Mound' in Lewes itself.

Perhaps the same can be said of the many other sites that seem, when you are in them, to be at the very centre of everything – places like the Withypool stone circle on Exmoor and the artificially flattened Dragon Hill below Uffington's White Horse in Oxfordshire. Such monuments are viewing points for natural features in the landscape, such as hilltops, which seem to arrange themselves (or to have been arranged by a benign deity) in perfect symmetry. Another example is the Tomnavery stone circle in Aberdeenshire (see plate 26). It is quite literally at the centre of its own world, for it stands on a hillock within an enormous glacial valley, entirely encircled by hills and mountains. We visited it below heavy rain clouds, but after a while these cleared and a ring of blue sky appeared directly overhead, enforcing the impression of being at the naval of the world. The clouds had probably cleared because of air being funnelled up around Tomnavery's hill, so the stone circle may have been constructed to mirror what happened regularly above. Like many stone circles in the Aberdeen area, Tomnavery includes a recumbent stone flanked by two uprights, creating a dramatic 'altar'. It faces the mountain of Lochnagar, whose peaks can be seen perhaps as another recumbent female deity. All these sites could have doubled as observatories where the rising and setting of the Moon and Sun along the horizon could be easily marked.

That some monuments were built for monitoring the movement of the heavens is beyond dispute. We happened to visit Brittany's Crucuno Quadrilateral towards sunset at the spring solstice, and my shadow, when standing in the rectangle's western 'gateway', pointed precisely to the north-eastern corner. The work of geo-archaeologists Richard and Robin Heath, whom we encountered deep in the woods measuring the nearby Manio Quadrilateral, which dates from about 3500 BC, shows very clearly that this was an observatory too, and a remarkably accurate one too. As the Neolithic advanced, astronomically aligned monuments became ever grander and more elaborate. The great passage tomb of Newgrange, Ireland (about 3100 to 2900 BC) was built so that, each winter solstice, the spiral-carved stones of its inner chamber are illuminated by the Sun shining directly down the passage that leads to it.

From about 3500 BC, while the climate was still milder than it is today, an extraordinary civilisation flourished in the Orkneys. With access to plenty of flattish stones and surely under the direction of a ruling elite – perhaps with distant trading and cultural links to the Mediterranean – a temple complex was built on the Ness of Brodgar, linked to the standing stones of Stennes (c. 3200 BC) and the later Ring of Brodgar (c. 2500 BC), all astronomically aligned.

Far to the south, on Wiltshire's Salisbury Plain, Stonehenge's earliest timber row, comprising four posts, aligned east-west perhaps to mark the rising and setting of the Sun, dates back to Mesolithic times, about 8000 BC. It is just to the north-west of where the stone rings stand now. There, a ring of posts was erected from about 2950 BC, followed by the small bluestone circle about 2600 BC. This may have been influenced by the building works of the Orkneys, because the people of Brodgar used 'grooved ware' pottery long before it appeared at Stonehenge in about 2600 BC. Stonehenge's final, colossal ring of local sarsens was put up about 2500 BC. Stones from this ring create a gateway for the midsummer sunrise and the midwinter sunset, surely making it a place to honour the dead and to try to understand and to claim some sort of ownership of the passage of time.

For all their building of stone circles to mark the seasons, the truly long stretches of time that we are now used to contemplating – thousands and even millions of years – were still alien concepts to the megalith builders. Yet, ironically, by surviving for thousands of years, the Neolithic monuments have come to symbolise all that is ancient. As fixed points in the landscape, they became focal points for later myths. Though built by those who first brought agriculture to

Britain, later generations saw them as the work of the giants whom the farmers were thought to have replaced – or thought they were giants, turned to stone.

The genetic legacy

We might wish to imagine the new farmers settling peacefully amongst the existing Mesolithic population, patiently teaching them the arts of herding and sowing. But the reality may have been less rosy. Aside from the possibility – or likelihood – of violence, there is also the question of disease. The great synthesis of Irish origin myths, the *Lebor Gabála Érenn* (*The Book of the Conquest of Ireland*), relates the coming of the mythological Partholon and his people from the Mediterranean to Ireland, only to be wiped out by a plague that they caught from the earlier inhabitants. But the experience of European settlers reaching the Americas suggests that the opposite is just as likely: the stag dancers of Star Carr would have been at terrible risk from diseases carried by the incoming farmers.

In the end, though, the populations did mix. The balance was heavily in favour of the new, Neolithic farming genes, but some genes from the Mesolithic Europeans, who were direct descendants of the Upper Palaeolithic people of north-west Europe, survived. Mainly, these survivals were through female lines, suggesting that the farming populations were happier to absorb hunter-gather women than men into their communities. It is the male-line Y chromosome, therefore, that best tells the story of colonisation.

The commonest haplogroup in Western Europe is R1b (M343). R1b increases as you go west through Europe to the extent that if a man in western Ireland does not test positive for R1b it comes as a genuine surprise. R1b accounts for 90 per cent of Basque, Welsh and Irish men, with percentages reducing as one moves east across Europe and into Asia, where it accounts for only 15 per cent of Turks and 10 per cent of Iraqis (presumably because its presence there was later overlain by many subsequent waves of immigration from the east).

Its root haplogroup, R, probably arose in the mountains of central Asia, perhaps the southern Urals, in Gravettian times, about 26,000 years ago. It is descended from P (M45), a descendant in turn of the IJK (L15/S137) group, which was in turn descended ultimately from the original 'out of Africa' lineage. Haplogroup R's first split was into R2 (M07), which spread into India, and R1 (M173). R1 spread from central Asia into Europe. 'Spread' means either that new hunter-gatherer bands who happened to carry this marker roamed west and interbred with the existing population, or that individual men joined bands already in Europe, and their genes just happened to proliferate at the expense of older male lineages. Either way, R1 became widespread within the European population. There is much argument over where the sub-haplogroup R1b originated, but one compelling view is that it emerged in the Middle East and spread into Europe because it happened to be the dominant Y chromosome subgroup of the Neolithic farmers.

R1b was discovered in 1999 by Dr James Wilson, who first published his findings in 2001. Professor Sykes wanted to mythologise it as 'the Atlantis gene' but it became known instead as the Atlantic Modal Haplotype. Since then, however, as genetic testing has become more precise, a great range of sub-branches of R1b have been found, of which the commonest in the West is in fact R1b1a2a1a (L11/S127/L151/P310). When geneticists speak now of the Atlantic Modal Haplotype, it is to this subgroup, which can also be written R (L11/S127/L151/P310), that they usually refer. It probably arose about 6,000 years ago and seems to have spread rapidly because of the advantages that farming brought to its early bearers. Unlike hunter-gatherers, women with stable hearths could have babies whilst also rearing very young children, so they could rear more children overall. The surplus produced by farming allowed more mouths to be fed, so more of these children could grow up healthy. Sons of farmers inevitably proliferated at the expense of the older hunter-gathering populations. These old populations survived and their genes (especially I, J and K) are still found scattered throughout Europe, but with nothing like the density of the Atlantic Modal Haplotype, which is dominant in Western Europe and particularly in the British Isles.

Any man having a simple genetic test of his SNP markers can find his place in the great pedigree of humanity as defined by the male-line Y chromosome. Any woman wishing to have the same information on her father's male line can have a test undertaken on a male-line relative, such as her father, brother, father's brother and so on. There are constant surprises and even groups A and B, the most originally African of all, turn up sometimes in ostensibly white families, such as some around the south-eastern Irish port of Waterford – they got there, perhaps, in the past thousand years, via Spanish traders who were themselves male-line descendants of Moors from North Africa. But the vast majority of tests show that people with British ancestry go back in the male line to R1b1a2a1a (L11/S127), the Atlantic Modal Haplotype, which was brought to Britain by the Neolithic farmers.

But while the Neolithic Britons were happily spreading their genes and building their long barrows and stone circles, great changes were underway in the Middle East.

Chapter 23

Our Ancestors in the Age of Troy

The rise of cities

Between the rivers Tigris and Euphrates lies the land the Greeks called Mesopotamia –'the land between the rivers', which is now Iraq. From about 6000 BC onwards permanent villages, with inhabitants skilled in the use of dykes and ditches to irrigate their fields with river water, became commonplace here. A style of pottery denoting Ubaid culture spread across the region in the 5000s BC. In southern Mesopotamia archaeologists have detected the emergence of a cultural elite, whose power probably rested on the control of harvested grain and of the religious buildings in which this was stored. In the settlement of Eridu, a series of buildings, each larger than the last, started being constructed on the site of what would become its great temple. Eridu, Ur, Uruk and other villages like them began likewise to expand in size during the 4000s and 3000s BC, with new satellite settlements appearing around them. They emerged in the 2000s BC as the great Sumerian city states, ruled by priest-kings at the head of a complex machinery of bureaucratic and military government. Meanwhile, the wheel was probably invented here about 3500 BC, followed by simple picture writing about 3400 BC, which developed into cuneiform script by 3100 BC.

From these early, civilised cities came federations of city states, out of which rose the Akkadian Empire (c. 2350 to c. 2100 BC), the first of the great empires destined to rule the region, which was followed by the successive empires of the Assyrians, Babylonians, Persians, Seleucids, Parthians and Sassanids, until the Arab conquest in the 600s AD.

Meanwhile, about the early 4000s BC, at Nabta Playa on the desert route between Lake Nasser and the springs of Bir Kiseiba, near what is now the Egypt-Sudan border, a nomadic campsite was delineated with standing stones and a stone oval was built. The stones are arranged in pairs, and one pair faces the Midsummer sunrise. Numerous flint arrowheads and stone axes have been found here too, along with grindstones and a sandstone monolith shaped deliberately to look like a cow. Out of such seasonal meeting places of herdsmen, who probably used the stone oval as a solar calendar to help time their migrations, grew Egyptian civilisation. Other significant sites are in the desert to the east of the Nile Valley, where rock engravings of animal hunts and gods travelling in sacred boats show how Palaeolithic rock art there evolved gracefully into the rich iconography of the land of the pharaohs. As the climate dried, the Neolithic nomads were forced into the Nile Valley and from about 3600 BC onwards cultural development speeded up, probably due to contact with the more advanced city-based culture of Mesopotamia. Cities grew and kingdoms developed in Upper and Lower Egypt, until in 2950 BC they were united by Narmer, the first ruler of united Egypt and founder of the First Dynasty.

Similar developments were taking place in the Indus Valley in Pakistan and India. Here the great cities of Mohenjo-daro and Harappa, set 500 miles apart on the river Indus in what is now Pakistan, were flourishing by about 2600 BC, but with village-based, agricultural roots stretching back to at least the 7000s BC. Civilisation had perhaps been seeded from Mesopotamia, though there are theories suggesting exactly the opposite and there may always have been trading and cultural links going both ways between the two, however sporadic. The spiritual landscape of the Indus Valley included, as John Mitchiner wrote, 'a widespread Mother Goddess cult, the veneration of certain animals, phallus worship, an emphasis on water and bathing, and what appears to be the worship of a Shiva-like deity who sits cross-legged in yogic posture'. From this evolved India's rich tapestry of mythology and religion.

China's civilisation followed a broadly parallel development too, based on the cultivation of rice and leading again to cities, hierarchies and their own character-based system of writing. Recent archaeological work in Peru has revealed that the civilisation of Norte Chico (also called Caral) was not lagging far behind. It was an agrarian society producing monumental buildings including stepped pyramids as far back as the mid-2000s BC. No evidence has been found to suggest a cross-seeding of civilisation here. In all probability, South American civilisation arose spontaneously and naturally as a result of agriculture, which was in turn a long-term result of the end of the Ice Age.

By the 2500s BC, when Stonehenge was being completed in southern Britain, there were fully formed city-based kingdoms in Peru, India and China, as well as in Egypt and Mesopotamia and all over the rest of the Middle East.

The Chalcolithic

We had evolved slowly from worms into cynodonts, and then into apes whose brain sizes increased as we learned to speak and use stone tools. From this came cave art, farming, the building of the Neolithic monuments that underpin the man-made landscape of Britain, and the rise of the cities and kingdoms of the Middle East. The basic trappings of civilisation, including the emergence of priest-kings, the building of big stone structures, and the practice of appalling cruelty to each other, may simply result from the way we humans are programmed to behave under the circumstances surrounding the emergence of efficient agriculture. Now, only one more development was needed to make the world into what it is, broadly, today: metalworking.

As early as the 4000s BC, the Mesopotamians were experimenting with soft metals such as gold and silver, which could easily be beaten, or heated and moulded, into plates, knives and jewellery. But more useful in the long term was copper, which could be melted fairly simply yet hardened into much more solid forms. Knives, swords, axe heads and arrow and spear tips could be fashioned with sharp edges, all superior to the stone tools that had served us so well for the past few million years. And so started the cultural phase known as the Chalcolithic – the age of copper.

The noise of smiths making copper tools was a constant feature of life in the early city states of Mesopotamia and Egypt, and the technology slowly spread further afield. The first worked copper in Europe – a copper axe – was found with the body of 'Ötzi the Iceman' (see plate 28). His frozen corpse was discovered in the Ötzal Alps, on the Austrian-Italian border, in 1991 and has been dated to about 3300 BC. His DNA has been studied intensively. His female-line mitochondrial DNA was haplotype K, and in 2011 Dr Eduard Egarter Vigl of Bolzano, who oversees the conservation of the remains, revealed that Ötzi's male-line genetic haplotype was G (M201), and later it was found that he belonged to subgroup G (L91). I wrote earlier that genetic test results can often prove very surprising: I took my test expecting to belong to haplogroup R, the commonest in Europe, but in fact I belong to haplogroup G (M201) as well. I belong to subgroup G (S2808), so Ötzi the Iceman, it turns out, was a distant cousin of my ancestor and we have male-line ancestors in common back in the Middle East. Ötzi's recent forebears had probably come from there, quite possibly carrying with them copper and the secrets of how to fashion tools from it.

Associated with early copper finds are distinctive bell-shaped, wide-necked clay beakers, hence the rather ridiculous byname of 'Beaker People' that was bestowed on the early copper workers by Lord Abercromby. They included the 'Amesbury Archer', who was buried below a round barrow near Stonehenge about 2300 BC. He was surrounded by almost a hundred personal possessions, including copper axe heads and a gold hair ring, some clearly fashioned in France and Spain. His tooth enamel, formed in early childhood, contains the chemical signatures of the soil and rocks of the Alps. His male-line DNA has not survived but perhaps he and Ötzi were related.

The Amesbury Archer helps us come closer to our Chalcolithic ancestors in Britain. So too, in a far less grand manner, does the so-called Dagenham Idol, now in Colchester Museum, with a replica in the Museum of London. Made of

Scots pine, it was found in Rainham Marshes in 1922, and was carbon dated to 2459 to 2110 BC. It is a crudely carved image of a human without arms, with a hole that could have been a vagina or for inserting a peg-penis (or both). It has a crude but recognisable human face. Whatever its purpose, it is a representation of someone, and if that someone was anyone in particular then the Dagenham Idol could well be an ancestral image for us all.

The Trojan War

The Chalcolithic was relatively short-lived because, back in the Middle East about 3300 BC, smiths discovered that a 10 per cent addition of tin to copper would create a much harder, brighter metal – bronze.

The term 'Bronze Age' was coined by museum curator C.J. Thomsen in 1848. Bronze working, and its associated trade in copper and tin, spread rapidly through the new civilisations of the Middle East, the Levant, Egypt and beyond. The civilisations of the Levant and Egypt between them stimulated the rise of the great Bronze Age civilisation of Minoan Crete, recalled in the Greek myth of Theseus and the Minotaur and unearthed at Knossos by the spade of Sir Arthur Evans at the start of the twentieth century – the first city, they say, in Europe. Minoan civilisation flourished from 2700 BC, with its ancient cults of snake and bull. Its palaces were flattened by a terrible earthquake about 1750 BC, only to be rebuilt, stronger and greater, with Knossos pre-eminent at the island's heart. Cretan fleets dominated the eastern Mediterranean and their culture spread to Greece, but in about 1400 BC Mount Thera on Santorini erupted and the Minoan civilisation collapsed under multiple assault from earthquakes, giant waves and choking clouds of acidic ash. In their wake, their former Achaean vassals on mainland Greece rose to pre-eminence under the Mycenaeans – they who went to war with Troy.

The Achaeans who dominated Greece at the time of Crete's collapse were relatively recent newcomers; barbarians from the north who had invaded the mainland about 1700 BC. At first their chieftains probably worked as mercenaries for the Minoans, and the Egyptians too, no doubt. But once Crete fell, they became masters of Greece and the architects of their own culture. Instead of Minoan palaces, which were curiously lacking in substantial defences, they built fortified cities such as Mycenae (see plate 29), Gla and Tiryns, using such great boulders (literally, 'mega liths') that later generations attributed their city walls to the work of the gigantic Cyclopses. If the Cretans' religion had been based on bull and snake cults, and ecstatic, almost shamanistic rituals in caves, the Achaean Greece's religion was centred on ancestor worship, as suggested by Mycenae's (megalithic-style) grave circles and enormous tholos tombs, clearly intended to promote the status of the great kings buried inside them. Mycenaean civilisation was as great and as golden as Homer portrayed it but it was not yet all that Classical Greece would become: as Samivel writes, 'The world conjured up by [Homer] ... strangely resembles our own Middle Ages. In it we read of boar hunts, neglected wives or mistresses and, finally, of a great host setting forth on a Crusade: the Trojan War.'

Homer's *Iliad*, the first piece of European literature, was probably composed about 800 BC. Its tale of the siege of Troy may contain echoes of a real war that, if it took place at all, is generally dated to 1194 to 1184 BC, in which the Mycenaean Greeks sailed across the Aegean to lay siege to the city of Troy. In the story, it was all about the love of Helen. In reality, it may have had more to do with Troy's stranglehold on the Dardanelles and thus the trading route to the Black Sea.

The war ended with the sack of Troy, but the effort to destroy it depleted the Mycenaeans' resources. Earthquakes struck and the barbaric Dorians swept in from the north. It was in the recovery from this catastrophe that Classical Greece emerged, and with it the gods we now think of as typically Greek, those 'certain divine beings', as Samivel wrote, who 'took the lead of all the others, catalysing the fears, aspirations and religious instincts of the race' and thus meriting great temples as their houses, an idea imported (in the course of trade, centred on the Greek island of Euboea) from the Middle East.

Bronze Age Britain

Like farming and copper working before it, the art of smelting bronze spread slowly into Europe, reaching Galicia about 2500 BC and Britain a few centuries after the Amesbury Archer's time, about 2000 BC. Britain was blessed with rich deposits of the two components of bronze – tin and copper. It is from this time (as opposed to the Chalcolithic period that preceded it) that copper mining really took off in Britain, particularly at Great Orme, above what is now Llandudno, Caernarvonshire on the north coast of Wales, where extensive mining activity started about 2000 BC. Over the next thousand years, its sophisticated system of deep shafts, with wooden gutters and ventilation shafts, would unearth up to 238 tons of copper.

But in general, life in Bronze Age Europe was very different to life in the palaces of Bronze Age Troy or Mycenae. Unlike the stone used in the Neolithic for dolmens, we built houses for the living out of wood, wattle and daub, and thatch. Our ancestors preferred the high ground, but with easy access to lower-lying areas for water and grazing. Most houses were circular or oval, though some square ones have been found. We were farmers, keeping pigs, sheep and goats, and relying ever more on the milk, cheese and butter that we obtained from our livestock. We also grew wheat and rye, turnips, beans, peas and lentils, but still gathered many wild fruits and nuts, catching and eating fish and molluscs and hunting in the woods. We wove clothes (as evidenced by finds of loom weights) and made the bell beakers so distinctive of the early age of metalworking.

The age of metalworking brought to an end the old egalilty of the communal Neolithic long barrows. The new, Bronze Age culture of Europe favoured smaller earthen mounds for burying individual members of the elite – like that earlier burial of the Amesbury Archer – or small, stone-built cists, some of which contain the trappings of the new, metal-using upper class, including metal weapons and archers' wrist bands. From the plain of Troy, where Homer's *Iliad* anticipates the interment of Achilles's body below a magnificent barrow, to the chalk uplands of Britain, burial mounds remain the most tangible reminders of our Bronze Age ancestors. They generally lack the draw of the older Neolithic long barrows, but not always. The Soerfon (Seven) Barrows, which sit grandly near the end of Avebury's much more ancient megalith-lined Avenue, gaze out across the Kennet valley to the (again, far more ancient) West Kennet long barrow. It is difficult not to imagine a dynasty of local kings being buried, side by side, amidst the grand solitude of the Marlborough Downs. Along the downs above Firle in Sussex is a similar string of barrows. We had no Homer to sing the deeds of our Bronze Age kings, but their barrows remain as eloquent testimony to their otherwise forgotten glories.

From the late Neolithic, through the Chalcolithic and into the Bronze Age, our ancestors in western Europe left behind traces of their thoughts through rock art. At Fylingdales Top, Yorkshire, many Bronze Age artefacts were excavated in 2004. Nearby are rock carvings, presumably from the same period, showing lines, squares and zigzags, which have been interpreted as early attempts at landscape drawing. The flat, exposed rocks of Argyll are rich in cups and rings, as are those of Galicia in north-western Spain, whose stones also boast deer, mazes, serpents, boats and horsemen. On the large rock of Auga da Laze near Gondomar, not far from Pontevedra, are unmistakable Bronze Age swords and halberds, too, points all upwards, together with what appear to be shields – a true sign that the age of the Bronze Age warrior had dawned in Europe.

At Grimspound on Dartmoor, Devon, you can walk amongst the ruins of Bronze Age round houses encircled by a stone wall. The site lies in a shallow saddle of land between two dominating hills, one of which is Hookner Tor, surmounted by exposed rocks. The physical location of the site is peculiarly similar to Mycenae in Greece and the two sites are contemporary. But although a handful of people may have gone from one to the other, particularly to trade in the tin that is plentiful on Dartmoor, the similarities are probably largely coincidental.

Both sites are abandoned. Weakened by its ruinous war with Troy, Mycenae was abandoned and ruined. Grimspound's downfall was more prosaic: farming activities there ruined the soil and, as the climate cooled, the land became ever more acidic and boggy. Now Grimspound's remaining stones lie deserted amidst the barren moorland.

Bronze Age deities

For about 40,000 years, since we first evolved the mental capacity to do so, imaginings and invocations of the female power represented by Venus figurines had probably accompanied the birth of each generation of our ancestors. But now, with the Bronze Age – or rather in the memories of the Bronze Age that lingered on in Homer's words – she becomes known to us, not as one deity, but fragmented by the Greek sunshine into many: Gaia the Earth Mother; Dione; Demeter; Kybele; Artemis; Hera of Argos and her daughter Eleithyia, who had special care of childbirth; and lovely Aphrodite, who was claimed as the mother of the Trojan prince Aeneas, from whom the Caesars and later the kings of Dark Age Wales claimed descent. Eventually these goddesses' crowns and mantles were assumed by another deity, the Virgin Mary, with the overseeing of pregnancy and childbirth delegated to a handful of saints, particularly St Margaret of Antioch, to whom millions of soon-to-be Catholic mothers all over the world continue to pray to this day.

In Britain, the Orkadian Venuses were part of the continuum of the goddesses' mythology here, but we have to wait until Roman times for any names to be recorded. Then, we know, the whole island had a female deity, Bride or Brigid, whom the Romans called Britannia and who lives on in Christian guise, too, as St Brigid, one of the patron saints of Ireland. Bride was probably worshipped in different guises across the land, not least in Brigantia, the realm covering what is now northern England, whose last warrior queen, Cartimunda, betrayed Caratacus to Claudius's Romans. The Iceni of East Anglia had their queen Boudica too, and the ancient Irish had mighty Queen Medb (Maeve), heroine of *The Cattle Raid of Cooley*.

The Picts of north-eastern Scotland continued to focus their society around a dynasty of queens until the time of Kenneth Mac Alpine (d. AD 858). Any man who would be king had to marry a female member of the royal dynasty, whose royal blood came through her mother. Whilst Pictish beliefs can be seen now only through the distorting glass of Christian records, it seems highly likely that this female-line dynasty claimed descent from the goddess Bride. Though Kenneth was a king of the Scots, his mother was a Pictish princess and it was through her that his rule over the Picts was justified. So it could fairly be argued that the

Scottish kings' ancestry and authority (and thus the authority of our modern Royal Family, as rulers of Scotland) was derived, ultimately, from the Upper Palaeolithic precursors of the Mother Goddess herself.

But whilst such beliefs survived a long time in northern Britain, the age of metalworking and metal weapons was tilting the balance towards a society dominated by men. With this sea change arose male gods who had once perhaps been no more than goddesses' consorts. These newly empowered male deities reduced the goddess to, at best, the status of mothers, wives, sisters or daughters (or an incestuous combination thereof). Thus arose Anu and Marduk in Mesopotamia; Zeus and his brothers and sons in Greece; and the Hebrew Jehovah or Yahweh, he who became the only god of the Jews.

Chapter 24

'… And All That'

The Celts

Smelting iron requires a much higher temperature than working copper or tin. It began as a secret art developed by the Hittites, whose empire was based in Anatolia (modern Turkey) and included the land of Troy. For a while the Hittites' unbreakable iron weapons gave them a fearsome advantage over their foes. But iron did not, ultimately, hold their empire together. It fragmented about 1200 BC, allowing Troy to become the free city state that so incurred the jealousy of Mycenaean Greece. Over the ensuing centuries, the mysteries of ironworking spread and the new technology swept across the world.

In central Europe from the 700s BC, the efficiency of iron weapons engendered what is termed Hallstatt culture – a social order dominated by violent young warriors whose faith in the druidic concept of reincarnation made them virtually fearless in battle. Contact with the Classical world stimulated the more sophisticated La Tène culture from about 450 BC. It was characterised by the use of two-wheeled chariots, a method of warfare imported ultimately from Mesopotamia. Spreading rapidly outwards from the Alps, the La Tène warriors, and those who adopted their behaviour, are termed Gauls, Galatians, Gaels or, generally, 'Celts'. They were not a race who had appeared in Europe from somewhere else: they were descended like everyone else from Neolithic farmers and the older, hunter-gatherer population, but now they had transformed themselves into a warrior elite, fiercely armed with iron.

Ironworking reached Britain about 400 BC. With it came endemic warfare and the need for imposing hill forts like Maiden Castle, Dorset (see plate 30) and Uffington Castle, Oxfordshire (see plate 31). The Victorian notion of the entire population of Britain and Ireland being replaced wholesale by Celts has long since been disproved. Britain's 'Celtic' languages are simply the native ones that had been here all along, and their affinity to those spoken on the Continent is due to their common roots in the far more distant past. But there was undoubtedly an influx of Celts into southern Britain and Ireland connected with the spread of Iron Age technology. Some of the southern British tribes, such as the Cantii in Kent, were probably founded by La Tène warriors from Europe. Meanwhile, in north-eastern France and Belgium, the mixture of La Tène Celts with Germanic peoples there bred the hybrid warrior race known to Caesar as the Belgae. Some of the Belgic tribes, particularly the Catuvellauni and Atrebates, made violent incursions into south-eastern Britain, much to the indignation of now-established 'native' tribes such as the Cantii, and they also account for the Fir Bolg, whom Irish tradition recalls settling in south-eastern Ireland too.

The Atlantic Modal Haplotype

All this testosterone-fuelled activity had a great effect on Europe's genes. The male-line haplogroup R (L11/S127/L151/P310), the Atlantic Modal Haplotype, had already spread throughout Europe because of Neolithic farming. But it gained its extraordinary dominance over other male-line lineages in Europe through the bloody ages of Bronze and Iron that ensued. Many clans of interrelated male warriors just so happened to carry this widespread marker, and as they slaughtered their way around Europe they inadvertently extinguished many older male-line genetic makers. Their actions probably had little effect on the female population and the old dominance of the female-line mitochondrial DNA haplogroup H probably remained unchanged since long before the Neolithic: instead of being killed by the incoming warriors, women were forced simply to swap one husband, one master, one rapist, for another.

Through both hostile action and economic advantage, Bronze and Iron Age warriors caused the dominance of their particular subgroups of the Atlantic Modal Haplotype. The vast majority of British male lineages belong to two major subgroups of the Atlantic Modal Haplotype – R (P312), and R (M405/U106).

R (P312) accounts for almost three quarters of all native British men. It is most common in the western British Isles, so is best associated with the original Neolithic incomers, whose genes were once prevalent across the whole of Britain. Out of that population, the specific lineages that survived, and survived so well, were those who took up the lifestyle of the Iron Age warrior. Studies of Irish lineages and the many Scottish lines claiming descent from Irish kings have produced fascinatingly clear results. Many Mac and O' surnames commemorate eponymous founding ancestors (MacDermot means 'son of Dermot' and O'Farrell means 'descendant of Farrell' and so on). Many of these eponymous founders (Dermot, Farrell and so on) are recorded in old Gaelic pedigrees that connect them back to Irish kings of impeccable Iron Age stock. Large groups of families with such surnames claim male-line descent from the same ancestral kings. By and large, genetic studies of the male-line Y chromosomes of the modern bearers of such surnames have confirmed that many do indeed share the same genetic signatures within R (P312). Traditional Gaelic pedigrees, though obviously manipulated to some extent, seem to contain considerable degrees of genetic truth. Thus, many families claiming descent from the Dal Cassians, the people of the great High King Brian Boru (d 1014 AD) are found to belong to a subgroup of R (P312) identified as R (L226). Their great rivals, the Ui Neill of Ulster, are generally from R (M222), which is another subgroup of R (P312). Within this latter subgroup are many surnames, such as O'Doherty, McLoughlin, O'Flanagan, McGovern, MacDermot and Crowley, whose founders were descended from the family of Niall of the Nine Hostages, the greatest of the Irish High Kings, who died about AD 405.

And all the rest ...

About the 900s or 800s BC, a few centuries after the Mycenaean Empire had collapsed in the aftermath of the Trojan War, Greek civilisation was revitalised by renewed contact with the Near East. The next few centuries saw the rise of the Greek city states, which in turn seeded colonies and civilisation in Sicily and southern Italy. Opposition to these Greek incomers stimulated the rise of Rome, whose traditional foundation date is 753 BC. Rome's empire spread and its legions conquered most of Britain in AD 43. Contact between Britain and the civilised world of the Mediterranean had existed all along, but spasmodically and often via indirect trading links. But from AD 43 onwards, all of Britain save the far north was the Roman province of Britannia.

Early in 2013, Dr Jim Wilson announced the results of a study of 45,000 British men. He found that 6.5 per cent of men in England and Wales, 4.3 per cent in Scotland and 1.8 per cent in Ireland belong to a subgroup of R coded S28, which is found in 13 per cent of men in Italy. On that basis Wilson theorised that R (S28) could be from the Romans in Britain. If so it would suggest that about 1.6 million men in England and Wales could have direct male-line descents from Romans (and then there were three other markers also identified as Italian, which bunks the total up to about 4 million).

When Rome's empire collapsed at the start of the AD 400s, power in England shifted to the Germanic Angles, Saxons and Jutes from the adjacent coasts of Denmark and Germany. They had been employed by the Romans in Britain as mercenaries, but now they encouraged their cousins to settle here in greater numbers. They gradually battled the Romano-British back – a conquest opposed unsuccessfully by Arthur – into Cornwall, Wales and south-western Scotland, where they established their own kingdoms.

Then, in the AD 800s and 900s, came the Vikings from Scandinavia, who forged their own kingdoms across the British Isles. A branch of them settled in northern France, too, where they became known as Normans. William of Normandy invaded England in 1066 – one human amongst many, a descendant of apes, cynodonts, fish, worms and ultimately of the single-celled life forms from which all life on Earth had evolved. His descendants sit on the British throne to this very day, and a vast number of Britons are descended from him, whether they know it through their genealogical research or not.

The male-line genetic marker R (M405/U106), which accounts for almost all of the other quarter of Britain's population referred to above, was probably brought to Britain by these numerous waves of invaders and immigrants who came into Britain from northern Europe, such as the Hallstatt Celts, Belgic Gauls, Saxons, Vikings and Normans.

The rest of Britain's story is, as the title of W.C. Sellar and R.J. Yeatman's 1930 satirical book on British history put it, *1066 and All That*. In terms of the human population, Britain's recent history has seen a series of relatively small but nonetheless significant waves of migration: Flemish weavers in the Middle Ages; Protestant refugees (Huguenots) in the sixteenth and seventeenth centuries; eastern European Jews in the eighteenth and nineteenth centuries; and Irish immigrants fleeing the Potato Famine from the mid-nineteenth century onwards. From the sixteenth century onwards came what Sir Anthony Wagner once termed the 'backwash of Empire', sailors, soldiers, servants and later free immigrants from, particularly, Africa, India, China and the Caribbean, whose population is descended from a mixture of African slaves and white slave owners, with a touch of native American blood as well. These immigrants from all over the world introduced, and continue to introduce, their genetic haplotypes into the British mix, resulting in many more people being born in Britain with the male-line signatures E, D, C, B and even A, the original, African male line of the 'genetic Adam'. Most recently, with the loosening of restrictions on movements within the European Union, has come an influx of Eastern Europeans. Throughout there have been occasional immigrations by western Europeans: my own Adolph ancestors settled in London in 1833, for example, as indigo merchants from north-western Germany. Each immigrant, each genetic line, has its story: all, together, contribute to the rich tapestry that is modern Britain.

Each family line can be traced back a certain way. Some link back through female lines into other, longer pedigrees, a few of which stretch back as far as 1066. A handful go further back into the Dark Ages, especially those of the Welsh, Scottish and Irish warlords. A couple of lines purport to go back from them to kings who ruled here in the Iron Age. That is a subject I have examined in detail in *Tracing Your Aristocratic Ancestors* (Pen & Sword, 2013), which explains that you certainly don't have to be aristocratic now to find a family link back to such illustrious lineages. For according to Joseph T. Chang's calculations, the ancient war lords recorded in our oldest pedigrees must be the ancestors of absolutely everybody alive now, many times over.

Until the next discovery

Any rational, modern view of our past, focused on Britain, must follow broadly the lines of the preceding chapters. Almost any paragraph in this book could be expanded into a whole book in its own right and indeed there is now a wealth of books, papers and articles focusing on every single detail covered in these pages.

As scientific research presses on, details will be honed. Speaking about tetrapod evolution on BBC4's *Beautiful Minds* in May 2012, Professor Jenny Clack commented that 'all this knowledge is provisional'. We are highly unlikely to find anything truly extraordinary – that humans interbred with lions; that dinosaurs lived in ancient Rome; that viruses possess a secret intelligence that controls the world. But we are bound to find more fossils to infill details of our ancestral journey, and genetics will allow us to trace our human family tree in even more detail than is possible now. Maybe, one day, we will gain a greater insight into what happened before the Big Bang itself. Or we will find that our world is merely one of many possible Earths amidst a universe of infinite possibilities. The most important thing from the point of view of the search for our ancient ancestors is what science may yet discover concerning the origins of life itself. Did our family tree of life definitely start here on Earth, or does our lineage go back, via the simplest amino acids, to somewhere else in the Universe?

But having traced the history of humans down from the dawn of life to the human settlement of Britain, a further consideration presents itself. As they developed and spread and settled, these creatures, these human ancestors of ours, did something that no animal has ever done before, initiating a chain of events down the millennia that led eventually to the writing of this book. They began to wonder where they came from, and to tell each other stories about their origins. But what were those stories, and how can we make sense of them now?

Part Five

Book of Myths

Chapter 25

Looking Back in Wonder

Doorways into the past

We have traced the ancestry of humans from the dawn of life right down to historical times. In the course of the story we have seen how our *Homo sapiens* ancestors suddenly started expressing themselves through sophisticated art about 40,000 years ago. It seems reasonable to assume there was some link between artistic expression (with its implied spiritual dimension) and our ancestors' ability – or inclination – to think about who they really were and how they stood in relation to time and place. These are not, after all, questions that seem to bother cows or dogs. Even our closest cousins, the chimpanzees and gorillas, seem blissfully rooted in the present and have no discernible curiosity about their origins. As far as we know, our obsessive fascination with where we come from and what lies in the future is unique to us, and has been part of our nature for no more than the last 40,000 years.

It is therefore interesting to think about what our ancestors over the past 40,000 years may have thought about their origins, before science came along with its new set of answers. By doing so we might understand how the origin myths enshrined in the holy books of the great religions arose. By pondering our ancestors' interest in the past we might also learn something new about our own, Western obsession with our origins, both in terms of the scientific account of the world, and our own family trees, which, through records and genetics, helps connect us back to that greater story.

Before science came of age, origin myths were the only information available to our ancestors concerning what happened in the distant past and how the world had come to be. Such origin myths were taken as seriously as John Lightfoot took them when he used the Bible to calculate that the world began on 23 October 4004 BC. Had things not changed, then people of the intellect of David Attenborough and Richard Dawkins would doubtless still be refining that same calculation now. Until science came along to tell us otherwise, origin myths were pondered over intensely, dissected, analysed and interrogated for truths, or traces of truths, about who we are and where we came from.

The innumerable contradictions between different myths, or even between different versions of the same myth, caused constant headaches but they also offered vast scope for new theories. Even today, some writers indulge in such theorising. The blurb for Paul A. LaViolette's 2004 *Genesis of the Cosmos*, for instance, claims that 'Many thinkers have speculated that the remnants of an ancient science survive today in mythology and esoteric lore, but until now the scientific basis for this belief has remained cloaked in mystery.' But now that science has provided a reasonably compelling account of where we came from, we no longer need to treat origin myths (or indeed any myths) as vehicles for hidden truths. We can recognise them as the products of active, questing human minds, sometimes stimulated by religious trances and religious drug use. We can relax and enjoy them for the fantastic stories they really are. We can also quarry them for some indication of what our ancestors over the last 40,000 years may have thought about their origins, without subjecting them to the unrealistic expectation of being true.

The recording of origin myths

Origin myths can reach us through oral tradition or ancient texts. Such texts may be based on older, oral traditions, but they generally bear the hallmarks of intellectual, literate interference. They might, for instance, show the compiler's attempt to combine more than one myth, to synthesise the beliefs of different peoples, or to emphasise a particular moral point. The trick here is to look through the words to try to find the earlier, underlying tales on which they may have been based.

Homer, for all his great tales of heroism and endurance, makes only passing references to the origin myths of Greece, and it was clearly not a subject that greatly excited him. But for his near-contemporary, Hesiod, origin myths were the foundation upon which all other knowledge could be based. The world's first identifiable genealogist, Hesiod lived in Boetia, just north of the Gulf of Corinth, about the 700s BC. His main work was his *Theogony*, a great family history of the gods. It seems ancient and immutable, but in fact his account, like most of ancient Greek mythology, was a fusion of native traditions with stories heard from the Near East and Mesopotamia. These stories probably arrived, orally, in two waves, one during the Mycenaean era (c 1600 to 1100 BC) and the other in the early centuries of the first millennia BC, just before Hesiod's time.

Mesopotamia's best-preserved creation myth is the *Enûma Eliš* (so named from its first two words, meaning 'when above'). Fragments of various versions of it have been excavated, at Assur (from about 1000 BC), Kish and Uruk, for example, but the most complete is from the ruins of King Ashurbanipal's library at Nineveh, which dates from the mid-600s BC. The epic exalts Marduk, who had emerged over the preceding few centuries as the dominant god of Babylon.

But comparison with other origin myths, deciphered from inscriptions found across the region, suggests that Marduk had been inserted into far older stories, in which the gods identified as his ancestors had once taken centre stage. Thus, the rise of Zeus to power as king of the gods in Greek mythology has many earlier parallels in Middle Eastern myth.

This reminds us that studies of origin myths are built upon shifting sands. What seems ancient and immutable was not always so. Thus, the Hebrew *Old Testament* had its origins too. Biblical scholars generally agree that it was compiled about the 500s BC. When Jerusalem fell to Nebuchadnezzar in 597 BC, King Jeconiah and many of his people were taken as prisoners to Babylon, in the heart of Mesopotamia. The Jews' unusually monotheistic religion had been developing over the preceding centuries, having grown out of a mythology of warring gods and great floods common to the entire Middle East. In Babylon, the Jews were re-exposed to many such old stories and also to literacy, and thus to a recent literary invention from Greece – Hesiod's *Theogony*, which reworked much ancient mythology around the strong central structure of a genealogical line. This, scholars argue, was the background to the writing of the *Book of Genesis*, a literary synthesis of Jewish beliefs structured around a genealogical line coming down from Adam and Eve to the Jewish kings and incorporating many Middle Eastern themes such as the Great Flood. Everything, as this was a Jewish book, emphasised the power of their one, universal god, Yahweh.

Genesis's ensuring power comes partly from the knowing, intellectual manner of its composition – it is certainly not a naïve tribal tale – and from its writers' insistence that, although humans penned it, it is nonetheless the unadulterated word of God himself. Part of its potency comes from its conscious echoing and synthesis of older origin myths, but with a moral slant promising eternal salvation for those who believe in it.

It then so happened that Judaism, of all religions, was the religious and cultural background of Jesus and most of his early followers. Christianity offered a new sort of religion altogether, based on love of one's neighbour, but no religious system is complete without an origin myth. Rather than using the Greek origin myth in Hesiod's *Theogony*, or synthesising a new one (which may in retrospect have been a better idea), the early Christians chose to use the *Old Testament*, complete with *Genesis*. And thus the West inherited *Genesis* – and has been locked in an intellectual struggle with it ever since.

To those who have only studied *Genesis*, its origin myth may seem all-encompassing, but readings of other origin myths from around the world provide a sense of perspective, enabling us to see it, if we wish, as simply the Hebrew version of a much older, simpler story that, as we will see, seems almost universal to our ancestors all around the world.

To the east of the Middle East, and periodically connected to it by trade, the ancient civilisation of the Indus Valley developed a rich mythology that was overlaid by the beliefs of the incoming Indo-Aryans about 1750 BC. The hymns of these invaders, with their great emphasis on sacrifice, were collected in the *Rig Veda*, the oldest of the Hindu scriptures and arguably the oldest religious text in the world. Following these in importance are the *Upanishads*, a collection of the writings of mystics, composed about 700 to 500 BC and laying great emphasis on meditation and asceticism. The other chief books of Hinduism are the great epics, the *Mahabharata* and *Ramayana* and a collection of traditions called *Puranas*: all these were composed about 300 BC to AD 500. Out of this wealth of literature came fully fledged Hinduism. There is no orthodoxy of Hindu belief and the texts contain many origin myths – but most agree on the main points, which are not, as we shall see, so very different in essence to those of their Middle Eastern neighbours.

Further east still, China ought to have a rich treasury of origin myths, all meticulously recorded, but in their efforts to make the teachings of Confucius universal, the Han dynasty (206 BC to AD 220) eradicated a lot of native nature worship and shamanism, and settled upon an orthodox origin myth, based on the figure of Pangu, which, again, is not so different to the myths found further west. In the Americas, the Mayan civilisation, which flourished in Central America from 500 BC until it was conquered by the Spanish in AD 1524, recorded its origin myths in the *Popol Vuh*. What we have now is a Latin version transcribed by a missionary, so the possibility of some Christian influence cannot be entirely discounted, but it seems mostly genuine and valid for comparison with the others.

Native traditions?

The power and endurance of the Greek and Hebrew origin myths in the West comes mainly from their having been written down long ago. A combined assault from both, starting with the Classical mythology brought by the Romans, followed a few centuries later by Christianity, managed to obliterate the native beliefs and myths of many parts of Western Europe almost entirely. The British Isles must once have been awash with origin myths, from Upper Palaeolithic times right down to the Iron Age, but these were overlain by the mythology of the Classical world and then swept away by Christianity. Ireland's *Lebor Gabála Érenn* (*The Book of the Conquest of Ireland*) had the potential for being a rich treasury of native origin myths, but instead the monks who composed it planted its roots very firmly in *Genesis*: it speaks of many ancient Irish gods, who are referred to as the Tuatha de Danann, but what the Irish had thought about the gods' beginnings has been replaced by a tall tale of their origins in Thrace, designed specifically to disempower them by giving them mundanely human origins. A story about Hu Gadarn and his oxen, which sounds like the vestige of a British origin myth, was in fact made up by Iolo Morganwg, alias Edward Williams (1747–1826), presumably because he felt so keenly the loss of any genuinely old stories: it has no roots in antiquity at all.

We might hope to find something closer to an original Western European origin myth when we come to the Germanic peoples who included the Norsemen, or Vikings. But their myths were only recorded after the arrival of Christianity. The best source is Snorri Sturluson's *Gylfaginning* of the early AD 1200s. His writings lack much of a Christian bias, but they seem deeply influenced by Classical mythology. Though their lands were far removed from the Mediterranean world, there had been prolonged contact between the two via the rivers of Russia, the Black Sea and Constantinople, where the Vikings went to trade and to serve as the Byzantine emperors' Varangian guardsmen. Through such routes Classical elements seeped into Norse myth. Indeed, Snorri drew many conscious parallels between the two, claiming, for example, that the siege and fall of Asgard, the home of the gods, was a retelling of the Greek myth of the siege of Troy.

Oral histories

Beside such old, literary compositions we also have more recent oral tradition, as passed down by word of mouth from one generation to another by native peoples around the world – and ultimately written down by missionaries, travellers and anthropologists. From such accounts we have many origin myths from the Americas, the depths of Siberia, Australia and elsewhere. Oral myths change constantly, and despite their tellers learning them by rote, they cannot help but mutate, slowly, with each telling, so each family, let alone each tribe, may have told its own subtle variants of a story. The personal bias of the person who recorded the stories affects what we think we know too, especially when that person was a Christian monk or missionary interested in proving that primitive peoples had an innate belief in one creating god.

Indeed, some origin myths, as recorded by missionaries, sound like their own, Christian teaching being filtered back to them through a few layers of native misunderstanding. Thus, we hear of the Aboriginals of south-eastern Australia believing in an All-Father, Baiame, and his consort Birrahgnooloo, the Mother-of-All, who fashioned the world and its people. That is quite at odds with the beliefs of the rest of the continent. Similarly, we hear of Pygmy origin myths that seems to include a Garden of Eden and a tree of knowledge. In this version the first man, Efe, was created from clay by the angel of the Moon, at the instigation the One God. That sounds like what the missionaries had told the Pygmies, garbled back to them. A more authentic-sounding Pygmy origin myth holds that the first man and woman were released from a tree, in a gush of water, by a chameleon.

Despite the dangers of oral traditions having been contaminated by literary sources, the native myths as recorded across the world have some striking similarities to each other that can help to highlight simple themes underlying the more complex literary myths. They can suggest, perhaps, what the earlier origin myths of our more distant ancestors may have sounded like.

Many origin myths seem to deal sequentially with the creation of the Universe; the appearance of the Earth; the genesis of the present ruling deities; the appearance of plants and animals; and (usually towards the end of the sequence) the birth of mankind, followed by something to link those first humans to us. That sequence is not too different to the order of events as suggested by science and as described in this book, except that the scientific view places the invention of gods towards the end, as the products of our human ancestors' fertile imaginations.

The first stage is the hardest: the creation of the Universe. For, as modern science itself is still asking itself, how do you create something out of nothing?

Chapter 26

Out of the Chasm

Conceiving nothingness

In *The Marriage of Cadmus and Harmony*, Roberto Calasso reimagined the way the Orphic mystics of northern Greece in the 500s BC had imagined what Zeus would have seen had he gone right back to the start of everything.

'Space no longer existed. In its place was a convex surface clad with thousands upon thousands of scales. It extended beyond anything the eye could see. Looking downward along the scales, he realized that they were attached to other scales, the same colour, interwoven with them in knot after knot, each one tighter than before. The eye became confused, could no longer tell which of the coiling bodies the scales belonged to. As he looked up again, towards the heads of the two knotted snakes, the body of the first snake rose, and its scales merged into something that no longer partook of the nature of a snake: it was the face of a god … and on either side of it were two other huge heads, one a lion and the other a bull, while from the shoulders opened immense, airy wings.'

Yet of course, as with most imaginings of nothing, this is not nothing at all: it is merely something, made as strange as possible.

The vexed question of how the world emerged out of nothingness is generally avoided by the native weavers of oral origin myths: they tended to pick up at some point later in the story, with the clap of a raven's wings, in the case of the Inuit, from which everything else follows. The origin myths of the Upper Palaeolithic and of ancient Britain probably evaded the question too. Why? Because the intellectual effort involved in delving right back to the beginning of everything is too great, too troubling. If the purpose of an oral myth is to root those listening around the communal fire in time and place, then the past cannot be made too giddyingly awful. It must be tamed, so it must start with something that can be imagined easily – such as a raven.

But for the more intellectual, literary origin myths, the problem of where the raven came from, and how anything could possibly have come out of nothingness, was as taxing then as the issue of what caused the Big Bang is for science now.

Some literary origin myths tackled the problem by arguing there had never been a beginning. The Chinese sages imagined that the Universe had always existed in a state of duality, *yin* (dark, cool, passive, female) and *yang* (light, warm, active, male). The opposition of these two forces gave rise to an egg containing chaos and Pangu. He was a rather fierce, Herculean figure, usually depicted with long, unkempt hair and with a muscular body clad only in a loin cloth. In order to bring order to chaos, Pangu broke out of the egg. Once the egg had broken, *yin* sank down to become the Earth and *yang* rose up to become the sky.

The Zoroastrians of eastern Persia (Iran) emerged about 1000 BC, but their creation myth seems to have incorporated older stories from south-western Asia. They envisaged a timeless, beginningless realm of light in which lived the wise Ahura Mazda, and an endless realm of darkness, inhabited by the evil Ahriman. One day, Ahura Mazda created a world, first the sky, then the sea, then the flat Earth. Similar, perhaps, is the timeless creator god Yahweh in St John's Gospel, 'In the beginning was the word, and the word was with God, and the word was God', where the implication is that the speaker of the word, God, was as timeless and beginningless as *yin* and *yang*: no explanation was required for how God began, because he had always been.

In other origin myths that dare penetrate so far back, there is a moment like the Big Bang, where things began, without any input from a pre-existing god. Hesiod's *Theogony* starts in this way, with a chasm of chaos, out of which emerged Gaia (the Earth), Tartaros (the Underworld) and Eros, the primal sexual urge. What came after was a series of couplings, all inspired by Eros, to produce everything else. But what caused the chasm to 'come to be', as he put it, Hesiod did not know, nor did he care to speculate.

But Orpheus did, he who had gone down into the Underworld in search of Eurydice and returned enlightened – or else it was the Orphic mystics, who claimed that their philosophy was derived from him. Orphism expanded the role of Eros into that of the Phanes Protogenos, the great bull-headed serpent who was the prime mover of the Universe. It was through intercourse with himself that Phanes produced a snakey daughter, and from their serpentine coupling together came Hesiod's chasm.

An eternal cycle

Most of these myths are unsatisfactory: they simply move back the problem of how all things began, and if we do not accept the premise that anything is genuinely beginningless, then we still do not know how 'eternal' forces such as *yin* and *yang* or Yahweh or Phanes Protogenos started. So some origin myths adopted an elegant solution – which can also be seen as an avoidance of the question – that there never had been a single, one-off starting point for the world. Instead, the Universe has been created and destroyed many times in an eternal cycle. That is an idea that some Western scientists are now considering for their

An eternal Orphic cycle, copied from a reimagining of it in Abraham Eleazar's *Uraltes chymisches Werk* (1760).

own explanation of this probably unsolvable problem of our ultimate origins. The Orphics imagined Phanes Protogenos devouring his own tail, thus forming an eternal circle and making him, by definition, without beginning or end. And in India, where Hindu sages spent longer than most meditating on the problem, there emerged the idea that the lifetime or *kalpa* of an entire universe is but one day in the life of the creator god, Brahma. Brahma is part of the Hindu Trinity of deities, who are distinct from each other and yet also one: the other two are Vishnu, the protector of universal order (who is also Buddha and Krishna), and Shiva, the deity of chaos. Once each *kalpa* has run its course, Shiva dances his terrible dance of death and, as Rudra, he destroys the Universe, gods and all, first with fire and then with a terrible flood. Everything – light, sky, death, even time – are eliminated, leaving nothing, but that nothingness has a watery nature and from that primal water everything is born anew.

The story varied, depending on who was telling it and who was listening: for an audience of villagers it was more than enough to say that the destruction of one world entailed sowing the seeds of new life for the next. But amongst themselves, the mystics stretched their minds to their furthest extent to conceive how anything could come from nothing, even within an eternal cycle of birth and destruction. The great *rishi* or sage Jamadagni said (as quoted in Roberto Calasso's *Ka*), 'Everything, among the gods and before the gods, as likewise, in the end, among men, happened within the mind. Hence the first substance the world was made of must have been none other than that element from which the mind emerged. But what was that? A subtle heat, a hidden simmering, a burning beneath the surface, which sometimes flares up, with images, words and emotions clutching at its seething crest, but above all: there blossomed the naked sensation of consciousness, like an incandescent point.' That is one, Hindu view (or perhaps an avoidance of a genuine view) of how the world could be born out of nothing.

Far from dusty India in the frozen northlands, Snorri Sturluson retold the Vikings' origin myth in the AD 1200s along strikingly similar lines to the Hindu story of a cyclical universe and Shiva's dance of death. Above the wracked surface of the Vigrid plain, Thor's lightning bolts seared the blood-red sky. It was the end of the world, and the frost giants were destroying almost everything in the great battle of Ragnarok. The gods' splendid palace of Asgard was torn down and engulfed in flames. One fearsome wolf swallowed the Sun and another, the baleful

Vidar slaying Fenris at the end of the world and before the dawn of the next, as imagined by Lorenz Frolich.

Fenris, bore down on Odin, king of the gods, and tore him to pieces. Mighty Thor slew the dreadful Jormungand serpent, only to stagger away nine paces and collapse, stricken by the serpent's poison. Everywhere across the blood-washed rocks, giants, gods, heroes and monsters were being slaughtered. Now Fenris bore down, howling with blood-lust, upon Vidar. Fair-haired and tall, the heroic son of Odin poised his spear, waiting. As the wolf's ghastly jaws roared open, Vidar stepped forward, pinning the lower jaw to the ground. As the upper jaw snapped down, Vidar plunged down his spear, straight between the beast's fiery eyes. Vidar staggered back, exhausted but alive. In the sky, the daughter of the devoured sun flickered back into life and new grass sprang up from the bloodied rocks. And the whole world began afresh, and would run its course until the time came for another epically destructive battle, and another rebirth.

That was the inspiration for the climax of Wagner's *Götterdämmerung*, which also ends with the destruction of Valhalla and the rebirth of a new world: the opera feels as if it encompasses everything because, for the Germans, it did.

So from India to the northlands, time and the Universe could be imagined as an endless cycle, whilst other cultures imagined everything emerging from a beginningless something, or just appearing out of nothing, or they side-stepped the question altogether. But having danced around the problem of how something came from nothing, how did the Earth as we know it now come to be? How did our ancestors imagine *that*?

Chapter 27

'Upon the Face of the Waters'

Out of the primal waters

Of all the elements with which to begin the world – air, fire, earth or liquid – it is striking how many origin myths chose water. *The Egyptian Book of the Dead*, which dates back to at least 1550 BC, starts with Nun, 'the great god who creates himself; he is water, he is Nun, father of the gods'. And according to Toby Wilkinson, one of Egypt's earliest creation myths relates how 'the waters of Nun receded to reveal a mound of earth'. Here sat Atum-Ra, the all-seeing creator deity wearing the double crown of Egyptian kingship, whose name meant both 'totality' and 'nonexistence'. Another version of the Egyptians' origin myth relates how a blue lotus opened on the waters of Nun, and out of its unfurling petals emerged falcon-headed Ra. And yet another relates how the celestial god, Ra or Horus, flew down in the form of a falcon and perched on a reed that grew out of a mound that stood out from the eternal waters. Throughout ancient Egypt's history every temple included a replica of that original mound, as a reminder to everyone of how all things had begun.

For the Hindus, Shiva's destruction of the last *kalpa* generated seeds of life, which lay dormant in a watery nothingness. Then, says the *Rig Veda* (10.129.1–4), echoing Hesiod's statement that Eros was amongst the very first entities to emerge from the chasm, 'Desire, the primal seed and germ of Spirit' kick-started the recreation of the world. The *Satapatha Brahmana* (11.1.6.1) relates that 'in the beginning this (universe) was water, nothing but a sea of water. The waters desired, "How can we be reproduced?" They toiled and performed fervid devotions [and] when they were becoming heated, a golden egg was produced.' After a year (despite time, technically, not yet existing) the egg hatched and from it emerged Prajapati, who is an incarnation of Vishnu, or Brahma, two members of the Hindu Trinity. At the end of a year, Prajapati spoke: 'He said "bhûh": this [word] became this Earth;--"bhuvah": this became this air;--"svah": this became yonder sky' (11.1.6.33). Then from the breath of his mouth he created the gods and the Earth, created from his spoken word.

The Incas, who were the successors of civilisations that had flourished in Peru since at least 2500 BC, shared a belief with their predecessors, the Tiahuanaco, that the world had been created out of nothing by a god called Con Ticci Viracocha.

But in the version recorded by John de Betanzos this deity had himself arisen out of the waters of Lake Titicaca – out, in other words, of the primal waters.

The Mayans thought that once there was only sea and sky, all plunged in darkness. The gods spoke to each other below the surface of the waters, and raised up the land. Similarly, in *Genesis*, at the very dawn of creation 'darkness covered the deep waters. The Spirit of Yahweh moved upon the face of the waters.' The events of the creation are divided into six days (with Yahweh resting on the seventh): light was separated from darkness on the first day, the waters from the sky on the second and the Earth rose up out of the waters on the third, and fruiting trees and seed-bearing grass grew on it.

Hesiod's *Theogony* does not follow this trend, for here Gaia, the Earth, appears first, and the seas and Ocean were amongst her earliest offspring. However, in Homer's *Iliad* (14.244–50), which probably predates it, Zeus's consort Hera refers in passing to Ocean, the 'fountainhead of the gods' and his consort Tethys. That may be an echo of a more watery origin myth from Mycenaean times. A watery origin is also recalled in the Greek pedigrees that derive famous heroes and dynasties from rivers. The mythological Mycenaean dynasty of Perseus and Hercules, for example, was deduced ultimately from the deity of the river Inachus, which flowed through the Argolid plain just south of Mycenae. And Inachus, like all rivers, was a son of mighty Ocean. So Hesiod seems to buck the trend, but when he envisaged Gaia emerging out of the chasm, perhaps he envisaged dry land rising *up* out of the chaotic chasm. And that chaos may, on reflection, have been of a watery nature.

In Hesiod, unlike the biblical account, the separation of the sky from what lay below came after the land had appeared. Gaia gave birth to the sky god Uranos and he lay on her, making her pregnant with the Titans and one-eyed Cyclopses. But so heavily did he lie on Gaia that these children could not emerge. Therefore, Gaia armed her eldest son, the Titan Kronos, with a sickle, which he used to castrate Uranos. Uranos recoiled, upwards, rising up to become the overarching, starry heavens (and from the last spurt of his fertile seed, which fell on the seas, was born Aphrodite).

The earthly body

In China, Pangu, that Herculean first-born being in the Universe, spent 18,000 years gradually pushing the sky up off the watery surface of the world until it reached its present height. Once he had done so, Pangu lay down, exhausted, and died. His body became the land, his feet became the western mountains and his head became the mountains in the east, which, together, continued to hold up the sky. Pangu's left eye formed the Sun and his right eye became the

Moon. His flesh became soil, his blood the rivers and seas, his teeth the minerals in the ground; his hairs the trees and flowers and the parasites crawling on his body became the fish and animals: everything in the world was made from parts of Pangu's dead body. So Pangu became the Earth, and he had emerged, let us remember, from an egg in the primal seas.

This Chinese idea that the Earth had been the body of a primal deity chimes with Hesiod's Gaia, who was both the physical Earth and also a fertile deity who gave birth to many elements of our world. The Norse myths imagined the Earth as a body too. They imagined the world beginning with a chasm, probably borrowed direct from Hesiod: they called it Ginnungagap, and from it emerged fire and water, the former becoming the blazing southern realm of Muspelheim ('destroyer's home') and the latter forming the bitterly cold, northern land of Niflheim ('the home of fog'). The heat of one melted the cold of the other and formed the frost giant Ymir, whose sweat created more frost giants. Then, out of the ice there thawed the primal cow, Audhumla. She licked a salty block of ice and out of it emerged a male deity called Buri. Buri had a son, Bor, who married a frost giant called Bestla and had in turn three children, Odin, Vili and Ve, the first of the gods. Odin and his brothers slew the frost giant Ymir and flung his body into Ginnungagap. Here, Ymir's body became the Earth; his bones became the mountains; his blood the seas; his hair the trees; his skull the sky; and his brains the clouds. A great ash tree grew up through the world, with its roots below the Earth and its branches spreading over the heavens. It is a complex story, but at its heart the Earth (Ymir's body) had emerged out of primal water, which, as this is a northern myth, had been appropriately frozen.

The Toltecs, who flourished in Mexico about AD 900 to 1200, had a myth that, in the beginning, the world was nothing but water in which there lay a nameless goddess. Whenever the gods created anything, this watery goddess devoured it. In the end, the gods Quetzalcoatl and Tezcatlipoca turned themselves into serpents and tore the goddess apart. Her lower half became the Earth and her upper half became the heavens. Another version calls the water goddess Coatlicue and says she gave birth to the Earth goddess Coyolxauhqui and the Sun god Huitzilopochtli. He severed his sister Coyolxauhqui in half: half became the heavens and the other rested on the sea to become the Earth.

This idea of the Earth being a body may come from hills, mountains and islands that look, to the imaginative eye, like living things – a herd of colossal mammoths with their domed heads and humped backs, or a recumbent figure, usually a woman, where the peaks are her foot, knee, pubis, breast and head. They may seem relatively small to us, as we know the world is enormous: but to people who spent their whole lives within sight of a particular mountain like this, such an apparently petrified giant body could easily seem like the centre, and starting point, of the Earth.

Tiâmat

The Mesopotamian origin myths are diverse, but they contain strong elements of a watery origin, and sometimes of the idea of the Earth being made from a deity's body. A late, Greek-influenced version of their origin myth, said to have been written by Berossus, a priest in Marduk's temple in Babylon about 275 BC, states that, originally, 'all was darkness and water'. This dark, chaotic world was presided over by the goddess Omorka or Thamte ('the sea'). It was peopled by strange, hermaphroditic beings who were part human, part animal – man-headed bulls; fish-tailed dogs; goat-legged men. Then came Bêl (Marduk), who clove Thamte in two to create, from her severed halves, the Earth and the heavens.

Mesopotamia's *Enûma Eliš*, similarly, starts with Apsû, the deity of fresh water, and Tiâmat (i.e., Thamte), the deity of both salt water and chaos. There was no land and 'not a reed marsh was to be seen'. But then the mingling of the two types of water produced Mummu, who was the mist and clouds rising from the waters. Then Apsû and Tiâmat coupled again and produced Lahmu and Lahâmu, who were the parents of Anshar and Kishar. Anshar and Kishar had Anu, who was father (by his sister, presumably) of Nudimmud, who was also called Ea or Enki. Ea became the leader of the gods, but the noise he and his fellows made infuriated Apsû, who conspired with Mummu to destroy them. But Ea was too clever for his ancestor and used spells to send Apsû to sleep, whereupon he slew him. Then an evil god called Kingu goaded Tiâmat (who was probably his mother) into avenging her husband's death. So fearsome was Tiâmat that neither Anshar nor Anu could withstand her, so Ea decided to send his own splendid son, Marduk, against her. The gods made Marduk their king and he set forth in his storm chariot, armed with his bow and arrow, with which he shot Tiâmat dead through her open mouth. Then Marduk cut Tiâmat in two. He made one half of her into the sky, the realm of Anu, and the other half onto the Earth, all of whose sweet waters he gave to Ea. He gave the surface of the Earth and the air above to Enlil (who was either a son or brother of Anu). Marduk then created the constellations and the Moon. What happened next, we do not know because the rest of the tablet on which it was written is broken off.

Though a Babylonian myth, most of the names in the *Enûma Eliš* are ancient Sumerian. It seems likely that the story of Marduk's rise to power has been superimposed onto a considerably older creation myth from Sumer, from the dawn of city-based civilisation itself. Before Marduk, the god who separated Earth and the heavens was surely Enlil himself. But it had all started with the primal waters.

Though found in a library, incidentally, we know that this was a living myth. It was re-enacted at the annual flooding of the Tigris and Euphrates by the king and his priests, who symbolically restored order from the watery chaos of Tiâmat.

Of Sely and Dyabdar

Sometimes, in Mesopotamia, with its man-made dykes, canals and cities, the Earth was imagined as the body of a humanlike deity, and it was the way it was due to the action of other humanlike deities. But a bilingual, Babylonian and Sumerian inscription recorded in the 500s BC and found at Sippar, where the Euphrates piled up silt at the head of the Persian Gulf, states that at first all was water, and the god Marduk created dry land by building a reed frame on the waters and pouring earth into it. That sounds like an older, simpler version of the story, before the idea of the Earth being a body had been developed. In many other cultures, the Earth emerged in similar manner, as earth, out of the primal waters, but through the agency of animals. We have echoes of such tales in the involvement of a cow in the Norse myth and serpents in the Toltec one, but in others, animals play a yet more prominent role.

Many Hindu origin myths imagine the Earth lying in the fathomless depths. The *Taittiriya Samhita* (7.1.5.1) describes how Prajapati, moving above the waters in the form of the wind, saw the Earth submerged, far below. He assumed the form of a boar and dived down into the water, so as to raise the Earth up to the surface. In the *Ramayana*, it is Brahma who takes the form of a boar and dives down to rescue the Earth. The *Vishnu Purana* tells how Narayana (a name for Vishnu) assumed the form of a boar, who plunged into the water and the submerged Earth bowed reverently to him as he raised it up to float on the surface of the water. The *Kalika Purana* develops the story further: Vishnu takes the form of a boar and dives into the waters, scooping up earth on his tusk in order to drag it up to the surface. Then he takes the form of a seven-headed serpent, Ananta, and supports the Earth on his hood. As a boar again, he couples with the Earth goddess: they become Varaha and Varahi, and between them they have three sons. These and the boar create trouble for the Earth, so Vishnu tells Shiva to kill the boar, who was, of course, a manifestation of Vishnu himself. In some versions, then, Earth is a body, in others it was simply earth – but its emergence from the water was always caused by an animal.

The Yoruba people of Nigeria had a sophisticated, city-based culture dating back to at least 300 BC. They imagined a primal universe of sky and water. Having obtained permission from the supreme deity, Olorun, the god Obatala commissioned a golden chain from the goldsmith of the gods, and climbed down it until he reached the sea. He sprinkled sand into the waters to create an island. He then released a white hen onto the island, and the hen's scratching enlarged the island to create Africa. The Maidu people of northern California have a similar myth: they envisaged a watery world too, and a turtle. The god Kodoyanpe climbed down from the sky on a rope made of feathers, and told the turtle to dive down into the sea to bring up soil to build the Earth.

These myths imagine the Earth being raised up from the primal waters through the agency of a god, but the real work in all cases is undertaken by boar, chicken or turtle – suggesting that these are sophisticated versions of older myths in which the animal alone made the world. And in some cultures these simpler, older myths survive. The Algonquian people who live around the Great Lakes of North America believed that the world was once all water, and a great hare called Michabo dived down and brought up a single grain of sand, and from this grew the Earth.

Their very distant cousins in Siberia had similar tales. Long into the nineteenth century and even into the twentieth, Siberian tribes led a nomadic lifestyle, not much altered since the days of their ancestors in Upper Palaeolithic times. True, they used metal and herded animals, but in most other respects their survival skills and beliefs had probably changed very little in 40,000 years. Their spiritual life, like that of the cave painters of Ice Age France, centred upon shamans, whose trance experiences (of imagined sinking and flying) probably underpinned their stories of the nature of the Universe. They imagined this as a series of tiers, with our world in the middle. The deities and spirits of the dead were above and the evil ones were below. All was connected (like the Vikings' world) by the roots and branches of a great tree.

Our middle world was nothing but sea. In one Siberian origin myth, Otshirvani and Chagan-Shukuty came down from Heaven and dived down repeatedly to the bottom of the sea to bring up mud, which they piled on the back of a turtle, until dry land was created.

Similarly, the Evenk tribe, who inhabit great swathes of Siberia to the north and east of Lake Baikal, imagined the world to have emerged as a small island amidst the endless ocean. On the island were the primal serpent, Dyabdar, and the primal mammoth, Sely. In one version, as told to M.I. Osharov by an Evenk tribesman called Moronenok in 1923, Sely the mammoth dived down repeatedly into the water and carried ever more sand, clay and rocks up to the surface to build the Earth. That story appears in M.G. Voskoboinikov's *About Evenk cosmogonic legends* (1981), which also contains another version of the story, as told to A.F. Anisimov by an Evenk called Vasiliy Sharemiktal on the Yudokon River, a tributary of the Stony Tunguska River, who again affirmed that the world had been dredged up out of the watery depths by Sely the mammoth.

This was a living myth. Sely's story was recalled in the layout of Evenk shamans' tents, constructed for the *ikenipke* festivals in the Tunguska region. These comprised three parts, the *dulu* or 'middle world' tent, with two galleries, east (*darpe*) and west (*ongang*), the latter containing a large image of a mammoth, and representing (amongst many other things) the lower world. The *ikenipke* festival included a dance around the shaman's tent, in which participants might not only perceive the future, but also return to the 'land of light', which existed at the start of the world. And the agents for the forming of the world were a snake and a mammoth.

The looming presence of mammoths in these Siberian stories must owe a lot to the periodic reappearance of their ancient, frozen corpses, melting out of the permafrost. But it is possible that such reappearances did not so much cause these stories, as keep old ones

A mammoth from the 'Grand Plafond', Rouffignac cave.

alive – very old ones, perhaps, dating back to the time when their ancestors and ours hunted mammoths across the tundra of Siberia and Europe. These stories take us straight back to the painted caves of Pech Merle and Rouffignac, where mammoths seem to have been revered. And the placing of animal imagery in Rouffignac is not random. In six places, groups of them are near natural wells leading down to lower storeys (where there is no art). It has been suggested that they are linked to the way down to the underworld. Maybe the pictures in these locations depict the animal ancestors who had brought the substance of the world up out of the depths in the first place.

Maybe it is possible to boil all these origin myths from around the world down to a simple origin, shared by all our Ice Age ancestors as they spread around the world – that the world had started as eternal, primal waters. Sea and sky were separated. And animal deities, such as the primal mammoth and the primal serpent, dredged up soil to create the Earth.

Chapter 28

The World Shapers

The Rainbow Serpent's journey

The world began and the Earth was raised out of the primal waters. Our ancestors' next concern was how the land gained the precise form it has now. Our scientific explanation focuses on plate tectonics and volcanos, but for our ancestors the answer lay with those benevolent creatures who had built the Earth for them in the first place. Moronenok's Siberian myth tells us that, by writhing over the newly formed Earth, the serpent Dyabdar created the river valleys. The world was inhabited by animals and people (whose origin is not specified, but they had probably been born out of the Earth). Unfortunately, the swift flowing of the rivers became out of hand. Whilst the other creatures took refuge in the hills, Sely and Dyabdar were both swept away into the lower world. Sharemiktal's version, meanwhile, relates how, having built the world, Sely and Dyabdar were attacked by the monster Chulugdy. During their primordial struggle, Sely's pounding feet created the lakes and bogs and her tusks threw up the mountains, whilst Dyabdar's writhings scoured out the valleys. Eventually, the mammoth and snake succeeded in casting Chulugdy down into the lower world, but in doing so they were dragged down there themselves too.

Many Aboriginal origin myths focus on the Dreamtime, a timeless state that exists independently of the material world, from which our spirits came and to which they will return. Perhaps it is similar to the 'land of light' of the Siberian shamans. Unlike many other cultures, there is no discernible echo in the Aboriginal myth of the Earth being dredged up out of the sea: maybe, as a people who inhabited great stretches of the waterless Outback, such tales, if they had ever existed there, had simply evaporated. What was left, instead of the primal seas, was an eternal, flat, barren plain. Nothing stirred but plumes of red dust, blown up from the featureless desert by the breeze. But below the arid earth there slept the ancestors of all living things. The first of these to awaken was the Rainbow Serpent. She pushed her way up through the soil and began to explore her new world. As she travelled, her coiling body dug out the valleys and pushed up the mountains.

Wherever you go in the world, you don't have to stray very far from the beginning of everything before you notice a serpent, coiling magnificently through the story. The name of Quetzalcoatl, the great benefactor of mankind across Central America, means 'feathered serpent'; Orphism started the whole of creation with a self-replicating snake; and in Hinduism the seven-headed serpent Ananta supports the Earth on his hood. Most often, as with the Aboriginal myth, the serpent also plays an important role in shaping the land.

In north-eastern Vietnam, where the erosion of limestone in Halong Bay has created an other-worldly landscape of high-domed islands jutting up out of the serene waters, legend speaks of the Mother Dragon and her children who were sent by the Jade Emperor of China to help the local people repel seaborne invaders. Descending on the bay, these flying serpents scattered emerald teeth out of their mouths to sink and trap the enemy fleet, and the emeralds became the islands. In China itself, the scooping out of the valleys was attributed to the serpent-tailed goddess Nugua or Nüwa, as she glided over the nearly formed world, just like Dyabdar and the Rainbow Serpent.

Much of Greece's landscape was formed by volcano and earthquake. The wracked landscape was sometimes attributed to the infernal battle between Zeus and the serpent-tailed monster Typhon. The chaotic, jagged volcanic landscape of the Pallene Peninsula in Greece was attributed to the Gigantomachy, the terrible battle between the Olympian gods and the giants. But the Pallene Peninsula is littered with the preserved remains of mammoth bones and mammoth tusks. Maybe the original myth related how the peninsula's wracked landscape was caused by a battle fought by the primal mammoth, similar to the Siberian myth in which Sely battled the monster Chulugdy. Only much later was the battle reimagined as a scene in the story of the Olympian gods, and the animals were recast as giant humans. Fascinatingly, many Greek depictions of giants show that the transformation was not even complete: many of them had long, curved serpents' tails instead of legs – memories also, perhaps, of the sweeping trunks or tusks of the mammoths themselves.

At Delphi we encounter the world-shaping snake most clearly, for here was born the Python, a vast serpent, son of Gaia, the Earth. He was said to have emerged out of the rocky cleft above the Kastallian Spring, which is said to resemble a vagina. His writhing doubtless accounted, in the original myth, for the dramatic mountains and valley north of the Corinthian Gulf. Looking down from Delphi today it's not hard to imagine the imprint of the Python's great, serpentine body as it coiled through the deep, winding Pleistos Vale. Originally, the Python was the benevolent guardian of Gaia's spring there, but in time he was demonised, and became the deserving victim of Apollo, the Sun god, who made his scaly body bristle with shining arrows. By this means Apollo became the supreme, oracular god at Delphi – a metaphor, perhaps, for the Sun 'dispelling the vapours of reptilian Chaos', as Samivel put it.

It's no surprise, after all this, to find the serpent lingering about near the beginning of *Genesis*. Once, perhaps, the ancient Israelites had told stories of

The great Pleistos Vale below Delphi looks as if it was gouged out by the passage of a giant serpent, as imagined in this sketch.

the Earth emerging from the waters with the serpent performing the beneficial role of shaping the land for humans to inhabit. But once Yahweh had become supreme in their imaginations, only he could have shaped the world. So the serpent – who would not go away – was demonised into a malevolent sneak, tempting Eve with his juicy apple, an instrument of pure evil. The story seems deliberately contrived to ensure that the world-shaping serpent would never be thought about in a positive light again.

Succession battles in Heaven

Probably, most early origin myths focused on animals, not human-shaped deities, as the makers of the world. But as the Neolithic passed and mankind wrought ever greater changes to the landscape, animals lost their wild nobility as they became ever more subservient to humans, and their role in origin myths started being assumed by gods in human form. Often, there are two phases of these: the primal deities who embodied eternity itself, like Phanes Protogenos and Ra and Prajapati, and then later gods, derived from these originals, who were altogether more human and more closely involved in human affairs.

Once the Earth had been raised up out of the primal waters in Egyptian myth, for instance, falcon-headed Ra spat out some saliva, which became the air god

Shu and the water goddess Tefnut – though another version says they were born from the vomit of Atum. Shu and Tefnut were the primeval, divine couple, whose children were Nut, the sky goddess, and Geb, the Earth god, from whom all else emerged. And in Hindu myth, once Prajapati had created the world and time, all through the power of his mind, he began to produce beings out of his body. From his buttocks, Prajapati produced the demons. Then he cast off his body, creating night. He then adopted a new body and brought forth the gods from his face and then he cast aside that body, creating light.

There are several Aztec traditions concerning the origins of Quetzalcoatl. Some make him the son of a creator god, Tonacateuctli, others the son of Coatlicue, the goddess of the primal waters, who became pregnant by swallowing a ball of feathers on Coatepec, 'the serpent mountain'. Others report a woman, Chimalman, standing naked in front of a god, usually Mixcoatl, the deity of the Milky Way, inviting him to impregnate her. The god fired an arrow up between her legs, and made her pregnant. When she gave birth, there slithered out a long green serpent, its multi-coloured feathers damp and matted, the infant Quetzalcoatl. As with many other mythological systems, the Aztec heavens could be a dangerous place for gods: Mixcoatl was murdered by his brothers and in some versions Quetzalcoatl dismembered his sister Coyolxauhqui to make the Earth in the first place. The slaying of older gods by younger ones seems cruel, but how else can human stories of gods explain the rise of new ones in the place of old, when all the protagonists concerned were otherwise immortal?

Many other cultures' myths involve bitter wars of succession between succeeding generations of gods. A cuneiform tablet (B.M. 74329, described by Lambert and Walcott) from about 600 to 300 BC, which describes itself as a copy of an original 'of Bab[ylon] and Assur', perhaps as old as 2000 BC, describes a visceral soap opera of intergenerational war and incest. The surviving section starts with a primal pair called Hain and Earth, who had a son Amakandu (or Sumuqan, the deity of livestock). Amakandu created his sister, the Sea, with a stroke of the plough (which presumably filled with water) and built the city of Dunnu. Then, Earth 'cast her eyes on Amakandu, her son', saw how shapely his body was, and felt herself filled with desire for him. 'Come, let me make love to you', she said to him. Then 'Amakandu married Earth, his mother, and Hain his father he killed.' Amakandu became lord of the world and proceeded to marry his sister, the Sea, who killed her mother, Earth. Amakandu and the Sea gave birth to Lahar and River, who overthrew and killed their parents. They were overthrown and killed in turn by their own children, an unknown male and Ga'um, who in turn fell victim to their own children, an unknown male deity and his sister, Ningestinna. In the Mesopotamian *Enûma Eliš*, a similar intergenerational fracas culminates in Marduk slaying his great-great-great grandmother, Tiâmat, the primal sea, and severing her in two to create Heaven and Earth.

Profoundly influenced by such Mesopotamian myths, the Mycenaean Greeks and their successors told – as echoed in Homer's *Iliad* and Hesiod's *Theogony* – how Kronos (he who had castrated his father, Uranos) married his own sister, Rhea. Fearing a similar fate to his father's, Kronos swallowed all but one of their children, but Rhea spirited their son Zeus away to Crete, where he grew up and was eventually able to overthrow his father and release his sibling gods from Kronos's stomach. Kronos then sent the serpent-tailed Typhon to destroy his son, but Zeus killed it and imprisoned his father, either below the Earth, or far out in the western ocean. In the *Iliad* (15.23–30) we hear how Zeus then took the sky and Mount Olympos for himself, assigning the rest to his brothers – to Hades he gave the realms below the Earth, and to Poseidon, the seas. British mythology was probably once full of similarly incestuous succession battles: the only echoes we have of them now are the garbled accounts of the wars between the godlike Tuatha de Danann and the giant Fomorians in Ireland's *Lebor Gabála*.

No such succession wars appear in the *Old Testament*, naturally, for there was only one god, who could not very well fight amongst himself. But it is now fairly well established amongst biblical scholars that the trend from polytheism to monotheism took place slowly, between about 1000 BC and 500 BC. It was probably based in practicality, for a nomadic tribe must carry statues and shrines of its gods with it, so the fewer gods there were, the lighter the load. Unusually, though, the Jews came to see their god Yahweh not just as the only god of their own people, but as the only god *of anyone*. But before that transformation was complete, Yahweh was probably imagined in similar fashion to the other ruling gods of the region. Biblical scholars such as Raphael Patai and Dr Fransesca Stavrakopoulou have argued that he had a consort, Asherah, who was almost but not entirely expunged from the sacred texts. In 2 *Kings* 21:7, for example, Josiah's grandfather Manasseh builds her a statue. In *Expedition* (20, Summer 1978), Ze'ev Meshel describes how a storage jar was unearthed at Kuntillet Ajrud, and from it was deciphered the inscription 'Yahweh … and his Asherah'. And a god with a wife suggests children, and parents, and perhaps a war of succession no different to those imagined for their gods by the Jews' neighbours. Just as Marduk battled with his monstrous ancestress Tiâmat and Kronos sent the dreadful monster Typhon to try to destroy Zeus, the Canaan storm god Baal had to fight the serpent monster Litanu or Lotan, 'the tyrant of seven heads', as related in tablets from Ras Shamra from about the 1200s BC. Was Yahweh ever faced with similar peril, sent by his own, wrathful father? Perhaps, yes, for in Psalm 74 we hear of Yahweh smashing 'the heads of [the monster] Leviathan in pieces'.

Do we hear in that phrase the last echo of the succession battle through which Yahweh had risen to become the supreme god? That, at least, is what some scholars suggest now.

Chapter 29

The Birth of Mankind

In the early Middle Ages, the craftsmen who created the Romanesque church of Saint-Savin-sur-Gartempe, near Poitou in France, finished their work by painting a series of scenes along the vaulted ceiling of the nave. Each depicted a Bible story, so that the congregation, few of whom could understand the Latin in which the mass was being said, could gaze up and fill their minds with appropriately religious thoughts. There are masons, just like those who built Saint-Sevan, constructing the Tower of Babel. There are apocalyptic beasts and winged horses with human heads, charging terrifyingly across the world. There is father Noah, safe in his Ark, crossing the Flood in search of Mount Ararat. And there, up near the altar, is a robed, bearded figure with a large halo, bending over the recumbent form of a man who lies thin and awkward, more like a mannequin than a real human.

Suddenly it dawns on us that we are witnessing God in the very act of making Adam. And just as we grow used to this, we realise that more is going on. God seems to be doing something to Adam's bare chest: he is extracting a rib, in order to make Eve. And so it is, for next to this scene is another: Adam has gained some weight and stands, naked and well built, next to his robed creator, who strokes his stubbly chin. On the other side of God stands the product of the rib – Eve. Needless to say, as our eyes continue to be drawn to the right, we see Eve turning away from God to consort with that most malignant of beings, the Serpent, below the Tree of Knowledge.

It's not so unusual to see depictions of Adam and Eve with the tree and the serpent. But to see God himself in the act of creating them – to go back in time in biblical imagination to witness the creation of our first human ancestors – that is much rarer.

All around the world, origin myths fall into two halves: the emergence and shaping of the world and its gods, and then the creation of our own, human ancestors. *Genesis* presents one story. Other cultures have their own views. It is striking though, how many agree that the world came into existence first, before humans appeared. We may have been an arrogant species who thought the world was created for our benefit – but we were seldom so arrogant as to imagine that we had existed first.

The serpent's song

The Rainbow Serpent, say the Aborigines, was the first of the Dreamtime ancestors to awake below the red earth of Australia. As she coiled her way across the arid plain, carving out the river valleys, she sang. Down into the Earth went the beautiful reverberations of her song, awaking the other ancestors, who came burrowing up, bleary-eyed, to the surface. The first to come to the surface were the frogs, who laughed so much with delight that they coughed up the water inside them. This flowed away down the channels made by the serpent's journey, which became rivers. As the water seeped out into the earth, plant seeds germinated and the land blushed green. While this was happening, a terrible squawking was heard as the crane and the emu fell into a furious argument. In a moment of inspired anger, the crane flung the emu's egg up into the sky, where it smashed. Its bright yellow yolk ignited and blazed forth as the Sun.

Amongst the newly emerged ancestors who blinked up for the first time at the blazing sun were those of the humans. The Australian myths may be typical of the hunter-gatherer myths that once existed right across the world, and they are fascinating because many of them draw little differentiation between humans and animals. The human ancestors had been sleeping below the ground along with the spider ancestors, the kangaroo ancestors, the kookaburra ancestors and all the rest, and just like them they awoke to the serpent's song and roamed the world, naked and filled with wonder.

All the same, these were stories told by humans. The divide between humans and animals is often blurred because in many versions the animal ancestors have two forms: one resembles the animal concerned but the other – its true, spiritual form – is human shaped. Thus when Aboriginals imagined the spirit ancestor of an animal, that spirit might well resemble a human, but with animal characteristics. In some versions, too, the humans received special treatment from the Rainbow Serpent, who permitted them to eat other animals, provided each tribe avoided devouring their own totem animal. The Rainbow Serpent also turned some of the primal ancestors into rocks, to watch over the human tribes.

In some parts of Australia, stories of the appearance of mankind have grown more human-centric. Some tribes envisage the animal ancestors carving the original humans out of rock. Others, especially in the south-east, have stories of ancestors who came down from the sky to create the world and its human inhabitants. Some northern tribes tell of two female ancestors coming across the seas from the Land of the Dead, which lies to the north, perhaps recalling genuine migrations of humans into Australia from the Malay Peninsula. But still, the commonest Australian myth is that mankind was awoken out of the Earth by the Rainbow Serpent.

Out of a pod of vetch

In ancient Greece, Adonis (whose cult was of Middle Eastern origin) was said to have been born out of the body of his mother, Myrrha, who had been turned into a myrrh tree. That story might be an echo of a string of beliefs, coiling round the world like tendrils of ivy, which imagined vegetal origins for many of our ancestors.

All around the northern ice sheet, in Alaska, Canada, Greenland and Russia, live the people called variously Inuit, Yupik, Aleut and Eskimo. They too believe that animals have a disguised, spiritual, human form. The raven, for instance, disguised its human-shaped spirit by pulling a beak down over its face. Once the raven had created sea, land and mountains by beating its wings, it created plants, including the wild vetches, which produce seeds in pods. Wild vetches spread across the Earth, and to the raven's surprise, one of the vetch seed pods split open and a man was seen to struggle out. When the raven realised the man was hungry, he made animals and fish out of clay for him to hunt, and a woman to keep the man company. As the humans started increasing, the raven also made bears, to hold the burgeoning population in check. Then, the raven flew away to a faraway land and stole a piece of the light that blazed there, bringing it back as the Sun, to illuminate the Inuit lands.

This idea of humans having vegetal origins reappears in the origin myth of the Maidu people of northern California. They believed that their creator god, Kodoyanpe, fashioned humans out of wood, but they would not come to life and remained buried in the earth. Suspecting the Coyote of causing this problem, Kodoyanpe attacked him. In the great battle that ensued, Kodoyanpe was killed but the result was that the wooden figures came to life and humanity was born.

Back in the northlands, and naturally akin to the Inuit story, the Vikings' myths told how, once the primal cow Audhumla had thawed the ice and the body of Ymir the frost giant had become the earth, maggots started appearing in Ymir's flesh, which became the dwarves who live below the earth. Odin roamed the world, accompanied by his two raven companions, Hugin and Munin, and his brothers, Vili and Ve. Finding an ash and an elm growing out of the earth, they created the first man out of the ash and called him Ask, and from the elm they made Embla, the first woman. The gods created separate homes on the Earth for the men, giants and gods, called Midgard, Jotunheim and Asgard, respectively. In the next cycle, after this world is destroyed at the Battle of Ragnarok, Vidar will remake the world and the first humans will be born out of the 'world tree', Yggdrasil: their names will be Lif and Lifthrasir. Odin's companionship with ravens may be significant here. The Vikings were a sophisticated, farming people, far removed from the old days of hunting and gathering. But were their gods interlopers here? Had the original agent for the birth of the first humans out of the trees been the ravens alone?

In Zoroastrianism, Ahura Mazda, who had created the world, made Gayomart the Primal Man and gave him the primal bull and fire. Gayomart and the bull stood by the river Daiti, which flowed from the centre of the world, where they were killed by the evil demon Ahriman. But from the bull's blood sprung vegetation, whilst his sperm spurted up to the crescent moon and from the union of the two were born the animals. And from the slain Gayomart's sperm there grew a plant that split and revealed the first man and the first woman. Again, this sounds like an older myth (that the first man and woman grew out of a plant) wrapped up in a more sophisticated one (that the plant had grown from a man's sperm). And here again is an animal, a bull this time, playing a significant role in the story, just as Sely the mammoth played his key role in the myths of Siberia.

The Navajo imagined five worlds, piled on top of each other. Insects from the first, black world found their way up into the second, which was blue and full of birds, so they fled up into the third, yellow world, which was inhabited by animals. In this world, four spirits (white, blue, yellow and black) fashioned the first humans out of ears of corn. These humans elected to be ruled by four animals: bluebird, lion, hummingbird and wolf. When food ran short the animals and humans of the third world, who were known collectively as the First People, took the advice of the four animal rulers and flew up into the fourth, black and white world, where they became the bird people, the animal people, the insect people and the Navajo. They found other people living in this world – the Apache, Hopi, Comanche and so on. Then the Coyote enraged the water monster, who flooded the fourth world. All the people climbed up the stem of a plant that grew on the highest mountain and reached the fifth world, the one in which we live now. This bizarrely complex story is probably underpinned by shamanistic experiences of flying, which go right back to Upper Palaeolithic times. But again we have animals playing key roles, and a birth of mankind out of plants.

We're only made of clay

Many of our ancestors probably believed, therefore, that they were descended from spirit ancestors who had awoken in the body of the Earth, or from a primal man and woman who had been born from plants that had grown in turn out of the earth. The animal deities who shaped the world may also have played a role in the first humans' appearance. But as myths became more sophisticated, the role of animals reduced and humanlike gods assumed the role of making our ancestors.

The Incas said that the god Viracocha had caused the world to be reborn out of the waters of a great flood. He made the animals anew, then carved the first humans out of stone and painted them. Viracocha planted these stone humans below the soil and, much later, he called on them to rise up and start living. The Greeks had similar beliefs: for them, humans were the children of Gaia, the Earth. Instead of a single pair of progenitors, they envisaged the different peoples as autochthones, born from the soil where they now lived. Some races like the Athenians had sprung up of their own volition. Others had been sown on the Earth – the body of Gaia – by a higher power. The Spartoi of Thebes (see plate 33), for instance, had grown from dragon's teeth sown on the fields of Fokida by Cadmus (who was a human grandson of the god Poseidon), whilst the Leleges had sprouted up from stones sown by Deucalion and Pyrrha (who were descended from Titans).

In China, after the world had been created out of the disembodied body of the giant Pangu, the serpent-tailed goddess Nugua or Nüwa, whose gliding over the Earth had carved out the valleys, realised the world lacked intelligent life. She stopped by the Yellow River and fashioned humans out of the clay from its bed. Nugua breathed life into them, making some *yin* (women) and others *yang* (men). Growing tired of fashioning such perfect humans, Nugua made the rest by dipping a rope in the river and then shaking the clay off it, each drop becoming a lesser human (thus providing a nice allegory for the distinction between the ancestors of the aristocracy, and those of the common people).

A similar story appears in Nigeria. After he had created the Earth in the midst of the primal seas, Obatala created the Sun and planted a palm nut, so that the land became clothed with jungle. Then Obatala created humans from clay, but whilst he did so he consumed too much palm wine and became drunk, so his creations – we humans – were as flawed as we really are.

An Egyptian myth asserts that Khnum or Khnemu, the god of the source of the Nile, was also 'the Divine Potter'. He scooped up some soft clay from the bank of the Nile, placed it on his potter's wheel, and fashioned the first human children. It is a tale little different to that told by the Dogon in Mali, who imagined the Sun, Moon, Earth and humans all being moulded by the creator god out of clay.

In the Mayans' *Popol Vuh* we hear how the gods created animals and plants but were dissatisfied that these living things could not praise their creators. Therefore, the gods used clay to make the first man and woman, but these clay people had no intelligence, so the gods destroyed them. The gods then made a human couple from wood, but these had no souls either, so became monkeys. Then, at the suggestion of the jaguar, the coyote, the crow and the parrot, they made four people, the First Fathers, out of cornmeal dough. These people were almost as perfect as the gods themselves. The gods then made the four First

Mothers in the same way. These first people asked the gods for light, so the Sun, Moon and stars were created. The gods clouded our ancestors' minds, so that they would not rival their creators. In contrast to the Nigerians, who blamed our short-sightedness on alcohol, the Mayans held that, by ingesting hallucinogenic plants, we can defy the gods and perceive the universe as it truly is.

The divine spirit

There is a progression, then, from older myths, which may be close to what our hunter-gatherer ancestors believed, which imagine our ancestors being born of the Earth, or from plants growing on it, to those that envisage us being made by gods. These latter tend to be the myths of the more self-important cultures. But there is a further step up, which envisages our origins both in the clay of the Earth *and* in the divinity of the gods. Perhaps we should not be too surprised by this, for it offers some consolation: we may possess mortal, clayish bodies, but our spirits come from the immortal gods. How else, after all, could a creature fashioned from the substance of the world end up with a spiritual dimension?

The myths of Mesopotamia return to this idea persistently. In the *Enûma Eliš*, Marduk forced the evil god Kingu and his henchmen to be slaves to the other gods, growing food to burn in sacrifice to the higher gods. But eventually the complaints of these slave gods wore Marduk down and he decided that his father, Ea, should create mankind to do this work instead. Ea killed Kingu and made mankind out of his blood. Finally, the gods built Marduk the great temple of Esagila, with the city of Babylon around it. A tablet found at Babylon, the beginning of which is lost, starts 'when Anu had created the heavens' and relates how Nudimmud (another name for Ea) created the minor gods, reeds, forests, mountains, seas, priests, kings and finally mankind 'for doing of the service of the gods'. A badly worn tablet from 1700s BC Babylon relates, alternatively, how Enki (Ea) asked the goddess Mami (or Nintu) to fashion mankind out of clay and the blood of a god he had ordered to be slain for this purpose.

Another tablet of about 800 BC, found in the ruins of Assur, records an old Sumerian story that, once sky and land had been separated and the courses of the Tigris and Euphrates had been fixed, Anu, Enlil, Ea and Shamash, the Sun god, sat in their exalted sanctuary, wondering what to do next. They decided to create mankind to serve the gods by working in the fields, maintaining the drainage ditches for the fields and celebrating the gods' festivals. In Uzamua, the sacred area in the city of Nippur, they slew two of the Lamga or craftsmen gods and made the first man and woman, Ulligarra and Zalgarra, out of their blood.

Berossus's version was that, once Bêl (Marduk) had cleft Tiâmat in two, separating Earth from sky, light flooded in between and the monsters who had inhabited the world died. To repopulate the world, Bêl ordered another god to behead himself, and from the blood Marduk made men *and* animals. It is rare in the Middle East to find humans and animals sharing the same origins, and we must remember that Berossus's version was a highly intellectualised one, disconnected by many steps from truly indigenous stories.

In *Genesis*, which owes a great debt to the older stories of the Middle East, the appearance of mankind is the final and greatest act of the creating god. On the fourth day Yahweh created the planets and stars and on the fifth he caused the waters to produce the fish, whales and birds. On the sixth day he caused the land to yield forth the animals and then he made Adam in his own image, forming him from 'the dust of the ground'. The very name 'Adam' may be derived from the Hebrew *adamah*, 'earth'. God then breathed life – the soul – in through Adam's nostrils. God took one of Adam's ribs and out of it he made Eve, as a companion for the man.

In Rome, Ovid's *Metamorphoses* admitted uncertainty over human origins: once the Earth had been populated with plants and animals, the creating god (about whose identity Ovid is non-committal) had perhaps made us from a 'divine seed', or else we were born from clay sprinkled with raindrops by the Titan Prometheus, and metamorphosed into bipedal creatures, more cerebral, more holy than anything that had come before.

The tears of the gods

Finally, and rising right up the scale of human self-confidence, are origin myths that dispense with worldly origins altogether and place humanity almost on a par with the gods. An Egyptian myth tells how Ra discovered that his first-born children, Shu (air) and Tefnut (water) were lost in the big wide world. When eventually he found them again he cried with joy. From the tears he shed appeared the first humans (though, if the tears hit the Earth first, then this is a precursor to the Greek stories of humans being 'seeded' in the soil).

In Central America, the Aztecs believed that, once he had created the world, Quetzalcoatl turned himself into an ant and stored up enough grain to feed the humans he was about to create. With the help of the female snake deity Cihuacoatl he created humans from the powdered bones either of his father or of earlier, now destroyed, races of humans, and then wounded parts of his own body, including his penis, and let the blood flow into the bones to imbue them with life.

In Hinduism, the primal being Prajapati, having created the whole world out of his mind, started peopling it, first with gods and demons and then with living things, each born of a new body of his, first, they say, the humans and rakshasas (man–eating beings), then the snakes and birds, followed by the animals and then the plants, which he created from his hair. That is a most unusual myth because it envisages humans existing *before* the plant and animal life that surrounds us: almost always, the order is reversed and we come, blinking in astonishment, into a fully populated world where we live out our short life, before the cold hand of death closes on us all.

Chapter 30

The Great Flood

The King of Uruk seeks answers

The Mesopotamians had a variety of origin myths, recorded on their cuneiform tablets, all hovering around a central theme: that the gods made the Earth, one way or another, out of the primal waters, and then made mankind to serve them. This region also produced the earliest written account of a human wanting to find any of this out, in the form of the epic tale of Gilgamesh, King of Uruk. The earliest version we have now was written in Babylon about 1200 BC, but it is believed to be based on much older tales, surely from ancient Uruk itself.

Gilgamesh befriends Enkidu, a hairy hunter who seems like a memory of the wilder, hunter-gatherer origins of humanity. When Enkidu dies, Gilgamesh becomes deeply troubled by human mortality and sets out on an epic journey in order to trace his own ancient ancestry. On an island at the edge of the world he finds his forebear Uta–Napishtim, who had survived the Great Flood, from whom he hopes to learn the truth about humanity. Uta–Napishtim confirms Gilgamesh's pessimistic view of the human condition: 'You exhaust yourself with ceaseless toil, you fill your sinews with sorrow ... the comely young man, the pretty young woman – all too soon in their prime Death abducts them!'

Death tends to abduct most of us a little later in life now than it did in Mesopotamian times, when surviving into one's forties was considered a rare achievement. But the general sentiment is one with which few people might disagree today. Uta–Napishtim, uniquely, knows why death exists. Long ago, he tells Gilgamesh, the lesser gods, tired of labouring in the fields, had rebelled. Ea (or Enki) resolved the dispute by making men out of clay to undertake the work instead, filling them with spirit from the rebellion's executed instigator. The scheme worked for a while, but humans were immortal and bred too quickly: soon the world was aswarm with them and their noise kept the gods awake at night. The gods sent a great flood to destroy humanity, but Ea warned Uta–Napishtim to build a great boat, in which he saved himself, his family and servants. Ea then persuaded the other gods to allow these select few people and their descendants to survive. But their numbers were to be held in check by infant mortality, infertility, religious celibacy and old age: only Uta–Napishtim and his wife were allowed to retain their immortality.

Having met his ancestor and learned both the true origins of humanity and why death is necessary, Gilgamesh returns home to Uruk, resigned at last to the human condition.

Surviving the Great Flood

Genesis has its flood myth, too, almost certainly based on the stories told in Mesopotamia (see plate 32). The Greeks adopted one as well, albeit rather half-heartedly, trying to segue it into their narrative of Greek mythological history. An earlier myth of the origins of a Greek people called the Leleges claimed that they had grown from seeds sown on the Earth by Deucalion and Pyrrha. This was adapted to make this couple the survivors of the flood (their ark having landed on Mount Parnassos), and from the seed they sowed had grown the ancestors of all humans.

Some versions of the Chinese origin myth contain flood stories, too – whether influenced by Mesopotamia and the Bible or not we do not know. In one, serpent-tailed Nüwa and her equally serpent-tailed brother Fu Xi lived amongst the people they had fashioned out of clay until the monster Gong-gong tried to destroy the world with fire and flood. Nüwa and Fu Xi were the only survivors. The flood broke the pillars that held the Earth above the primal seas, so they replaced them with legs cut off a turtle. Then, they repopulated the world by making men out of clay afresh.

The Incas thought that, long ago, Viracocha the creator god presided over a dark world inhabited by animals and giants. Viracocha then turned the giants into stone and destroyed his creation with a flood, which probably poured out of Lake Titicaca. When the flood waters receded, he caused the Sun to be born on an island in Lake Titicaca and remade humanity afresh.

In Aztec mythology, the humans who had been created by serpent-tailed Quetzalcoatl lived happily in the world that had been made through the dismemberment of the original, watery goddess of the seas. But she remained hungry for sacrifice, and because the people did not make these sacrifices properly, she flooded the world. The same process happened three more times and then our, fifth, world was created, in which the Aztecs had finally learned to make the correct sacrifices, and thus stave off further, watery disaster (or so they believed: the last of the Incas' bloody sacrifices was made almost 600 years ago, and the goddess has not destroyed us all – yet).

The origins of the Great Flood

Science finds no evidence for a universal flood, but it is possible that local inundations may have helped enforce flood stories in origin myths. The Mesopotamian flood myth was powerful because it recalled both the springtime flooding of the Tigris and Euphrates, and also a singular event in the Neolithic past. Back in about 5800 BC the whole Black Sea region had been subject to a collosal inundation when the Sea of Marmara, fed by the rising level of the Mediterranean (caused in turn by the melting of the polar ice caps after the end of the Ice Age) burst over the hills that the lay to the north of it. The water gouged out the Bosporus and cascaded north to flood what became the Black Sea. The flooded area included much Neolithic farmland and the peoples displaced may have included some of the ancestors of the Mesopotamians. It is no surprise, then, that floodwaters were never far from the Mesopotamians' mythmaking. But that can only be part of the reason why flood stories were popular in that region, and it does not explain why they are sometimes found much further afield.

One possible explanation is that flood stories do not recall great floods at all. Instead, they are simply a narrative device enabling storytellers to add a prehistory to the watery origins of the world, or to combine more than one origin myth into a single narrative. Many origin myths start with the Earth appearing out of the waters, after which mankind appears. But what if the desire arose to explain where the waters had come from? That required a backstory for those primal waters, and this caused what mythographers call 'doubling' – the use of what is essentially the same story more than once in the same narrative. The primal waters are doubled, and on their second appearance they are not primal waters any more, but waters covering the Earth due to a great flood. So we have the watery beginning for the world, followed by some activity on the part of deities and a false start in which humans appear and proliferate. Then comes a destructive flood, after which the world as we know it emerges from the waters and the flood survivor and his descendants *re*populate the world (whereas in the original story, they may have been the first ever people).

Thus, we read in Gilgamesh's epic of Uta–Napishtim's world being submerged by a flood only to appear back out of the receding waters. But perhaps what we are reading here is the last vestige of an Uruk creation myth that had *started* with Uta–Napishtim being created as the first man on the first ever dry land that had ever emerged out of the primal waters, and to which a backstory (probably derived from another Mesopotamian city, such as Babylon) was added later. The resulting, more complex story satisfied the Mesopotamians' philosophical desire to probe into the ever more distant past, and also combined two older, simpler origin myths (perhaps of Uruk and Babylon in this case) into one longer story.

It all seems like irresponsible myth-making, but it arose out of a pressing need to explain how and why the complex world we inhabit could possibly have come to be and the desire to synthesise different origin myths. It is not so very different to the way modern science tries to piece together the story of our own, ancient beginnings. Having said that the Universe began with the Big Bang, the explanation becomes unsatisfactory as nobody knows what caused it. Maybe in a few decades' time, science will tell us that the Big Bang was not the ultimate beginning of everything, but a destructive event – a great flood, in effect – that brought to an end an earlier and now lost world. Who knows?

How to make an origin myth

Wherever we go in the world, and as far back into the past as ancient texts allow us to penetrate, we hear of origin myths. From the Arctic Circle to Aboriginal Australia, from Africa to Central America, Siberia and Europe, and from the earliest literate societies in the Middle East to tribespeople interviewed in the twentieth century – everyone, it seems, had myths of how their ancient ancestors came to be. The phenomenon is so widespread that it appears to be an innate part of our human make-up, a natural result of our having evolved enquiring minds in the first place.

Origin myths helped our ancestors, and still help us now, to try to answer many deep-seated human needs, not least our desire to overcome our fear of death. Gilgamesh brought back a clear explanation of why we must die. Later myths like the Norse ones promise the rebirth of the world after the death of this one. But in part, at least, these myths exist for the most obvious purpose – to try to satisfy our desire to know who we are and where we come from.

Whilst each myth is different, there are certain elements that recur repeatedly, all around the world. Usually, there were primal waters, standing for a state of chaos, and the Earth that emerges from them promises more order. Usually, animals were involved in making and shaping the world. The serpent is arguably the most prevalent, whilst birds, boars and mammoths are amongst the other creatures involved. As farming cultures developed, many of these Earth-shaping animals morphed into human-shaped gods. In the ages of Bronze and Iron, cultures such as the Greeks and the Jews who placed supreme confidence in humanlike deities diffused any surviving myths about Earth-shaping animals by asserting that these creatures, particularly the Earth-shaping serpent, were not beneficial originators, but malevolent interlopers. Usually, humans came into existence after the world had been formed, and often there is a sense that it had been created for our benefit. Usually, the first humans owed their existence to the beneficial agency of animal deities. Later myths turned these animal-helpers into human-shaped gods too. Often, origin myths included great floods that helped define the borders between the remote past and more manageable, recent history. These flood stories were usually created by the doubling-up of two origin myths, each involving a watery origin, the second one being altered into a flood, after which the modern world begins.

Thus, as Mount Ararat emerges out of the receding flood waters in the biblical origin myth, we may question whether we are really looking at a mountain that survived the flood at all. Is it, in fact, that primal mound that, in some much earlier, almost forgotten Middle Eastern origin myth, was believed to have been the very first land ever to rise up out of the primal seas, at the very beginning of the world?

From figurine to deity

In Upper Palaeolithic culture, the many Venus figurines that we encountered in earlier chapters were primarily emblems of female fertility used by women in childbirthing, usually quite distinct from the animal deities depicted on the cave walls, which may have been believed to have made the world. In all probability, the figurines were imagined as the personification of their owners' own ancestral human mother, one of the first pair of humans who had been awoken in the earth (or from a plant growing from the earth) during the Dreamtime by the benevolent animal deities.

Over a long period of time, the figurines may have become mentally associated with female animal deities or with the fertility of the Earth itself. In farming cultures, the role of the female principle embodied in the Venus figurines may have expanded to take in these other aspects of our ancestors' perceived cosmos. She became a deity, perhaps herself instrumental in shaping or making the world. She became the primal oceans (Tethys, Tiâmat) or the Earth itself (Gaia). Although the mother figure depicted in the figurines had originally been awoken out of the Earth, she now assumed the role of the fertile spirit of the Earth itself. Her recumbent form was also seen in certain privileged places within the landscape itself, in certain mountains, whose peaks might resemble her face, breasts, pubis, bent knees and feet. As the Neolithic progressed, the goddess completed her transition from birthing aid and ancestral human mother into something more universal. Then, as the Bronze and Iron ages came, and the balance of power in many societies shifted from female to male, the power invested in the goddess shifted to gods (so gods are, in a sense, masculine forms of the goddess), and the husks of the goddesses, though still responsible for childbirth, were left to become the mere consorts of the now all-powerful male deities.

All in the mind

It seems that origin myths from around the world have a great deal in common with each other. If so, we find ourselves wondering whether they come from a common and very ancient origin.

Oral origin myths cannot be proved to be much older than the people who were recorded telling them. Written ones are only as old as the date of the recording, so at best we can refer back to written origin myths from Mesopotamia from a few thousand years BC. Before then, we can't prove there were any origin myths at all. However, the very widespread nature of origin myths and the themes they all have in common argues for their being considerably older than their earliest surviving recordings. Equally, whilst stories change a little with each telling, it seems reasonable to suppose that earlier, unrecorded versions of these myths were at least similar to their earliest recordings.

We might theorise that the world's origin myths are descended from stories that were told in Africa before the human race dispersed, about 80,000 years ago, and that each of the 'out of Africa' emigrants took their own versions of these primal stories with them, just as they took the roots of language and genetic haplogroups with them.

It's an appealing idea, but it doesn't square with the sudden appearance of art in Aurignacian Europe, about 40,000 years ago. David Lewis-Williams and others thought this was caused by a sudden change in human brains in Europe. This change may then have spread around the world through a potent mixture of cultural exchange and interbreeding (but not necessarily down direct male-to-male or female-to-female lines, so it need not have affected the modern distribution of male-line or female-line genetic haplotypes). We know from the statistical work of Joseph T. Chang that the most recent common ancestor of all people alive now may have lived less than 2,000 years ago. On that basis, the idea that the people of Aurignacian Europe, in which that sudden change in the human brain took place, could have been ancestors, one way or another, of everyone living anywhere in the world a few thousand years later, is not implausible – indeed, it is statistically likely. And if lines of descent could spread across the world, so too could a story. A single, original origin myth about watery origins could have started in Europe at some point after 40,000 years ago and spread all over the world with the awakening of full, human consciousness. Or, alternatively, such a story may have originated *anywhere* in the world and spread out all across the world, many thousands of years *after* the rise of full, human consciousness.

That is one theory. Another is that, when broken down into their component parts, origin myths are very simple. They tend to assume that we are the end product of a process that, working back, also gave rise to the animals, the plants, the gods, heavens, the solid earth and, at the very beginning of the process, the chaotic, formless substance of water. Maybe different origin myths came into our minds at different times, in different parts of the world, quite independently of each other, but all were similar because they are simply the sort of thing that a fully conscious human mind is likely to generate when forced to imagine how our world could possibly have come about. Perhaps the forming of a basic origin myth, which starts with formless water and ends with us, is simply a natural byproduct of our advanced human brains.

Chapter 31

An Origin Myth for Britain?

Silbury Hill

From the start of the first millennium AD, the dual assaults of Classical mythology and then Christianity swept away most traces of Britain's native origin myths. But having established now a clear outline of how world origin myths seem to work, is it possible to guess, at least, at what the inhabitants of Britain, and by extension their own ancestors in the caves of Ice Age France, may have thought about themselves and their origins?

Probably, they told of a world of primal water, out of which an animal deity had dredged the Earth. Maybe they pointed to a nearby hill or mountain and claimed that it was the original mound from which the rest of the world had grown. We know that sophisticated, city-based cultures such as that of the Egyptians deliberately built artificial mounds to remind themselves of the way the world had begun. There was a conical hill of ashes next to the temple of Zeus at Olympia, too, and it is striking how many Greek temples were within sight of natural, conical hills or mountains. We cannot suddenly attribute every mound associated with religious worship to this one myth, but it is interesting to speculate on how far such origin myths may have permeated into human consciousness and religious worship.

Not far from the great stone circle of Avebury, Wiltshire, stands Silbury Hill (see plate 36). Constructed about 2400 BC, it is 131 feet high, making it the tallest prehistoric monument in Europe, comparable in size to some of the smaller Egyptian pyramids. The latest research shows that it is entirely artificial. It was built up in stages, using different types of soil and stone, some brought from a considerable distance, probably by the different Neolithic communities of the region. In the low-lying area at the base of the mound, water often gathers and maybe Silbury Hill had once stood in the middle of an artificial lake.

Jim Leary has argued that the whole exercise of building Silbury Hill may have been a symbolic re-enactment of the creation of the world, with each tribe piling up earth just as the animal ancestors had done to make the dry land out of the primal waters in the first place. Perhaps Silbury Hill was indeed a symbolic primal mound, just like those of ancient Greece and ancient Egypt.

Memories of mammoths?

The prevalence of serpents in origin myths from around the world makes us wonder whether they played a similar part in the origin myths of Ice Age Europe or Neolithic Britain. It is possible, of course, but we have no real way of knowing. They are not a prominent feature of Ice Age art, but there may be more lines drawn on cave walls that were intended to represent snakes than we realise. A series of undulating lines on a small disc of mammoth ivory found in a boy's grave at Mal'ta, Siberia, from very approximately 20,000 years ago, has been interpreted as a depiction of snakes. Three fine and unmistakable serpents with big heads appear on a larger mammoth ivory plaque from the same grave (both items are in the Hermitage Museum, St Petersburg). On the back of this second plaque are patterns of dots and circles that have been interpreted as the cosmos. It might all represent an origin myth, but we cannot know that for sure. It's a leap from this to argue that the people of ancient Britain, gazing out across the valleys of the Thames or the Kennet, told themselves that the landscape had been scoured out by the journey of a great serpent at the beginning of the world, but such a story is always possible.

The mammoth known as Sely looms large in the Siberian origin myths. This is probably because the preserved corpses of mammoths are sometimes found there, thawing out from the permafrost. This may have caused Sely's myth in the first place, or it may have helped keep alive a much more ancient myth, dating back to Palaeolithic times. If so, then perhaps our ancestors in the rock shelters of the Vézère Valley and Cheddar Gorge and Creswell Crags told each other stories of a great mammoth like Sely, diving into the primal seas to dredge up the Earth. So when mammoths appear in painted caves, such as Rouffignac and Pech Merle, they may recall such origin myths.

Just as there is a diversity of animals depicted in Ice Age art and a diversity of animals in origin myths from around the world, it is likely that, if the people of Ice Age Europe and the Neolithic told themselves similar stories, each band, each tribe, had their own preferences. Just as pictures of certain sorts of animals dominate certain caves, so too may one band have told of the world being shaped by a primal horse, another by a bison, another by a mammoth and so on. And in Neolithic Britain, if such stories existed, maybe the creatures involved included the hares, boars, wolves and perhaps snakes too, which inhabited the land. And maybe sometimes the memory of mammoths lived on, transferred to the great aurochs, the wild cattle that lurked in the depths of the greenwood and who, our ancestors may have believed, had dredged the world up out of the primal waters at the beginning of time.

From animal to Devil

If our ancient ancestors had imagined the world being created out of the water and shaped by creatures such as mammoths and snakes, then what happened to these creatures in the later, more sophisticated myths of the city-based civilizations?

The trend from animal to human-shaped deities seems to have gone hand in hand with the advent of farming, city building and metalworking. The more advanced the civilisation, the further removed its people were from nature, and the less inclined they were to attribute the creation of the world to anything other than humans. The snake and mammoth survived, but in reduced forms. In Greece, for instance, the snake remained beneficial to mankind as the harbinger of the springtime and it regained its creative role as the great serpent at the beginning of the Universe in Orphic cosmology. But as human culture moved inexorably away from animal deities and towards human ones, the snake turned increasingly nasty, so elsewhere in Greek mythology we encounter the snakey monster Typhon who tried to destroy Zeus and the world, and it continued its inexorable slither towards the dark side as the serpent in the Garden of Eden.

The only origin myths to retain mammoths were those of Siberia. Elsewhere, maybe, stories of mammoths or other now extinct Ice Age animals such as bison and woolly rhinoceroses were all absorbed into stories about bulls. These loom large in Greek mythology: Zeus became one to abduct Europa from Tyre and carry her across the sea to Greece; Hercules subdued the Cretan bull and later Theseus killed it, just as he was later to slay its monstrous half-human, half-bull son, the Minotaur. One reason why bulls play such a large part in Greek mythology may be that they absorbed many ancient tales of other creatures, which were once much more benevolent, such as mammoths.

In the millennia after farming took hold, there was a trend away from imagining the world shapers as animals, and towards imagining them as being human shaped. Many features in the British landscape are attributed to this day in folklore to giants. In Somerset, the Avon Gorge was dug out by the giant Ghyston. The Cheddar Gorge was dug out by the giant Goram, and a clod of earth he threw out in the process became Brent Knoll. St Michael's Mount in Cornwall (see plate 37) was a rock dropped by the giantess Cormelia, and there are many, many more examples. Maybe each story arose independently and had always concerned a giant. Or perhaps these folk tales date back many thousands of years and had originally featured gigantic animals like Sely and Dyabdar, they who had built and shaped the world.

In other cases, the myths seemed to have morphed once again. Many other features of Britain's landscape are now attributed not to animals or giants, but to the Devil. The Devil's Dyke in Sussex, for instance, is said to have been gouged out by the Devil, who wanted to flood the Weald so as to wash away its churches (see plate 38). Chalk thrown out in the process created both the Isle of Wight and a rock lying in Goldstone Valley near Hove. But is this an original story, or had Christian clergymen tried to diffuse an older legend concerning giants, by turning a giant into the Devil? Is it possible that all such stories of the Devil forming the landscape go back, via the giants, to animal world shapers as well?

One natural feature in France said to have been created by the Devil is the Gouffre de Padirac, near Cahors. It is an enormous, dramatic hole in the ground. How the Devil may have made it is unclear, but it is not far from the painted cave of Pech Merle, which is full of images of mammoths. It is easy to imagine the hole resulting from a giant mammoth's tusk puncturing the Earth, or from a giant mammoth's stamping foot, as it battled a monster like Chulugdy. Is that, in fact, how the story originated?

So perhaps, like the Gouffre de Padirac in France, the Avon and Cheddar Gorges, St Michael's Mount and the Devil's Dyke, along with many other features of the British landscape that are now attributed to giants or the Devil, had once, in our ancient ancestors' imaginations, been gouged out by huge, world-shaping creatures such as snakes and mammoths. Whilst we have no surviving written records of what the pre-Roman inhabitants of Britain thought about the origins of the world, we may have some hints – in the earthen mound of Silbury Hill, and in the stories of giants and devils attached to the natural features of the landscape. Here in Britain, once, there may have been tales of an earth mound, raised up out of the primal seas by benevolent animal deities, of the sort remembered in Siberia as Sely the mammoth and Dyabdar the serpent, and then shaped by their activities into a fitting place for human to inhabit.

A British Adam?

The long barrow called Adam's Grave, which overlooks the Vale of Pewsey in Wiltshire, is one of a number of ancient British monuments now linked to Adam, the earliest human ancestor in the Bible (see plate 28). But that name is likely to have been applied to the barrow long after Christianity arrived in Britain, and probably has no bearing on how the mound was viewed in pre-Christian times. Whilst we can hypothesise that the Neolithic Britons who built Silbury Hill had a myth about the origins of the world, in which primal animals raised the Earth up out of the primal sea, we have no idea who they thought their earliest ancestors were, or how they had appeared. They may have imagined their ancestors being born from the oak and ash, or fashioned from the clay of the rivers, or woken from a timeless sleep beneath the British soil by the song of a primal serpent. But of the specifics we have no discernable trace. Nor do we know if they had a dramatic event in their mythology, like a great flood, to create a dividing line between the recent past and more ancient times, when the world was new. Maybe they did not at first, but if they developed one later we have no idea what it may have been. And that is as much as we can say on the matter. Nor do we know how they filled in the gap between those earliest, imagined ancestors and themselves. But we know a great deal about how other cultures bridged this gap and, later, how this bridging was achieved in Britain in the Iron Age and Dark Ages. That is a subject that takes us straight to the heart of genealogy.

Chapter 32

Tendrils from the Past

Linking the past to the present

The final element of origin myths is a pressing concern for us all: the attempt to bring down tendrils from the past, from our earliest human ancestors, however they were imagined, to our own hazy memories of our long-dead great-grandparents. Before about 40,000 years ago it is likely that our ancestors, like all other living creatures, gave little or no consideration at all to who we are or where we came from. But, as our newly improved minds started churning, notions of origins began to form, and with these came the problem of how to connect those origins with us now.

The closest we have now to the way they all thought – from the jungles of South America to the caves of Ice Age Britain – has probably survived best in the Australian idea of the Dreamtime. Bruce Chatwin described it as an ever present force in Aboriginal life, with greater reality than the here and now. Indeed, Aboriginals sometimes say that our world exists only in the dreams of our ancestors who live in the Dreamtime.

In the Dreamtime, the animal deities Father Cockatoo, Father Spider, Father Kangaroo, Father Man and so on, walked across the Outback and left their 'songlines' or 'dreaming tracks' behind them, each pair of footsteps corresponding to a couplet in the songs they were singing. These couplets have lain in the ground ever since. Whenever a pregnant creature steps on one, the couplet leaps up into her feet and into her womb, giving spirit life to her unborn baby. Thus, the Dreamtime ancestors are seen as the spiritual fathers of each animal and human alive now.

As part of the rite of passage into adulthood, and no doubt after suitable inducement by the shamans, adolescent Aboriginals dream of the spirit animal ancestor from whose footsteps they had gained their spirit life. They spend the rest of their lives revering this ancestor as their totem and spirit father. They are encouraged to follow the songlines, traversing Australia on 'walkabout', seeking other people who share the same spirit father. Sometimes, many members of the same spiritual clan might meet in a place sacred to their spirit father, to sing their ancestral song, each contributing their own allotted couplets in strict order.

For the Aboriginals, then, human spirits are simply earthly manifestations of the eternal ancestors who occupy the Dreamtime. Aboriginals will not depict true likenesses of themselves or their ancestors, lest they trap their spirits in the present. Nor will they utter the names of the dead, for the same reason. They recognise immediate family ties amongst the living, of course, but they place a higher importance in being the spiritual children of specific Dreamtime animal ancestors. This creates a network of spiritual family ties superior to considerations of biological kinship. It also creates a compact, manageable belief system, eminently suitable for a roving, non-literate society. The world began, the animal ancestors were born, and from these were born each of our human ancestors and each of us as well.

If your own father-spirit originated in the Dreamtime and was one of those that awoke when the primal song of the Rainbow Serpent was first heard, reverberating down through the red soil, then your relationship with the distant past is as clear and immediate as can be. The names of the dead cannot be spoken, but there is no need for genealogies to connect you to the past because your personal origins are timeless.

In the West, we have grown used to thinking in terms of hundreds, thousands or even millions of years. It's almost impossible to imagine what it was like not to think in this way. But for a goldfish, with its miniscule brain, the world might seem to have existed for about five minutes. When each of us was four, a time span of even four years was virtually inconceivable to us. Of course, a wise old hunter-gatherer was never so innocent, but still, most hunter-gatherers simply didn't think in terms of vast spans of time. For our ancestors in the Upper Palaeolithic, the world was probably imagined to have existed for no more than a handful of generations.

The dawn of genealogy

A sort of Dreamtime was probably imagined by our ancestors all over the world, including those in Britain and France in Upper Palaeolithic times. But the onset of Neolithic farming led to a change in our ancestors' way of thinking about time and their relationship to it. Time, as conceived by humans, started to expand. The convenient notion of the world only being a few generations old was harder to support when people's homes became fixed to one spot and bones began to pile up, generation upon generation, in their burial places. The decorated skulls from 'Ain Ghazal, Jordan, made about 7,200 BC, seem to illustrate the way attitudes began to change: instead of the uttering of the names of the dead being taboo, they decorated their ancestors' skulls to make them seem as if they were still alive. Farming and the building of permanent homes led to more complex tribal or city-based societies that required more complicated ways of ordering human relationships and that is probably one reason why lists of ancestors – or pedigrees – became important. The individual burials of members of the Bronze Age elite must be relevant too: if you retained your own identity after death then presumably your own name *could* be spoken after death, and pedigrees could start to be remembered that recounted the descent of the living from the dead heroes who lay in the round barrows.

As the skulls in a settlement's burial places piled up, the number of barrows on the hill increased or the remembered rulers of the city grew ever greater in number, it became impossible to avoid acknowledging that time had been going on for more than just a handful of generations. This produced the urgent need for some explanation of what had happened in the intervening time. Recalling the names of ancestors was a way of answering that need.

Once true writing started, in Sumer about 3100 BC, the names of kings were recorded in lists and we can see exactly how the people then stood in relation to the passage of time, and the widening gap between the origins of the world and the present. They had their origin myth that told of the world emerging out of the watery chaos of Tiâmat, and the fashioning of the first humans out of clay by the gods, and then of the Great Flood, which Uta-Napishtim had survived. To fill the gap down from the first man to Uta-Napishtim they created a list of ten kings, starting with the primal Alulim, who ruled in succession, each for enormous spans of time. This list is found at the beginning of Mesopotamian King Lists, which exists in a number of variants, such as the 'Weld-Blundell Prism', in the Ashmolean Museum, Oxford:

Alulim of Eridu, 64,800 years
Alagar, 72,000 years
Kidunnu, 72,000 years
Alimma, 21,600 years
Enmenluanna, 21,600 years
Dumuzi, 28,800 years
Ensipazianna, 36,000 years
Enmenduranna, 72,000 years
Sukuriam, 28,800 years
Ziusudra, 36,000 years up to the flood

Ziusudra in this version is identical with Uta-Napishtim, the man who survived the flood in Gilgamesh's story.

Lists like this formed the prologue to the recorded histories of each of the Mesopotamian cities. Having thus dealt with pre-history, they had to account for the time between the flood and the present. They did this by recording further lists of kings. Usually they wrote out lists of the kings of the most prominent cities, followed by a list of the kings of the city in which the list was made: the final name on the list would be the present ruler of that city. They could regard this as a complete system, accounting for all time from the birth of humanity to now. It was a system that many cultures would later try to emulate. It confirmed the suspicions of city dwellers that time had been rolling on for a long time, but it also made that huge span of time manageable by identifying the rulers who had presided over it.

The people were reminded by the myth that their ancestors had been created to serve the gods, so they too must work hard. Cheekily, the kings themselves, besides claiming to be the senior heirs of Uta-Napishtim, usually obtained a more exalted pedigree for themselves by claiming that their fathers had been consorts of the goddess known variously as Inanna or Ishtar (a spiritual descendant of the Upper Palaeolithic Venus figurines). The body of the mortal woman who bore the king's heir, they claimed, had been inhabited by the goddess, so each generation of kings considered themselves to be goddess-born. The world might be old, but each king was the son of the goddess who had been there right from the very start. Similar claims, which elevate kings above normal mortals, are common across the ancient world. Each Egyptian pharaoh, for example, was held individually to be the son of a god, usually the creating god, Ra. Such a conceit seems far removed from the Australian Aboriginals, but they believed that their mothers had been made pregnant by the song of a Dreamtime ancestor who may just as well, when seen in this light, have been a deity. The only difference is that, away from the egalitarian world of the Aboriginals, this spiritual ancestry became the exclusive preserve of the elite.

As the Bronze and Iron Ages took hold, experiments in filling the gap between the distant past and the present proliferated. Whilst the Mesopotamian system relied on King Lists that may or may not have included genealogical connections between the men named, most later systems were based very explicitly on pedigrees, in which the earliest ancestor was rooted firmly in the distant past and the descendants at the bottom were those living now. Genealogy, we might say, was the deal our Bronze Age ancestors struck with time. It rooted them in the beginning of the world, and also helped ensure their immortality: you can take our lives, they thought, but we will live on forever in our descendants' genealogies.

Heroic ancestry

Our view of what the Greeks believed must not be clouded by Hesiod's *Works and Days*. He had encountered a story that was probably no more than a morality tale, probably of Middle Eastern origin, but for some reason he took it seriously and tried to incorporate it into Greek mythology – with decidedly confusing results. The original story probably told that humanity had been created four times, first from gold, then silver, then bronze, then as men of iron (ourselves), and was intended to reconcile us with the humdrum drudgery of our daily lives. But Hesiod retold it as if it were an established part of Greek mythology. Because the Golden Age of Heroes was just before our own time, he said that humanity had been created five times, first from gold, then silver, then bronze, then as heroes, and finally as us, the men of iron. The downward progression was thus illogically interrupted, for the race of god-born heroes was nothing if not golden. But this story had no real bearing on how the Greeks saw themselves.

The Greeks believed that races were autochthonous, with ancestors born (like the Aboriginals) from the land where they lived. They lacked recorded genealogies, so when proudly autochthonous races like the Athenians wanted to chronicle their story since the start of the world, they had to invent a chronology based on lists of city officials and the like. True, Deucalion and Pyrrha (whose parents were Titans) were said to have been the parents of Hellenos, who can be seen as an eponymous ancestor for all the Greeks, but originally the term 'Hellenic' was used only of the people of a small part of Greece near the Gulf of Malia. It is likely that it was only these people's rulers who laid serious claim to Hellenos as their forebear. In common with other royals and aristocrats across Greece (and those with pretentions to aristocratic ancestry), these rulers both distanced themselves from the common herd and also provided their people with a vicarious sense of connectedness with the past by claiming descent from deities. Most did so by claiming descent from heroes born from the unions of gods or goddesses with mortals.

In the height of the Bronze Age, those unions were probably as immediate as those imagined by the Egyptian pharaohs and the Mesopotamian kings, but by Homer's time the inexorable march of history had forced even kings to acknowledge that their godly connections lay in the past, and that it was not they but their ancestors that had been god- or goddess-born (Alexander the Great in the 300s BC was a later exception who proved this rule, when he claimed that, when he was conceived, the body of his biological father, Philip II of Macedon, had been inhabited by Zeus). Usually, the ancestor was a male Olympian god or a river god, who coupled with daughters of Titans, nymphs or women whose own origins went back to other godly unions. Thus, Hesiod, the author of the *Theogony*, claimed descent from Zeus, and at various times Homer was given a descent from either Odysseus or Orpheus, both heroes with godly ancestry. Dardanos, ancestor of Aeneas and the Trojan kings, was the son of Zeus and Elektra, daughter of the Titan Atlas. Later, the Macedonian kings, including Philip II of Macedon, claimed descent from Hercules, who was born of the union of Zeus and a mortal woman (herself of godly descent) and the kings of Epiros claimed descent from Achilles, whose mother Thetys was daughter of the god Nereus, a grandson of Gaia, the Earth.

The Iron Age Greeks looked back to those born of such godly unions as the shining heroes of the Golden Age (which, in our estimation of time, was the Bronze Age). Their descendants might be mortal, and ostensibly human, but in Greek eyes their humanity was of a far more exalted nature than that of the proletarian descendants of autochthones. Each river god was a son of Ocean and he, along with the other Titans and gods had their place in the divine genealogy set out in Hesiod's *Theogony* – they were all ultimately descended from Gaia (the Earth) and Uranos (the heavens) near the beginning of the world.

Bridging the gap

The Iron Age was characterised by elitist bands of aristocratic warriors, and in such a world pedigrees came into their own. Within warlike tribes, the chieftain was chosen from the immediate male-line kin group of the previous chief. In Ireland this kin group was termed the *derbfine*, and comprised the male-line grandchildren and great-grandchildren, and sometimes also the great-great-grandchildren, of former chiefs. Everything depended upon your genealogy and the incentive to remember pedigrees was enormous – but only back for a handful of generations. Before then, in pre-literate societies, the past was still largely undefined and the rest of eternity was accounted for by the gods. Thus, most Iron Age pedigrees probably went back between ten or twenty generations at most, and were then capped with a hero who was the son of a god. When pedigrees became too long, some of the earlier, intervening generations would be quietly left out and forgotten. The hero and the god remained at the top, but the pedigree remained a convenient sort of length, despite the passing of the centuries.

Although many British and Irish pedigrees were manipulated shamelessly by Christian monks in order to extend them back, ultimately, to the family of Noah, glimpses of Iron Age beliefs shine through. There is a pedigree that deduces the ancient kings of Ulster from Conn Cétchathach, who surely started his career as a battle god, and a pedigree of Bran the Blessed, who was probably a late Iron Age king in Kent, which goes back to Aedd Mawr, the 'great fire', probably a Celtic version of Zeus.

It was only when cultures around the world acquired literacy and genealogies were written down that pedigrees started to grow inexorably longer. It was no longer possible to conveniently forget a few generations to keep the pedigrees at a manageable length. As a result, kings grew ever more distant from their godly ancestors. Perhaps that is one of the underlying and unspoken reasons why religions promising immediate, renewed contact with a saviour god, such as Christianity, became so popular.

Around the world, literate civilisations found themselves recording ever longer pedigrees. In China, almost all royal and aristocratic pedigrees go back up the male line to the early dynasties, which derived themselves from the mythical Emperor Huangdi, 'the Yellow Emperor' (2,697–2,597 BC). Huangdi was credited with having brought all the trappings of civilisation to the hitherto nomadic Chinese, and was the third of the Three Sovereigns, who founded the Chinese nation. The first of the three had been Fu Xi, the consort of the serpent goddess Nüwa, who between them had fashioned humanity out of clay. Thus, many Chinese people now, whose pedigrees survived the destruction of the Cultural Revolution, can trace their lines back to Huangdi, near the start of everything.

In northern Vietnam, the dragons that had created the islands in Halong Bay remained living there. A legend describes how a dragon king, in union with the bird king's daughter, produced a hundred eggs, out of which came the Vietnamese, the first hatched being, of course, the first king, who was ancestor of the royal dynasty. That myth was later severely mangled in order to fabricate a genealogical link back to the early Chinese emperors, but at its root there was probably a simple descent from a world shaper in the form of a dragon.

Although we know less about the Incas, we hear that they believed the ancestors of all humans apart from themselves were born of stones planted in the earth by the god Viracocha. But they believed that their own ancestors were descended from the sun god.

All the Germanic and Norse peoples, including the Anglo-Saxon kings in England, deduced their royal and aristocratic dynasties either from Odin or from the goddess Freya. The British royal family, as heirs of the English kings and thus of the Saxon kings of Wessex, can trace back a family line through Alfred the Great to Cerdic, first king of Wessex, for whom was claimed a pedigree going back nine generations to Odin himself.

In India, the common run of humanity had been one of the many creations of Prajapati (who had created everything else too, from gods to pigs). But Prajapati, in his incarnation as Brahma, had a great-grandson, Vivasvat, the god of the Sun, and Vivasvat had a son, Manu Vivasvata, who survived a great flood. From Manu's sons were descended the ancestors of the kings who fought in the great battle recalled in the *Mahabharata*, and all the brahmins (priests), ksatriyas (warriors) and royal dynasties. This, as in China, is a living system. In a caste-bound society proof of descent was essential so records were maintained by the brahmin priests, generation by generation. Many higher caste Hindus today know their descent – albeit perhaps with some gaps – from Manu Vivasvata, great-great-grandson of the eternal Brahman.

Descents from Noah

These beliefs, each distinct and yet all revolving around the same ideas, provide some context for the Bible's own system for connecting the distant past to the present. God made Adam and Eve, and they had children – Cain, Abel, Seth and other 'sons and daughters'. They must have reproduced amongst themselves to produce the next generation. *Genesis* (6.1–4) also refers to 'the sons of God' taking 'the daughters of men' as their wives, resulting in 'the Gibborim who were of old, the men of renown'. This suggests that the Jews used to have a myth similar to the Greeks; that in the Golden Age there had existed a race of heroes, born for the most part from the union of mortal women and gods. But of that story the Bible provides only a diluted echo, with no further details.

The family line that matters most in *Genesis* runs down from Seth through Enos, Cainan, Mahalel, Jared, Enoch, Mathuselah and Lamech to Noah, who survived the Great Flood. Each of these patriarchs was very long-lived: Seth, for example, died aged 912. The ten generations down from Adam to Noah, together with their great ages, echoes the far older Mesopotamian King Lists, which also list ten immensely long-lived kings down to the time of their flood survivor, Uta-Napishtim. It seems likely that the writers of *Genesis* used the older lists as the inspiration for their own genealogy back to Adam.

In the Mesopotamian myths, the gods sent the flood because mankind had multiplied too quickly and was making too much noise. In *Genesis*, this same flood, like almost everything else, takes on a moral slant. We read that Yahweh sent it to wipe out mankind because we had grown wicked, and he wanted to start afresh with the only one who showed any piety, Noah. *Genesis* then goes into great detail about Noah's sons, grandsons and great-grandsons, each of whom was the eponymous ancestor of one of the different peoples of the world known to the writers of *Genesis*. Noah's great-grandson son Eli'shah, for example, was the eponymous ancestor of the Greeks (and his name was derived from the name Hellenes, which the Greeks had adopted for themselves). The narrative focuses on Noah's eldest son, Shem, ancestor of Eber, the eponymous progenitor of the Hebrews. It follows down the family line to Jacob, from whose sons the Jewish tribes claimed descent, and then on to David and Solomon, the stem to which Matthew and Luke later attached the genealogy of Jesus.

There exist Jewish genealogies that purport to link back into this grand pedigree and of course that was the point of its existence. The biblical genealogy exists within a book that also came to be used by Islam and Christianity too. As a result, at different times, people of these faiths have also connected their genealogies back to the biblical stem, starting with the Ethiopian Christians' claim that the Queen of Sheba had given birth to their first king after a night of passion with King Solomon.

However they managed it, different cultures around the world used genealogies to bridge the gap between the distant past and the present. It is, in fact, what genealogies were for. If a genealogical line does not answer that psychological need, it is not, ultimately, perhaps, of very much use.

From Noah to Britain

The Dark Age Christian kings of Wales wanted their descent from Noah just like everybody else. Their genealogists made up a pedigree connecting them back to an early British king called Beli Mawr, who, they claimed, had married a cousin of the Virgin Mary. Meanwhile, Brutus of Troy was invented as an eponymous ancestor for the British. He was made into a great-grandson of Aeneas, the prince who had survived the Fall of Troy

This woodcut from Jean Bouchet's *Les Anciens et Modernes Genealogies* (1531) shows Aeneas leading some of the surviving Trojans away from burning Troy. Within the layers of myth that built up around the Trojan story, Aeneas laid the foundations of the Roman Empire and his great-grandson Brutus later colonised Britain.

and settled in Italy. Aeneas's mother was the goddess Aphrodite and his father Anchises was a male-line descendant of Dardanos, the founder of the Trojan dynasty, whose own father was Zeus. The Christian monks made surprising use of the Trojan pedigree as a means of bridging the gap back to Noah's family. If there was but one true god, Zeus cannot have been a god, but merely a powerful Greek king. If all humans are descended from Noah, Zeus must have been too, so a short pedigree was invented to connect King Zeus of the Greeks back to Noah's son Japheth. Then, a further pedigree was fabricated coming down from Brutus to Beli Mawr. Thus, all the Welsh princes could claim descent, via Beli Mawr, from Brutus and thus from Noah. This rooted them and, vicariously, their subjects, in time and space. They knew how they fitted into the greater scheme of things as revealed by the biblical origin myth.

These genealogical connections could be presented in poetic form, such as the stories in Homer's *Iliad* (which describes the origins of many of the Greek heroes present at the Siege of Troy) and Virgil's *Aeneid* (which brought Aeneas from Troy to Italy), or else in prose, such as Geoffrey of Monmouth's *History of the Kings of Britain*, which developed the myth of Brutus into the form in which it was received throughout the Middle Ages. It is interesting to reflect how much of our early literature was concerned, one way or another, with our origins, either retelling origin myths or filling out the stories of the generations in between our earliest ancestors and the present. King Arthur's story saw its first major telling in Geoffrey's history, as a major link in the narrative chain between the Welsh princes and Beli Mawr (whom Geoffrey calls Heli). In many ways, the roots of our entire literary tradition lie in our ancestors' tales of their own origins.

The descent of the British from Brutus was believed, unquestioningly, for over a thousand years until Polydore Vergil shone the sceptical light of Renaissance scholarship onto the story in the 1500s. It was when belief in the Brutus myth and its connecting genealogies faded that enquiring minds set forth on their ongoing mission to discover the truth about our origins: to start searching for our real, ancient ancestors.

Chapter 33

Creation, Evolution or Aliens?

'The myth grows spiral-wise'

W hen an origin myth is told to a small child, whose world is no bigger than its home town, it seems profoundly true. That was certainly my experience, being told the stories of Adam, Eve and Noah in a Catholic school in the outer suburbs of London in the early 1970s. But when viewed against the immense backdrop of our evolutionary history, and once we have understood how our human consciousness might only have fledged into its modern form about 40,000 years ago, we can see origin myths in a new light. Maybe they are not so much eternal truths as the attempts of our fully conscious ancestors to comprehend and make sense of their world, in the absence of any better clues, and before anybody realised that the discovery of any such clues through science was possible.

In his 1963 book *Structural Anthropology* Claude Lévi-Strauss (1908–2009) wrote, 'The purpose of myth is to provide a logical model capable of overcoming a contradiction.' The myths keep on generating variations of themselves, each trying to cope with the contradiction: 'The myth grows spiral-wise until the intellectual impulse which has produced it is exhausted.'

It would be fair to say that the attempt of *Genesis* to provide a rational, fully believable explanation of the world around us was exhausted by the seventeenth century, when science was starting to unfurl like a springtime fern and educated Western Europeans were starting in earnest to try to decipher the secrets of the world around them. But besides its genealogical information and origin myth, the biblical story contains a moral code and the hope of salvation too, so many people, even some scientists, continued to believe in it. The legacy of this is that we now have not one narrative for life on Earth, but two – the old narratives of the creation myths and the new narrative of science.

Alien intervention?

The existence in the modern world of these two very different narratives was always likely to cause interbreeding, creating new, bizarre chimerical offspring. In the nineteenth century, Madame Blavatsky and her Theosophists tried to synthesize world religions (particularly Buddhism and Hinduism) with prevailing scientific theories, and came up with an extraordinary story of how we had evolved slowly from vast, spiritual beings – the true giants of old – who had lived on Earth's ancient continents. These ancient ancestors of ours gradually solidified and shrunk to become modern humans, and the Theosophists prophesied that the destiny of our enlightened descendants is to return to a purely spiritual form.

The most recent intermarriages of science and myth take the form of the 'alien intervention' theories. Robert Charroux wrote *One Hundred Thousand Years of Man's Unknown History* (1963), which inspired Erich von Däniken's better-know *Chariots of the Gods?* (1968), both claiming that human culture and biology had been influenced by aliens. Their approach took into account the scientific view of the Universe with its many stars and implied planets on which it was possible that life had evolved. But they also sought evidence in ancient myths. Any story or carving that imagined higher beings coming down from the sky, or humans (such as Ezekiel in his fiery chariot) ascending into the clouds, suddenly became startling new evidence for their claims.

Since then theories have built on each other and kept pace with scientific understanding: as human genetics became better understood, 'alien intervention' proponents started claiming that aliens had manipulated our genetic codes to make us what we are now. The ancient gods of many cultures have been reimagined as alien visitors, and those dynasties, Jewish and Gentile, which claimed descent from Adam and Eve, have, in various publications such as Laurence Gardner's *The Genesis of the Grail Kings* (1999), become dynasties of super-humans carrying alien genes. Instead of the reality of a dynasty rising to power and laying claim to biblical descent, their descent from the biblical stem is taken as being true, and thus their rise to power becomes an inevitable outcome of their superior, alien genetic makeup.

And so it goes on: Joseph P. Farrell's *Genes, Giants, Monsters and Men: the surviving elite of the Cosmic War and their hidden agenda* (2011) claims that 'the religious stories that have often been the core basis for mankind's understanding of where it belongs in the history of creation may actually reveal a planet occupied with tyrannical giants and an elite race bent on genetic mutation', and Graham Hancock told the magazine *Atlantis Rising* that 'the reason we are so screwed up at the beginning of a new century is that we are victims of a planetary amnesia [about alien intervention]. We have forgotten who we are.'

It's all superb nonsense, which has inspired much wonderfully imaginative science fiction. Our culture would be poorer without these new mythologies – but we must not become carried away by imagining any of them to be true. No hard evidence of aliens, let alone alien intervention, exists. The wonders of the ancient world were the works of our ancestors and their origin myths were the fruit of their own imaginations, unaided by external powers. To claim otherwise is to denigrate the extraordinary achievements of our ancestors' hands and minds. Science explains perfectly well how we evolved here, without the need for alien help.

And, in any case, if everything we have here on our planet – our advanced minds and our multifaceted culture – was all brought here by aliens from another planet, then how did *they* become so technologically advanced in the first place? How did *they* evolve? We had to evolve somewhere, so is it really more glamorous, more exciting, more meaningful, to imagine our ancestors coming here in an alien's test tube? Is not the true story, so far as we understand it, of our single-handed evolution right here, on our own planet, by far the nobler tale?

Creation vs evolution

Almost everything in this book concerns that vast stretch of time before the present, which most of us, most of the time, leave to the experts, priests or scientists to cogitate upon while we lead our lives in the here and now.

When we think of it at all, were are left with a choice between two stories about the origins of the world, and our own origins within it. We can willingly suspend our disbelief and opt for what our ancestors dreamed and what our white-robed bards and priests told us: wonderful stories of the Earth being built up out of the primal, chaotic waters, either by animal deities or humanlike gods, and of our first forefathers springing up from the Earth, or from pea pods or trees, or being fashioned out of clay by the hands of artisan gods, who then breathed our souls into us, after which a select few of their descendants survived a calamity such as the Great Flood and spread out to populate the world anew.

Or, we can chose to believe the new origin story fashioned over many patient generations by the white-coated scientists, that mysterious new priesthood of the laboratory: that the Earth was the product of the Big Bang at the beginning of the Universe; that the landscape was shaped by the forces of nature over millions of years; and that life evolved slowly, leading to our descent from the trees onto the savannahs of Africa and our ancestors' eventual spread around the world.

Or, instead of choosing one and throwing the other away in contempt, we can see them both, more clearly, as two different sorts of narrative by which we humans have tried to make sense of our origins. We can recognise that their aims, at least, are similar, and it is interesting to see how much they continue to affect each other.

Whilst hard cores of believers refuse to countenance the scientific narrative at all, many people, even Pope Francis himself in October 2014, now say they believe that the story of Adam and Eve is an allegory of the 'true' scientific explanation.

'Evolution in nature is not inconsistent with the notion of creation,' said the Pope, 'because evolution requires the creation of beings that evolve. ... The Big Bang, which today we hold to be the origin of the world, does not contradict the intervention of the divine creator but, rather, requires it.'

In other ways, origin myths are affecting science. In contemplating the complexities of how the world may have started, myth makers over the last 40,000 years have thought through a vast number of possible scenarios. Scientists are beginning to ponder such options too and to explore what used to be the exclusive preserve of origin myths – notions of a universe locked in an eternal cycle of creation and destruction and of non-linear time. It seems possible that rational, hard-headed science might soon ask us to believe that the true nature of the Universe might have something in common with the mind-bending concepts conceived by Eastern mystics, many generations ago.

The journey to find our true origins has yet to reach its goal, and the conversation between science and mythology is far from over. Perhaps the best approach is to appreciate each for its own merits. Science satisfies our intellects and origin myths feed our souls. Maybe we can all enjoy exploring the world that surrounds us using the scientific narrative, whilst also seeking spiritual solace from the origin myths left behind by our distant ancestors.

But if we choose to place our rational beliefs in the new scientific narrative and not in the old stories then we lose an important element of the origin myths – the fabulous old pedigrees that stretched down from the past to connect us to our human origins. So how do we fare in a modern world in which mainstream culture has cashiered our old origin myths and the fictitious pedigrees that went with them? Must we all resign ourselves to being post-modern orphans? Or can we, now, connect ourselves back in a similar way to the new, scientifically constructed origin myth?

We can, using genetics.

Epilogue

How You Fit Into the Story

Genetic testing

If you have not yet had a DNA test then the wonderworld of genetics may seem rather hypothetical. But once you have learned your male- and female-line genetic haplotypes, then you will see how immediately relevant this is to you.

Although the science of genetics is intensely complicated, its application to the study of our origins is simple. The two genes that are relevant here are the Y chromosome, which passes down from father to son, down from our earliest male ancestor, and the mitochondrial DNA inside the mother's egg, which passes down from mothers to all their children, but which is only passed on by daughters to their offspring. It runs back from our mothers to their mothers and so on back up the female line to our earliest female ancestor. Mutations in both lines result in identifiable haplogroups and sub-haplogroups, which together form two branching family trees of humanity, one following the male line and the other following the female line.

Of the two, mitochondrial DNA mutates much less often, but the Y chromosome mutates very frequently and results in a much more detailed tree, whose many sub-sub-sub-(etc)branches are still being identified.

We can all have a test on our mitochondrial DNA, but only men can have Y chromosome tests (because only men have Y chromosomes). Women are not excluded: you can have your father's Y chromosome tested, or if he is not alive you can have a test on your brothers', or your father's brothers', or their sons', or your father's father's brothers' sons' Y chromosomes – anyone in your family who shares the same male-line ancestry as your father will do.

The up-to-date details of the human pedigree, as defined by female-line mitochondrial DNA, is at www.phylotree.org/tree/main.htm. A detailed pedigree of humanity as defined by the male-line Y chromosome is on the website of the International Society of Genetic Genealogy: www.isogg.org/tree/. Both trees are constantly being modified and tweaked as new genetic evidence comes to light.

It is by complete chance that the most detailed way of finding our place within the extended family of humanity uses the Y chromosome, just as the old way of achieving this was by surnames, which were also, usually, transmitted down male lines. Whereas fifteen years ago the Y-chromosome tree was only detailed enough to group all men in the world into a couple of dozen branches, it should soon be possible to tell apart different branches of individual families just by studying their unique Y chromosome mutations.

Of course, surnames don't always follow male lines. Adopted children are given their adoptive father's surname without sharing his Y chromosome. Illegitimate children usually carry their mother's surname, and married women who have affairs can introduce their lover's Y chromosome into their husband's surname line. So surnames can be an unreliable way of identifying our wider family connections. But membership of Y chromosome sub-haplogroups is infallible. I belong to a subgroup of haplogroup G, which is coded G (S2808), and that's who I am. Other members of this subgroup are my close(ish) male-line relatives, regardless of surname, illegitimacy or adoption. Genetics reveals our true male-line origins, regardless of what surname we happen to have inherited.

Genealogical research, using oral history and surviving written records, used to be an end in itself, as that was the best we could do to trace our roots into the past, back towards the first humans. Now, it can best be used to clothe and put names to the recent generations of our much more reliable genetic lineages. And that genetic lineage can be used to prove our genealogies: I am G (S2808), so I assume my male-line Adolph ancestors were as well. If I trace a distant Adolph cousin, supposedly descended in the male line from Adolph ancestors we have in common, and find that he is G (S2808) as well then, barring a great coincidence, I can be certain that the genealogy is correct and that our common ancestor was also G (S2808).

Imagine a builder erecting a core of breeze blocks, and then bricklayers building up neat brick walls around that core to create a house. Geneticists create the breeze block core, and genealogists provide the elegant brickwork on the outside. Both breeze block and brick constitute the finished building: genetics and genealogy, together, help us define who we are and thus how we stand in relation to each other and to the past.

The surname line is special, because our surnames are one of the ways by which we define ourselves. But we can also research our other ancestral lines – our mother's male line, our two grandmothers' male lines, our four great-grandmothers' male lines and so on, and of course many family trees don't follow male lines rigidly. The Royal Family's is a case in point, where the line of succession passed from the Hanoverian to the Saxe-Coburg-Gotha dynasty through the marriage of Queen Victoria to Prince Albert, and will pass from that line to the Oldenburg dynasty when Elizabeth II's son Prince Charles inherits the throne. The Royal Family tree is often drawn as a single pedigree, but when viewed in terms of male lines and the Y chromosomes inherited down them, it is in fact several sections of different male-line pedigrees (and male-line genetic lineages) linked together by the marriages of daughters.

To learn the Y chromosome haplogroups of our different ancestors derived through female lines, we can have male line descendants of each line tested. I wanted to learn my mother's father's male-line haplogroup, for instance: he had died by then, and his only son did not want to have a test, so I had my grandfather's cousin (in the same male line) tested instead. He belonged to haplogroup R, so I can assume that my mother's father was also a member of this most frequent of European male-line haplogroups.

Organising your family tree

When geneticists draw diagrams of interconnected haplogroups and sub-haplogroups, they tend to do so in a scientific way, often left to right. Although these are family trees, geneticists don't often draw them that way, so it makes them difficult for genealogists and laymen to follow. Equally, most genealogists are still used to drawing up family trees showing the results of research in oral history and written records, and tend to ignore the results of DNA testing, mainly because genetic haplogroups are not traditional names. But what is a name but a collection of letters of the alphabet applied to a human? One of my ancestors was called Johannes Peter Adolph. But earlier still I have an ancestor whose name in real life has been long forgotten, but in whom arose the mutation for G (S2808). That may not be a traditional name, but it identifies this distant forebear of mine, nonetheless.

Therefore, I propose a new way of presenting our ancestral lines, combining both genetic results and genealogical results. The example I have used here is the Queen's family. The Royal Family have never made their male-line genetic signatures public, but the work of Bradley Larkin shows that a male-line Coburg cousin of Her Majesty's was tested a couple of years ago, and from this much can be inferred, as can the known genetic profile of some of Prince Philips's male-line cousins. Despite the small element of uncertainty caused by such inferences, I wanted to use the Royal Family as the example here because they lie at the heart of the British family and their male-line haplogroup, conveniently, is R, the most widespread in Britain. It is presented here merely as an example of how to draw up a pedigree combining genetic and genealogical results.

The example adapts the style of narrative pedigree that goes back, in spirit, to Hesiod's *Theogony*, but which was perfected in the nineteenth century by John Burke for his famous *Peerage*. It is a style that I hope will catch on. Throughout, the Queen's direct ancestors are marked in bold, and collateral lines are shown by indented, numbered paragraphs. You can write up a similar pedigree for yourself, following your own genetic haplotype down and then continuing the story with those ancestors of yours to whom you can put names using genealogical research.

The story of our descent from the earliest, single-celled life on Earth is told in this book and so this book provides a preface to each of our personal family histories, including the Queen's. This is, in some ways, the modern equivalent of the family bible, in which people took the book that included the origin myth in *Genesis* and wrote their own recent family details in the front or back – a way of bringing together our ancient and recent origins between the same covers. We pick up the story with:

Homo Erectus, who evolved out of earlier *homo* species (and thus from earlier mammals, cynodonts, labyrinthodonts, fish, worms and ultimately single-celled life-forms), perhaps in the Caucasus, about 1.8 million years ago, ancestor of:
1. Erectus ancestors of *Homo floresiensis*, nicknamed 'Hobbits', who lived in the island of Flores until at least 12,000 years ago.
2. *H. Heidelbergensis* (*see below*).

Homo Heidelbergensis, who evolved in Africa about 1 million years ago, ancestor of:
1. **Heidelbergensis people in Africa** (*see below*).
2. Heidelbergensis people in Europe, probably including those at Happisburgh, Norfolk, about 950,000 years ago, ancestors of:
   1. Heidelbergensis people in Asia, ancestors of:
      1. Denisovans, who evolved in Asia and interbred with the later *H. sapiens*, colonisers of south-eastern Asia.
   2. Heidelbergensis people Europe, probably including those at Boxgrove about 500,000 years ago, ancestors of:
      1. The people of Swanscombe, Kent, about 400,000 years ago, who were probably amongst the ancestors of:
         1. Neanderthals, who evolved in Europe about 250,000 years ago, and who later interbred with the early *H. sapiens* who came out of Africa.

Heidelbergensis people in Africa, who were ancestors of:

A00 (AF6/L1284), an archaic human male in Africa more than 200,000 years ago, in whose Y chromosome the A00 (AF6/L1284) genetic mutation arose, ancestor of:

1. A00 (AF6/L1284), whose descendant in Africa about 30,000 years ago bred with a *Homo sapiens* woman and left male-line descendants amongst the Mbo people of the Cameroons (with an African–American descendant carrying the same marker).
2. *Homo sapiens* (*see below*)

Homo sapiens, who evolved in Africa about 200,000 years ago, ancestors of the **Mitochondrial Eve** (who lived about 140,000 years ago and is now ancestor of all living humans through the female line) and of:

A0-T (L1085) the '**Genetic Adam**' (descended in the female line from the Mitochondrial Eve), an early *Homo sapiens* who lived in Africa about 80,000 years ago, ancestor of:
1. AO (L911), with descendants in Africa.
2. A1 **(L986/P305)** (*see below*).

A1 (L986/P305) who was ancestor of:
1. A1a (M31) with descendants in Africa.
2. A1b **(P108)** (*see below*).

A1b (P108), in Africa, ancestor of:
1. A1b1 (L419), in Africa.
2. **BT (M91/M42)** (*see below*)

BT (M91/M42) who emerged in North Africa about 60,000 years ago, ancestor of:
1. B (M60), ancestor of men with haplogroup B, mostly in Africa.
2. **CT (M168)** (*see below*)

CT (M168), probably in Ethiopia, ancestor of:
1. DE (M145/P205), ancestor of:
   1. D (M174, including many early migrants to southern India and the Andaman Islands.
2. E (M96), with many descendants in Africa, and a line reaching Corsica, where it was ancestral to Napoleon Bonaparte.
   2. **CF (P143)** (*see below*).

CF (P143), the main group who left Africa about 55,000 years ago, and interbred with **Neanderthals** in the Middle East, some of whose descendants also interbred with Denisovans further east in Asia, ancestor of:

1. C (M130), whose subgroups include:
    1. C (M347), early Aborigines in Australia about 42,000 years ago.
    2. C (M217), Chinese, Mongols (including Genghis Khan) and many native Americans.
    3. C (M338), in Indonesia and Polynesia.
    4. C (P55), in Indonesia and Polynesia.
2. **F (M89)** (*see below*).

F (M89), in the Middle East and south/south-western Asia about 48,000 years ago, before the start of the Aurignacian culture, the ancestor of:
1. F (M89), mainly in India.
2. **GHIJK (F1329)** (*see below*).

GHIJK (F1329) was ancestor of:
1. G (M201), in the Caucasus about 46,000 years ago, ancestor of G (P287); ancestor of the male-line ancestors of Richard III and also of G (L1259) about 15,700 years ago, ancestor both of G (PF3146), from which descended G (L91), the genetic subgroup of Ötzi the Iceman, and also of (L30), which was ancestral through a number of further mutations of G (S2808), from whom descends my earliest named male-line ancestor Johannes Peter Adolph in Litterscheid, Germany, in the late seventeenth century.
2. **HIJK (M578)** (*see below*).

HIJK (M578), ancestor of:
1. H (M2939), in southern Asia, especially India.
2. **IJK (L15)** (*see below*).

IJK (L15), in western Asia, c. 45,000 years ago, ancestor of:
1. IJ (M429), maybe in Iran about 40,000 years ago, ancestor of:
    1. I (M170) found in northern and eastern Europe and also south-eastern Asia.
    2. J(M304), found in the Middle East and south-eastern Europe, and also some in northern Africa.
2. **K (M9)** (*see below*).

K (M(9), in southern or western Asia, ancestor of:
1. K (M9).
2. **LT (L298)** (*see below*).

LT (L298), ancestor of:
1. L (M20), about 30,000 years ago Iran and India.
2. T (M184) in western Asia.
3. **NO (M214)** (*see below*).

NO (M214), about 35,000 years ago in Aurignacian times, by the Aral Sea, ancestor of:
1. N (M251) in north-eastern Europe and northern Asia.
2. O (M175 in south-eastern Asia, ancestor of:
    1. O (M175).
    2. M (P256).
    3. S (M230), in Papua New Guinea.
3. **P (P295)** (*see below*).

P (P295), in central Asia, ancestor of:
1. Q (M242) about 22,000 years ago in central Asia, also now found in America.
2. **R (M207)** (*see below*).

R (M207) in central or southern Asia about 26,000 years ago (in, by European standards, Magdalenian times), ancestor of:
1. **R1 (M173)** (*see below*).
2. R2 (L722/M479) in southern Asia.

R1 (M173) in Europe and Asia, ancestor of:
1. R1a (L146) which emerged in the Ukraine.
2. **R1b (M343)** (*see below*).

R1b (M343), which may have emerged in the Vézère Valley in Magdalenian times and spread throughout Europe and Asia with some lines returning to Africa. It was ancestral to my mother's Rietchel family, whose exact genetic profile below this level is not yet known, and of:

R1b1 (P25), ancestor of:

R (P297) (at which point we will drop the 'R1b1a/b' system and stick only to the simpler codes for the markers), ancestor of:

R (M269/L483/L150), ancestor of HRH Prince Philip (whose exact genetic profile below this level is not yet known) and of:

R (L23), ancestor of:

R (L51), ancestor of:

L151/L11/P310/S127, the 'Atlantic Modal Haplotype', ancestor of:
1. **R (M405/U106)** (*see below*).
2. R (P312), the mutation defining about three quarters of all British men, increasing in numbers as one goes west, ancestor of:
   1. R (L21), the ancestor of the Crowley family (whose exact genetic profile below this level is not yet known) and of:
      1. R (CTS241), ancestor of:
         1. R (S218), ancestor of R (S686), ancestor of R (L226), the genetic signature of the family of Brian Boru, High King of Ireland and his many male-line descendants including the O'Briens.
         2. R (DF49), ancestor of R (S6154), ancestor of R (S476), ancestor of R (DF23), ancestor of R (Z2961), ancestor of R (M222), the genetic marker of the family of Niall of the Nine Hostages and his many male line descendants.

R (M405/U106), ancestor of:

R (Z381), ancestor of:

R (156), ancestor of:

R (Z305/Z306/Z307), ancestor of:

R (L1/P89.2), the genetic marker of one of the Queen's Coburg cousins, which we may assume the Queen has also inherited down the male line. We may infer that the man in whom the genetic marker R (L1/P89.2) arose was the male-line ancestor of the Queen's earliest certain named male-line ancestor:

Dedi, Count of Hassegau, Saxony, Germany (d. 957), who was father of:

Dietrich, Count of Hassegau, who married **Jutta von Merseburg** and had:

Dedi I, Count of Hassegau (killed on 13 November 1009), who married **Thietberga von Haldensleben** and had:

Dietrich II, Count of Hassegau and Brehna (k. 1034) who married **Mathilde von Meissen** and was 6 x great grandfather in the male line of:

Frederick I, Landgrave of Thuringia and Margrave of Meissen (d. 1323), great-grandfather in the male line of:

Frederick I, Elector of Saxony (d. 1428), 5 x great grandfather in the male line of:

Ernest I 'the pious', Duke of Saxe-Gotha-Altenburg (d. 1675), 3 x great-grandfather in the male line of:

Albert of Saxe-Coburg-Gotha (who died at Windsor Castle in 1861), Prince Consort to **Victoria, Queen of Great Britain**. Through her father Queen Victoria has ancestral lines going back to the Welsh princes who claimed descent from Brutus of Troy, who was in turn said to be a descendant of the biblical Adam and Eve. Victoria and Albert were parents of:

Edward VII, King of Great Britain (d. 1910, who married **Alexandra of Denmark** and had:

George V, King of Great Britain (1865-1936), who married **Mary of Teck** and had:

George VI, King of Great Britain (1895-1952), who married **Lady Elizabeth Bowes-Lyon** and had:

Elizabeth II, Queen of Great Britain, born on 26 April 1926 at 17 Bruton Street, Mayfair. Here the Coburg male line ends, but we can continue down the male line of the Queen's consort **Prince Philip of Greece**, a member of the House of Oldenburg, whose male line ancestry is believed to be R (M269/L438/L150):

Charles, Prince of Wales (b. 1948), who married first to **Lady Diana Spencer** (and secondly to Camilla Parker-Bowles) and was father of:
   1. **William** (*see below*).
   2. Prince Henry of Wales (b. 1984).

William, Duke of Cambridge (b. 1982), who married **Catherine Elizabeth Middleton**, a descendant through the Fairfaxes of Suffolk of Edward III, and had:

Prince **George** of Wales (b. 22 July 2013).

The style suggested here is a robust one: you can write as much as you like under each ancestor and follow each collateral line of descendants down using numbered, indented paragraphs as far as you wish. It can be as flexible as you like (hence my adding on some of the Queen's descendants, even though, strictly speaking, they have a different recent male line ancestry). The ancestors of the women who married into the male line are best recorded in separate narrative pedigrees following exactly the same style as this.

By writing up such a narrative pedigree for yourself you will see clearly how you fit into the great family tree of humanity, which connects us all back into the greater family tree of life on Earth. It carries our ancestry right back to the very first organisms ever to live on our planet, who were our most ancient ancestors, about 3,500 million years ago. It connects each and every one of us back, in the most direct and meaningful manner possible, into the over-arching narrative of the story of the Earth, the Solar System and the Milky Way – right back to the dawn of time itself.

Your Family Tree

You can record a brief summary of your own family tree here, to show how you fit into the great family tree of humanity as defined by the male line:

Your male line (Y) genetic haplotype (A, B, C, etc):

_____

Your latest known (Y) genetic sub-haplotype ('A (M118)', etc):

_____

The origin of the surname used in your male line:

_____

Your earliest known male-line ancestor:

_____

His year and place of birth:

_____

Your grandfather's name:

_____

His year and place of birth:

_____

Your father's name:

_____

His year and place of birth:

_____

Your name:

_____

Your year and place of birth:

_____

Your female line (mt-DNA) haplotype:

_____

Your mother's name:

_____

Your mother's year and place of birth:

_____

Her father's male-line genetic haplogroup:

_____

Other family details:

_____

_____

_____

_____

_____

_____

Acknowledgements

This book could not have been written without the encouragement and help of Scott Crowley, whose many contributions include driving me to many of the places mentioned here, all over Europe and beyond. I am also most grateful to James Essinger of the Canterbury Literary Agency for his creative input, and Linne Matthews and Jonathan Wright of Pen & Sword for their foresight in agreeing to publish it, and again to Linne for her great care in editing it.

I should have kept a list of the many other people who have helped in different ways, particularly answering questions, and much regret not having done so, but I can remember a few and hope others will not be too offended at not being included here: my cousin William Adolph (for taking us to La Marche); Nick Crowe (for giving me *The Songlines*); Bennett Greenspan and Max Blankfeld of www.familytreedna.com for my genetic tests and reams of advice; Debbie Kennett for answering numerous questions about genetics; Ray Banks and Alice Fairhurst, architects of the ever evolving Y chromosome family tree of humanity; Rolf Langland of the Haplogroup G project; Denise McKinney for her stimulating ideas about the modern reception of genetic results; Angela Muthama for introducing us to the work of Benjamin Harrison; Dr Mike Hammer, who is both a leading geneticist and one of my genetic cousins; Professor Brian Cox, for explaining the origins of stars to me on the set of ITV's *This Morning* a decade ago; Joseph T. Chang, for allowing me early access to his groundbreaking statistical work. And finally, I wish to thank the Muses of Mount Helikon, they who inspired Hesiod to write his *Theogony* in the first place, and who played their own special part in the creation of this book.

Select Bibliography

Adolph, Anthony, *Tracing Your Aristocratic Ancestors*, Pen & Sword, 2013.

Adolph, William, *The Simplicity of Creation*, privately published, 1856.

Calasso, Roberto, *The Marriage of Cadmus and Harmony*, Vintage, 1994, quote p.199.

Calasso, Roberto, *Ka*, Vintage, 1999, quote p.177.

Castleden, Rodney, *The Wilmington Giant: The quest for a lost myth*, Turnstone, 1983.

Ceram, C.W., *Gods, Graves & Scholars: the story of archaeology*, Book Club Associates, 1971.

Chatwin, Bruce, *The Songlines*, Picador, 1987.

Cook, Jill, *Ice Age Art: the arrival of the modern mind*, British Museum Press, 2013.

Cope, Julian, *The Modern Antiquarian*, Thorsons, 1998, quote p.227.

Cunliffe, Barry, *Iron Age Communities in Britain*, Routledge, 2010.

Darville, Timothy, *Prehistoric Britain*, B.T. Batsford Ltd, 1987.

Davies, Paul, *The Origin of Life*, Penguin Books, 1999.

Dawkins, Richard, *Climbing Mount Improbable*, Penguin Books, 1997.

Dawkins, Richard, *The Ancestor's Tale*, Phoenix, 2004.

Desdemaines-Hugon, Christine, *Stepping Stones: a journey through the Ice Age caves of the Dordogne*, Yale UP, 2010, quotes on Cap Blanc, p.139, Bernifal, 177.

Dinnis, Rob and Stringer, Chris, *Britain: one million years of the human story*, Natural History Museum, 2014.

Fox, Robin Lane, *Travelling Heroes: Greeks and their myths in the epic age of Homer*, Allen Lane, 2008)

Heidel, Alexander, *The Babylonian Genesis*, University of Chicago Press, 1951.

James, Simon, *The Atlantic Celts*, British Museum Press, 1999.

Jones, Steve, *The Serpent's Promise*, Little, Brown, 2013.

Lambert, W.H. and Walcott, P., 'A New Babylonian Theogony and Hesiod', *Kadmos*, 4 (1965) 64–72.

Lane, Robin Lane, *Travelling Heroes: Greeks and their myths in the epic age of Homer*, Penguin, 2009.

Larkin, Bradley, 'Y-DNA of the British Monarchy', *Surname DNA Journal*, 2013.

Lawlor, Robert, *Voices of the First Day*, Inner Traditions International Ltd, 1991.

Leakey, Richard & Lewin, Roger, *Origins Reconsidered*, Little, Brown & Company, 1992.

Leakey, Richard E., *The Making of Mankind*, Michael Joseph, 1981.

Leary, Jim, 'Making sense of Silbury', *British Archaeology*, Issue 116, January/February 2011.

Lewis-Williams, David, *The Mind in the Cave*, Thames and Hudson, 2004, quotes 'social relations', p.109; 'zigzags', p.126.

Lévi-Strauss, Claude, *Structural Anthropology*, Basic Books, 1963.

Mayor, Adrienne, *The First Fossil Hunters*, Princeton UP, 2000.

Meirop, Marc van de, *A History of the Ancient Near East*, Blackwell Publishing, 2004.

Meshel, Ze'ev, 'Kuntillet Ajrud, An Israelite Religious Centre in Northern Sinai', *Expedition*, 20, Summer 1978.

Mitchiner, John, *Guru: The Search for Enlightenment*, Viking, 1992.

Mithen, Steven, *The Prehistory of the Mind*, Thames & Hudson, 1996.

Olson, Steve, *Mapping Human History: Discovering the Past Through Our Genes*, Mariner Books, 2002, quote p.138.

Oppenheimer, Stephen, *The Origins of the British*, Robinson, 2007.

Pargiter, F.E., *Ancient Indian Tradition*, Motilal Banarsidass Publishers, 1997.

Pryor, Francis, *Britain B*, Harper Collins Publishers, 2003.

Reed, A.W., *Aboriginal Myths, Legends & Fables*, Reed New Holland, 1999.

Rosenberg, Donna, *World Mythology*, Harrap, 1986.

Samivel, *The Glory of Greece*, Thames & Hudson, 1962, quotes on Minoans, p.22; on Middle Ages, p.46; on Python, p.65.

Snell, Daniel C., *Life in the ancient Near East*, Yale UP, 1997.

Tattersall, Ian, *The Fossil Trail*, OUP, 1995.

Vidal, James, 'Bones of Contention', *The Guardian*, 13 January 2005, *Life* section p.6.

Voskoboinikov, M.G., *About Evenk cosmogonic legends. Languages and folklore of Northern people*, Novosibirsk, 1981.

Wagner, Sir Anthony, *English Genealogy*, Phillimore, 1983.

Wells, H.G., 'The Grisly Folk', *Storyteller Magazine*, April 1921.

Wells, Spencer, *The Journey of Man: A Genetic Odyssey*, Penguin Allen Lane, 2002.

Wendt, Herbert, *From Ape to Adam*, Thames and Hudson, 1971 and 1972.

West, M.L., *Hesiod: Theogony & Works and Days*, OUP, 1988.

West, Martin, *The Hesiodic Catalogue of Women*, Clarendon Press, 1985.

Wilkinson, Toby, *The Rise and Fall of Ancient Egypt*, Bloomsbury, 2010.

Zimmer, Carl, *Evolution, the triumph of an idea*, William Heinemann, 2001.

Index

'Ain Ghazal, 139, 211
A Pedra do Mouro, 142
Aardvarks, 36
Abbots Bromley, 134
Abel, 217
Abercromby, Lord, 153
Abominable Snowman, 51
Aboriginals, 51, 73, 78, 80, 86, 120, 122, 147, 171, 185–6, 191, 201, 210, 213–14, 238, 292
Abri de Castanet, 100
Acanthostega, 28
Achaeans, 154
Acheulean culture, 49–51, 53
Achilles, 156, 215
Acropolis, the, 126, 140
Adam, vii, ix, 4, 6, 8–9, 61, 64, 67–9, 72, 89, 116, 145–6, 169, 190, 196, 208, 217, 220–2, 232
   genetic, 67–8, 162, 228
Adolph family, 162, 225–6, 229
Adolph, William, 7
Adonis, 192
Aedd Mawr, 215
Aegyptopithecus, 43
Aeneas, 3, 157, 214, 218–19
Afrotheres, 36–7
Agassiz, Louis, 72, 87
Ahrensburg culture, 133
Ahriman, 174, 193
Ahura Mazda, 174, 193
Akkadian Empire, 151
Aldène, cave, 101
Alexander the Great, 214
Alfred the Great, 216
Algae, 20–1, 27, 29
Algonquians, 183
Aliens, 18, 221–2
Allotheria, 33
Altamira, 88, 100, 115
Amakandu, 188
Amesbury Archer, 153, 155–6
Amesbury, 153, 155–6
amino acids, 18–19, 163
Ammonites, 35
Amoebas, 21
Amphibians, 11, 22, 29, 37, 59–60
Ananta, 182, 186
Anchises, 218
Andaman Islands, 72, 78, 228
Angels, 5, 7, 117, 124, 161, 171

Anisimov, A.F., 183
Anteaters, 34
Anthracosaur, 29
Ants, 4, 48, 138, 196
Anu, 158, 181, 195
Anubis, 119
Apes, 5, 9–11, 22, 41, 43–5, 47–8, 50, 65, 110, 125, 152, 161
Aphrodite, 157, 179, 218
Apollo, 186
Apsû, 181
Ararat, Mount, 190, 202
Archaean eon, 18
Archaeopteryxes, 36
Archosaurs, 35–6
Ardipithecuses, 44
Aristotle, 5, 65
Ark, the, 10, 190, 199
Armada, Spanish, 64
Armadillos, 36
Armstrong, Leslie, 130
Arrows, arrowheads, 56, 112, 118, 125, 134, 136, 145, 151, 153, 181, 186, 188
Art, 88–90, 96–8, 100–102, 104–106, 108, 111, 113, 116, 134, 120–6, 130, 132, 134, 139, 152, 155–6, 159, 167, 184, 203, 206
Artemis, 157
Arthropods, 23–4, 27–8
Arthur, King, 3, 27, 161, 219
Asgard, 171, 176, 192
Asherah, 189
Ashmolean Museum, 134, 139, 212
Ashurbanipal, 168
Askri, viii
Assur, 168, 188, 195
Assyrians, 151
Atapuerca hills, 52, 55, 80
Athens, 13, 141, 194, 214
Atlantic Modal Haplotype, 150, 160, 231
Atlas, 214
Atrebates, 160
Attenborough, Sir David, ix, 22, 167
Atum, 178, 188
Audhumla, 180, 192
Auga da Laze, 156
Aurignacian culture, 85, 87, 91–3, 95–7, 99–101, 103, 106, 116, 122, 125, 139, 203, 229–30

Aurochs, 55, 101, 105, 113, 120, 131, 145, 206
Australopithecuses, 45–6, 48, 50
Autochthones, 78, 194, 214–15
Avalonia, 26–7
Avebury, 145–6, 156, 205
Aveline's Hole, 134
Azilian culture, 133
Aztecs, 188, 196, 199

Baal, 189
Babel, 62, 190
Babylon, 151, 168–9, 181–2, 195, 198, 200
Bacho Kiro, 93
Bacon, Sir Francis, 4, 65
Bacteria, 19–20, 66, 137
Badegoulian culture, 108
Badgers, 33
Baiame, 171
Baikal, Lake, 183
Baker's Hole, 57
Bakola Pygmics, 69
Balanoglossi, 24
Bantu, 62
Barnfield Pit, 55
Barrows, 143–7, 150, 156, 212
Basque, 149
Bateson, William, 65
Bath, Marquess of, 132, 135
Beachy Head, 145
Bears, 51, 53, 69, 101, 111–12, 114, 129, 131–2, 168, 192
Beckhampton, 146
Beddoe, John, 64
Beeches Pit, 54
Beedings, 95
Bees, 37, 42, 65, 138
Beetles, 30, 36, 45
Bêl, 181, 195–6
Belas Knap, 145–6
Belgae, 160, 162
Beli Mawr, 218–19
Bell beakers, 153, 156
Bering Straits, 80
Bernifal, cave, 115–17, 237
Berossus, 181, 195–6
Berthoumeyrou, Gaston, 89
Betanzos, John de, 179
Beune Valley, 107, 111–13, 115
Biache-Saint-Vaast, 56

Bible, 3, 6–7, 16, 68, 167, 169, 179,
    189–90, 199, 202, 208, 217–18,
    220–1, 227, 232
Big Bang, x, 12, 15–18, 163, 173–4,
    201–203
Bilateria, 22–3
Bir Kiseiba, 151
Birds, 36–7, 118, 131, 143, 193, 196,
    201, 216
Birrahgnooloo, 171
Bison, 88–9, 98, 100–101, 104, 107,
    111–14, 116, 118–19, 122–3, 129,
    131, 135, 206–207
Black Cuillins, 41
Blavatsky, Madame, 220
Blombos, cave, 63
Boars, 145, 155, 182–3, 201, 206
Boetia, 168
Bonaparte, Napoleon, 10, 228
Bonobos, 44, 48
Borneo, 43, 116
Boron, Mount, 54
Bosporus, 200
Boudica, 157
Boxgrove, 53, 56, 85, 227
Brahma, 175, 178, 182, 216
Bran the Blessed, 215
Brassempouy, Dame de, 107
Brecon Beacons, 24
Breuil, Henri, 114, 121
Brian Boru, 161, 231
Bride, 157
Brigantia, 157
Brigid, St, 157
Britain and the British, vii, 3–4, 10,
    23, 29, 32, 35, 41, 43, 52, 54–5,
    57–8, 60, 64, 67, 75, 86, 99–100,
    104, 130–3, 135–9, 144–5, 149–50,
    152–3, 155–63, 170–1, 173, 205–11,
    215–16, 218–19, 226, 231–2, 237–8
Britannia, 157, 161
British Museum, 10, 130, 139
Brittany, 140–5, 148
Brixham, 8, 99
Brodgar, Ring of, 148
Brontosaurus, 35–6
Bronze, 67, 107, 113, 126, 154–7,
    160, 201–202, 212–15
Broom, Robert, 31, 48, 60
Brutus of Troy, mythical founder of
    Britain, 3–4, 144, 218–19, 232
Buckland, William, 87, 99
Buddha, Buddhism, 175, 221
Buffon, 6–7
Bulls, 33, 120, 154, 173–4, 181, 193,
    207
Bullón, Comte de, 104
Burins, 85, 103, 131
Burke's Peerage, 226
Butterflies, 37, 42
Bytham, river 53–4

Cadmus, 173, 194
Caesar, 104, 157, 160
Cahors, 90, 208
Cain, 217
Cairnholy chambered cairns, 146
Calasso, Roberto, 173, 176
Cambrian period, 23–4
Cameroons, the, 69, 77, 228
Canaan, 189
Canada do Inferno, 105
Candelabra Theory, 72–3
Canterbury, 145–6
Cantii, 159–60
Caratacus, 157
Carboniferous period, 17, 28–9
Carpathian Mountains, 101
Cartailhac, Émile, 89
Cartimunda, 157
Castel Merle, 94, 100
Castleden, Rodney, 147
Castlerigg stone circle, 145
Çatal Hüyük, 139–40, 144
Catholicism, ix, 3, 7, 13, 106, 157,
    220
Cats, 17, 36, 45, 53
Cattle, 36, 101, 104–105, 135, 157,
    206
Catuvellauni, 160
Caucasus, Caucasians, 50, 73, 78, 91,
    227, 229
Cavallo, Grotta del, 94
Caves, 20, 35, 45, 47, 51, 53–4, 56–7,
    61, 68, 74–5, 79–80, 85, 87–90,
    93–6, 98–105, 108, 110–21,
    122–6, 130–5, 152, 154, 183–4,
    202, 205–206, 208, 210
Celts, 134, 159, 162, 215
Cenancestor, 19
Cenozoic era, 17, 23, 41
Cerdic of Wessex, 216
Cernunnos, 135
Chad, Old Man of, 44, 48
Chagan-Shukuty, 183
Chalcolithic culture, 152–6
Chang, Joseph T., 86, 162, 203
Chardin, Teilhard de, 60
Charles, Prince of Wales, 232
Charnias, 21–3
Charroux, Robert, 221
Chasms, 13, 174, 178–80
Châtelperronian culture, 95–6
Chatwin, Bruce, 78, 210
Chauvet, cave, 101, 113, 115
Chazine, Jean-Michel, 116
Cheddar Gorge, 131, 134–5,
    206–208
Chicxulub crater, 37
Chilterns, 35
Chimpanzees, 11, 44–5, 47–8, 65,
    73, 167
Choanoflagellates, 20

Choirokitia, 139–40, 144
Chordata, 24
Christy, Henry, 56, 87–8, 111
Chromosomes, 20, 65–70, 72–3, 77,
    92, 149–50, 160, 224–7
Chulugdy, 185–6, 208
Churyumov-Gerasimenko comet, 18
Cihuacoatl, 196
Clack, Jenny, 28, 163
Clactonian culture, 54
Claudius, 157
Clovis culture, 109
Côa, Vale do, 105–106, 130–1
Coatlicue, 180, 188
Coelacanths, 25–6, 37, 125
Coldrum long barrow, 145–6
Coliboaia, cave, 101
Comanche, 193
Combarelles, cave, 111–12, 118
Comets, 16, 18, 29
Compton, Tim, 99
Con Ticci Viracocha, 178
Condover, 136
Confucius, 170
Conn Cétchathach, 215
Continental drift, 26–7
Coon, Charles Carleton, 73
Cope, Julian, 146
Cormelia, 207
Cornwall, 24, 161, 207
Corsica, 228
Cosnac, 95
Cosquer, cave, 115
Cotswolds, 32, 145
Cotylosaurs, 30
Cougnac, cave, 103, 116, 118
Courbet, cave, 116
Cox, Brian, 18
Coyolxauhqui, 180, 188
Coyotes, 192–4
Creffield Road, 57
Creswell Crags, 57, 75, 104, 129–30,
    206
Cretaceous period, 36–7, 138
Crete, 114, 126, 154, 189, 207
Crick, Francis, 65
Crocodiles, 28–9, 36–7
Crô-Magnon, 85, 87–8, 100, 103,
    105, 129, 137
Cromeleque dos Almendres, 142
Cromlechs, 143, 145
Crossopterygian fish, 25
Crowley family, 161, 231
Crucuno, 148
Crustaceans, 23, 37, 145
Cuneiform, 10, 151, 188, 198
Cunliffe, Barry, 237
Cyanobacteria, 20–1
Cycads, 30
Cyclopses, 137, 154, 179
Cynad, 37

Cynodonts, 32–3, 35, 60, 125, 152, 162, 227
Cynognathuses, 33, 35
Cyprus, 139

Dagenham, 153–4
Daleau, François 89–90
Danann, Tuatha de, 170, 189
Däniken, Erich von, 221
Dardanos, 4, 214, 218
Dart, Raymond, 48
Dartmoor, 144, 156
Darwin, Charles, 8–11, 47–8, 57, 65, 73, 87–89
Dawkins, Richard, 9, 167
Dawkins, Sir William Boyd, 130
Dawley, 29
Deer, 53, 55, 57, 65, 89, 101, 104, 111, 113–14, 118, 129, 134, 156
Delmarva Peninsula, 80, 109
Delphi, viii, 13, 186–7
Demeter, 126, 157
Denisovans, 79–80, 85, 227–8
Desdemaines-Hugon, Christine, 113, 117
Desmond, Richard, 48
Deucalion, 194, 199, 214
Deuterostomes, 24
Devil, the, 207–208
Devonian period, 25–9
Diamond, Jared, 48
Diana, Princess, 232
Diana, Triple, 117
Diapsids, 31, 35
Dicynodonts, 32
Dima, 137
Dimetrodon, 31
Dinosaurs, 22, 31–2, 35–7, 41, 163
Dione, 157
Dmanisi, 50
DNA, 19, 64–9, 71–3, 75, 77, 80, 91–2, 135, 153, 160, 224, 226, 235, 237
Doggerland, 53–4, 58, 99, 135
Dogon, 194
Dogs, 9, 32–3, 36, 48, 51, 111, 133, 138, 167, 181
Dolmen di Axeitos, 142
Dolmens, 110, 141–2, 144, 155
Dolní Věstonice, 106
Dorians, 155
Dragonflies, 30
Dragons, 147, 186, 194, 216
Druids, 144, 159
Dryas octopetala, 132
Dryas, Younger, 132, 135–6, 138
Dryopithecus, 43, 44, 87
Dubois, Eugene, 50
Dumuzi, 212
Duruthy, 113
Dwarves, 192

Dyabdar the serpent, 182–3, 185–6, 207–208

Ea, 181, 195, 198
Easter Aquhorthies, 146
Ebbsfeet, 57
Eber, 217
Ebu Gogo, 51
Echidnas, 34, 37
Echinoderms, 24
Eden, 29, 60, 72, 89, 120, 171, 207
Edinburgh, 27
Eels, 24
Eemian interglacial period, 58
Egypt, 10, 43–4, 119, 136, 139, 151–4, 178, 187, 196, 205, 213–14
Einsten, Albert, 13
El, 115
Eleithyia, 157
Elektra, 214
Elephants, 36, 41, 51, 53, 55, 114
Eleusis, 126
Elizabeth II, 225, 232
Elliott, T.S., 17
Emus, 191
England and the English, 3, 9, 26–7, 53–4, 57, 65, 74, 129, 137, 144, 157, 161, 216
Enki, 181, 195, 198
Enkidu, 198
Enlil, 181, 195
Enoch, 217
Enos, 217
Enuma Eliš, 168, 181, 188, 195
Eocene epoch, 41
Eomaia, 36
Epiros, kings of, 214
Epona, 113
Er Grah, 143
Erasmus, 8
Eridu, 151, 212
Eros, 13, 20, 174, 178
Esagila, 195
Eskimos, 80, 192
Esmark, Jens, 87
Ethiopia, 44–5, 49, 59, 61, 69, 217, 228
Euarchonta, 41
Euboea, 155
Eukaryotes, 20–1, 66
Euphrates, river, 151, 181–2, 195, 200
Europa, 207
Eurydice, 174
Eusthenopteron, 26
Eutheria, 36
Evans, Sir Arthur, 154
Eve, vii, ix, 4, 6, 61, 64, 67, 91, 105, 116, 146, 169, 187, 190, 196, 217, 220–2, 232
mitochondrial, 67–8, 91, 228

Evenk, 183, 238
Evolution, 3, 8–9, 11, 22, 26, 28–9, 31, 34, 36, 41, 46–8, 50, 52, 55, 59–61, 64–5, 85–6, 90, 96–7, 125, 163, 220, 222–3
Évora, 142
Exmoor, 147
Extinction, 29, 33, 35, 61, 70, 104, 114
Extremophiles, 20
Ezekiel, 221

Fadets, cave, 121
Fairfax family, 232
Feathers, 36–7, 182, 188
Fenni, 136
Fenris Wolf, 176–7
Ferns, 27–30, 32, 37, 53, 200
Feustal, Rudolph, 117
Fiji, 79
Finchley Road Tube Station, 54
Fir Bolg, 160
Firle Beacon, 146, 156
Fish, 11, 22–6, 28, 31, 59–60, 104–106, 122, 156, 162, 180–1, 192, 196, 227
Flandrian stage, 133
Flatworms, 23
Flint, 8, 47, 53, 56–7, 59, 87, 93–5, 10, 103, 106, 108, 111–12, 114, 131–3, 140, 145, 151
Floods, 4, 6, 10–11, 54, 56, 100, 139, 169, 175, 181, 190, 193–5, 198–202, 208–209, 212, 216–17, 222
Flores, 51, 73, 227
Fokida, 194
Fomorians, 189
Font de Gaume, cave, 89, 112, 115
Foraminifera, 35
Forth, Firth of, 27
Fossils, 21–4, 25–6, 28–9, 33, 35–7, 41–3, 45–6, 50–1, 64, 163
Foxhall Road, 54
Francis, Pope, 223
Freya, 216
Frogs, 28–30, 37, 65, 191
Frolich, Lorenz, 176
Fuhlrott, Johann Carl, 8
Fungi, 21, 111, 137–8
Fylingdales Top, 156

Ga'um, 188
Gabillou, cave, 118
Gaelic, Gaels, 62, 159, 160
Gaia, vii–viii, 13, 27, 29, 157, 174, 179–80, 186, 194, 202, 215
Galapagos Islands, 9
Galatians, 159
Galicia, 142, 155–6
Galilei, Galileo, 15

Garrod, Dorothy, 130
Gates of Grief, 71
Gayomart, 193
Geissenklösterle, 98–9
Genealogy, genealogists, vii, 6, 8–9,
    13–14, 59, 168, 209, 211, 213,
    215, 217–18, 224–6
Genes and genetics, ix, 19–20, 34,
    43, 48, 51–2, 55, 61–2, 64–71,
    72–3, 75–80, 86, 91–2, 97, 111,
    135, 149–50, 153, 160–3, 167,
    203, 221, 223–8, 235–6
Genesis, Book of, 4–5, 7, 10–11, 60,
    62, 72, 168–70, 179, 186, 190,
    196, 199, 217, 220–1, 227, 237
Genghis Khan, 79, 114, 229
George, Prince, 232
Gethsemane, 126
Ghanaians, 69
Ghyston, 207
Giants, 142, 149, 176–7, 180, 186,
    192, 199, 207–208
Gibbons, 43, 48
Gibborim, 217
Gibraltar, 44, 95
Gigantomachy, the, 186
Gilgamesh, 10, 198–201, 212
Ginkgos, 30, 37
Ginnungagap, 180
Gla, 154
Glaston, 95
Gmelin, Johann, 5
Goats, viii, 99, 104–105, 106, 155,
    181
Göbekli Tepe, 141
God, gods and goddesses, vii, 4–10,
    13, 15–16, 27, 60, 65, 106–108,
    113, 120, 126, 140–2, 145–6,
    151–2, 155, 157–8, 168–83,
    186–90, 192–6, 198–9, 201–202,
    204, 212–18, 221–2
Goethe, Johann von, 5, 87
Goldcliff, 136
Goldfish, 211
Goldstone Valley, 208
Gondomar, 156
Gondwanaland, 26–7, 35, 41–2
Gong-gong, 199
Goodman, Morris, 48
Goram, 207
Gorgonopsians, 32–3
Gorillas, 11, 44–5, 47–8, 65, 73, 167
Götterdämmerung, 177
Gouffre de Padirac, 208
Gough's Cave, 131–2, 135
Grail Kings, The Genesis of the, 221
Granville, Crô de, 114
Gravettian culture, 91, 103–108, 111,
    116, 149
Great Orme, 130, 155

Greece, vii–viii, 13, 89, 116, 124,
    126, 154–6, 158–9, 168–9, 173,
    186, 192, 205, 207, 214, 232
Griffins, 37
Grimaldi, 107
Grimspound, 156–7
Grotte Sous-Grand-Lac, 118
Guadalupe, 142
Guthrie, Dale, 123
Gylfaginning, 171
Gymnosperms, 30, 36

Hadean eon, 16–18
Hades, 189
Hadrian's Wall, 27
Hadrocodium wui, 33
Haeckel, Ernst, 11, 22, 31, 47, 50, 66
Hagfish, 24
Hallstatt culture, 159, 162
Hallucinations, 124–5, 195
Halong Bay, 186, 216
Hancock, Graham, 221
Hangenberg event, 29
Hanoverian dynasty, 225
Haplorrhini, 42
Happisburgh, 43, 53, 56, 85, 227
Harappa, 152
Harpoons, 93, 111, 134
Harrison, Benjamin, 57
Hartsoeker, Nicolas, 65
Hassegau, Counts of, 231
Hawaii, 79
Heath, Richard and Robin, 148
Hebrews, 158, 169–70, 196, 217
Heinrich events, 71, 93, 99, 104, 110
Helen of Troy, 155
Helikon, Mount, vii, x, 13
Hellenos, 214
Hercules, 15, 44, 174, 179, 207, 214
Heroes, 3, 44, 144–5, 147, 149, 177,
    179, 212, 214–15, 217, 219
Herto, 61–2
Hervey, William, 65
Hesiod, vii–x, 13, 17, 20, 168–9, 174,
    178–80, 189, 213–15, 226
Hetty Pegler's Tump, 145
Higham, Tom, 99
Himalayas, 41, 51
Hinduism, 48, 170, 175–6, 178, 182,
    186, 188, 196, 216, 221
Hittites, 159
Hobbits, 51, 73, 227
Hohle Fels, 98–9
Hohlenstein, 98, 125
Hollington, 35
Holmes, Arthur, 26
Holocene epoch, 17, 133
Homer, viii, 3–4, 17, 155–7, 168,
    179, 189, 214, 218
Hominiae &c., 48

Homo afarensis, 45; africanus, 46,
    48; antecessor, 52; erectus, 50–3,
    70, 85, 227; ergaster, 49–50;
    floresiensis, 50–1, 227; habilis,
    46, 49; heidelbergensis, 52–3,
    55, 57, 59, 73, 76, 79, 85, 227;
    helmei, 59; rudolfensis, 49;
    sapiens, 55–6, 58–9, 61–2, 64,
    66–8, 70–7, 80, 94–6, 99–100,
    110, 167, 227–8
Hookner Tor, 156
Hopi Indians, 193
Horne, John, 26
Horses, 36, 53, 58, 88–9, 101,
    103–106, 108, 111–14, 116, 118,
    129–31, 136, 147, 206
Horsetails, 30
Horus, 178
Hoxnian culture, 54–5
Hoyle, Fred, 13
Hu Gadarn, 171
Huangdi, 216
Hubble, Edwin, 15
Huguenots, 162
Huitzilopochtli, 180
Humboldt, Alexander von, 17, 26
Hummingbirds, 193
Hutton, James, 7
Huxley, Thomas, 10
Hyenas, 53, 85, 110, 132
Hylobatidae, 48
Hylonomus, 30
Hypocrene spring, vii–viii, x

Iapetus, 27
Ibexes, 89, 100–101, 111–12, 114,
    122
Ice Age, 21, 43–4, 47, 52, 54, 56,
    58–9, 61, 71, 78, 85–93, 98–100,
    110, 114, 126, 132–3, 135, 138–9,
    152, 183–4, 200, 205–207, 210
Iceni, 157
Ichthyosaurs, 35–6
Ichthyostegas, 28–9
Ictidosaur, 33
Ida, 42–3, 85, 126
Ightham, 57
Iguanodon, 35
Iliad, the, viii, 3, 155–6, 179, 189, 218
Inanna, 213
Incas, 178, 194, 199, 216
Indo-Aryans, 170
Indus Valley civilisation, 152, 170
Insects, 5, 23, 28–9, 36–7, 136, 138,
    193
Intermaxillary bone, 5
International Society of Genetic
    Genealogy (ISOGG), 224
Inuit, 173, 192
Iolo Morganwg, 171

reland and the Irish, 27, 29, 62, 64, 74, 86, 135, 144, 148–50, 157, 159–62, 170, 189, 215, 231
ron, 6, 15, 113, 117, 135, 145, 159–60, 162, 170, 201–202, 209, 213–15
shtar, 213
srael, 71, 74–5, 186
sturitz, 132
vo Eleru, 77

acob, 217
amadagni, 176
anusiscus schultzei, 25
apheth, 4, 218
ava, 50–1
econiah, 169
efferson, Thomas, 137
ehovah, 158
ericho, 139
ersey, 57
erusalem, 169
esus, 6, 126, 169, 217
ews, 158, 169, 162, 169, 189, 201, 217, 221
ohn o'Groats, 26
ulieberry's Grave, 146
upiter, 4
urassic period, 17, 22, 33–6
utes, 161

a, 176
alavasos-Tenta, 140
alimantan, cave, 116
angaroos, 118, 191, 210
aroo, 31–2
astallian Spring, 186
azantzakis, Nikos, 9
ebara, 74
eiller, Alexander, 146
ellwasser event, 29
endrick's Cave, 130
ennet, river, 206
ent, 55, 57, 145–6, 159, 215, 227
ent's Cavern, 8, 99
enyanthropuses, 45
enyapithecus, 43
eraterpeton galvani, 29
ercado, 143, 145–6
ermaro, 143
erzerho, 143
hnum, 194
horilatai, 114
ibish, 61
imberella, 23
ingu, 181, 195
ircher, Athanasias, 6
ish, 168
ishar, 181
nossos, 154
odoyanpe, 182, 192

Kostienki, 103
Krapina, 95
Krishna, 175
Kronos, 179, 189
Ksatriyas, 216
Kuntillet Ajrud, 189, 238
Kybele, 157

La Cotte de Saint Brelade, 57
La Ferrassie, 57
La Madeleine, La, cave, 87, 110
La Marche, 120–2, 130
La Mouthe, cave, 89
La Piletta, cave, 104–105
La Placard, cave, 132
La Sabeline Museum, 121
La Tène culture, 159
La Vache, cave, 120
Labyrinthodonts, 29–30, 60, 227
Lacorre, Ferdinand, 103
Laetoli, 45
Lagar Velho, cave, 74
Lahâmu, 181
Lamarck, Chevallier de, 7–8
Lamech, 217
Laming-Emperaire, Anette, 123
Lampreys, 24
Lancets, 24
Landsteiner, Karl, 64
Langurs, 43
Lapa de Gargantáns, 142
Larkin, Bradley, 226
Lartet, Édouard and Louis, 43, 56, 85, 87–8, 103, 110–11
Lascaux, cave, 100, 109, 111, 118, 122–3
Laugerie Basse, 117
Laurasia, 35, 41
Laurasiatheres, 36–7
Laurentia, 27
LaViolette, Paul A., 168
Lazaret, cave, 56
Le Moustier, 56–7, 95, 100
Le Roc de Marsal, 57
Leakey, Louis and Mary, 45, 49
Leary, Jim, 205, 237
Lebor Gabála Érenn, 149, 170, 189
Ledi-Geraru, 49
Lehringen, 58
Leipzig, 116
Leleges, 194, 199
Lemaître, Georges, 13
Lemmings, 57
Lemurs, 42
Leopards, 45
Les Eyzies-de-Tayac-Sireuil, 88–90, 100, 107–108, 110–12, 114, 117–18
Les Trois Frères, cave, 118–19, 134
Levallois culture, 59, 93
Lévi-Strauss, Claude, 220

Leviathan, 189
Lewes, 147
Lewis-Williams, 96, 123–4, 203
Liang Bua, cave, 51
Libby, William F., 90
Life on Earth, ix
Lightfoot, John, 6, 167
Limassos, 139
Linnaeus, Carl, 5, 7–9, 22, 72
Lions, 45, 53, 98–9, 101, 111, 121, 125, 163, 173, 193
Lister, Dr Adrian, 136
Liverworts, 27
Lizards, 32–3, 35, 37, 51
Llandudno, 155
Lobe-finned fish 25
Loch Ness, 35
Locmariaquer, 143
London, 7, 54, 57, 87, 153, 162, 220
Lorises, 42
Lotan, 189
Lowestoft, 53
Lowmoor, 29
LUCA, 19
Lucy, 45–6, 48
Lungfish, 26
Luther, Martin, 3
Lyell, Charles, 8, 10–11, 87
Lyme Regis, 36
Lynford Quarry, 58
Lystrosaurs, 32–3
Lyuba, 137

MacDermot family, 160–1
MacDonald family, 62
Macedonia, 140, 214
Maeve, Queen, 157
Magdalenian culture and people, 91, 108, 110–14, 116–18, 120–2, 125–6, 129–32, 134, 141, 230
Mahabharata, the, 170, 216
Mahalel, 217
Maiden Castle, 159
Malebranche, Nicholas, 65
Mammals, x, 5, 11, 22, 31–7, 41, 59–60, 227
Mammoths, 6, 8, 36, 47, 53, 57–8, 85, 87, 89–90, 93–5, 98–9, 101–104, 107, 110–18, 120–1, 129, 131–2, 135–7, 180, 183–6, 193, 201, 206–208
Manasseh, 189
Mandela, Nelson, 62
Mané Lud, 143
Manu Vivasvata, 216
Marduk, 158, 168–9, 181–2, 188–9, 195–6
Marean, Curtis W., 61
Marlborough Downs, 145, 156
Marmara, Sea of, 200
Marston, Alvin, 55

Marsupials, 34, 37
Mary, Virgin, 157, 218
Maryland, 80, 109
Mathuselah, 217
Mayans, 170, 179, 194–5
Mbo, 77, 228
McGovern family, 161
McLoughlin family, 161
Meadowcroft, 80
Megaliths, 140–2, 146, 148, 154, 156
Megalocephalus, 29
Megaloceros, 101, 103, 118
Megazostrodon, 34
Mendel, Gregor, 65
Mendips, 32, 131, 134
Menhirs, 142–3
Meshel, Ze'ev, 189
Mesolithic culture, 64, 133–6, 138, 148–9
Mesopotamia and Mesopotamians, 10–11, 16–17, 90, 151–3, 158–9, 168–9, 181–2, 195, 198–9, 200, 203, 212–14, 217
Mesozoic era, 23, 33
Metazoans, 21
Meteorites, 18–19, 37
Michabo, 183
Middleton, Catherine, Duchess of Cambridge, 232
Milankovitch cycles, 52
Milky Way, 14–15, 188, 233
Millar, Hugh, 25
Millipedes, 27, 30
Minoans, 126, 154, 238
Minotaur, 114, 119, 154, 207
Miocene epoch, 43
Miremont, Grote de, 114
Mitchiner, Dr John, 152
Mithen, Steven, 96
Mither Tap, 146
Mitochondrial DNA, 66–9, 71–3, 77–8, 91–2, 135, 153, 160, 224, 228
Mixcoatl, 188
Mohenjo-daro, 152
Moles, 5, 32, 36, 137
Molluscs, 23, 156
Mongols, Mongolia, 73, 79, 114, 229
Monkeys, 10, 42–3, 89, 118, 121, 194
Monmouth, Geoffrey of, 144, 219
Monotremes, 34
Moon, the, 15–16, 107, 120, 137, 148, 171, 179, 181, 193–4, 195
Moore, John, 134
Morbihan, 141
Morgan, Thomas Hunt, 65
Morganucodont, 33–4
Moro, Abbé, 6
Moronenok, 183, 185
Morris, Desmond, 48
Morwood, Michael, 51
Mossel Bay, 61, 63, 68

Mourant, Arthur, 64
Mousterian culture, 56–7, 59, 90, 95
Mudskippers, 28
Multiregionalism, 72
Mungo, Lake, 78
Munin, 192
Muses, the, viii, 13
Mushrooms, 21, 124–5, 144
Muspelheim, 180
Mycenae, Mycenaeans, 154–7, 159, 161, 168, 179, 189
Myrrha, 192

Nabta Playa, 151
Narayana, 182
Narmer, 152
Natuf, Wadi al, Natifians, 138–9, 144
Navajo, 193
Neanderthals, 8, 47, 52, 55–9, 61, 71, 73–7, 79–81, 85–7, 90, 94–6, 104, 227–8
Nebra, 116
Nebuchadnezzar, 169
Nematode worms, 23
Neolithic culture, 107, 124, 138–43, 145–50, 152, 155–6, 159–60, 187, 200, 202, 205–206, 208, 211
Neptunism, 6
Nereus, 215
Nerja, caves, 95
Nevali Cori, 141
Newgrange, 148
Newts, 28, 30, 37
Niaux, Grotte de, 100, 112, 120, 122–3
Nile, river, 151–2, 194
Nineveh, 168
Ningestinna, 188
Nintu, 195
Nippur, 195
Noah, 4, 10, 73, 190, 215, 217–18, 220
Normans, 161–2
Norsemen, 171, 180, 182, 201, 216
Norte Chico, 152
Notland, 147
Nudimmud, 181, 195
Nummulites, 20
Nut, 188
Nüwa, 186, 194, 199, 216
Nymphs, 13, 214

O'Doherty, 161
O'Farrell family, 160, 221
O'Flanagan family, 161
Oak trees, 8, 20, 41, 43, 137, 208
Obatala, 182, 194
Ochre, 57, 63, 75, 78, 95, 99, 101, 103–107, 116, 130, 132
Odin, 145, 177, 180, 192, 216
Odysseus, 214
Odyssey, the, viii
Oldbury Hill, 55, 57, 75

Oldenburg, House of, 225, 232
Oldowan culture, 49
Oligocene epoch, 43
Olorun, 182
Olson, Steve, 62
Olympia, 205
Olympos, Mount, viii, 15, 140, 189
Omorka, 181
Oppenheimer, Stephen, 97
Orang–utan, 43, 48, 73
Ordovician period, 24, 27
Orion-Cygnus arm of the Milky Way, 14
Orkneys, 147–8, 157
Orpheus, Orphism, 173–5, 185, 207, 214
Orrorin tugenensis, 44
Orrorins, 44
Osharov, M.I., 183
Osteichthyes, 25
Ostrachoderms, 24
Otshirvani, 183
Ötzi the Iceman, 153, 229
Ovid, vii
Owen, Richard, 32
Oxygen, 20–1, 26, 29, 66, 124

Pääbo, Svante, 75, 80
Pair-non-Pair, 89–90, 100–101, 110, 112
Pakefield, 53, 56, 85
Palaeolithic culture, 49, 53, 59, 85–6, 88–91, 94, 100, 102, 105, 110–11, 113, 119–25, 132–4, 136, 140, 143, 147, 149, 152, 158, 170, 173, 183, 193, 202, 206, 211, 213
Paleocene epoch, 41
Paleozoic era, 23
Palestine, 138–9
Pallene Peninsula, 186
Pan, 126
Pangea, 29, 31–3, 35
Pangu, 170, 174, 179–80, 194
Papua New Guinea, 75, 79, 230
Paranthropuses, 45
Parapithecus, 43
Parish registers, vii
Parnassos, Mount, 199
Parthians, 151
Partholon, 149
Partraighi, 135
Patai, Raphael, 189
Pataud, Abri de, 100, 107
Paviland, Red Lady of, 99–100
Pavlov, Moravia, 102, 107
Pech Merle, 90, 103, 113, 118, 184, 206, 208
Pécharmant, 100, 122
Pedigrees, 4, 10–11, 150, 160, 162, 179, 212–13, 215–18, 223–7, 233
Pedra Arca Piosa, 142

edra da Lebra, 142
elycosaurs, 31
eñascosa, 105
engelly, William, 8
ennines, 32, 145
ermian period, 31–2
erseus, 179
ersians, 151, 174, 182
erthes, Jacques Boucher de
    Crèvecoer de, 8
eyrony, Denis, 111–12, 115
hanes Protogenos, 174–5, 187
hilae probe, 18
hoenicians, 64
icts, 67, 157
ierolapithecus catalaunicus, 43–4
iggott, Stuart, 146
igs, 32, 140, 155, 216
ikaia, 24
iltdown Man, 47
innacle Point, 61
istachios, 138
ithecanthropus alalus, 47
lacoderms, 25
lankton, 24, 37
latypuses, 34, 37, 41
leistocene epoch, 49, 133
leistos Vale, 186–7
leniglacial period, Lower, 71
les, Mrs, 48
lesiadapis, 41
lesiosaurs, 35–6
liocene epoch, 44
liosauruses, 22
lutonism, 6–7
ongidae, 48
ontevedra, 156
ontnewydd, 57, 75
opol Vuh, 170, 194
oseidon, 189, 194
rajapati, 178, 182, 187–8, 196, 216
restwich, Joseph, 87
rimates, 41–2
rimatomorphs, 41
robainognaths, 33–4
roconsul, 43
rokaryotes, 19
rometheus, 196
roterozoic eon, 20
rotoceratops, 37
rotochordata, 24
rotozoa, 20–1, 32, 35, 60
silocybin, 124
sittacosaurus, 37
armigans, 122
erodactyl, 36
erosaurs, 36
uranas, 170, 182
gmies, 69, 171–2
yrrha, 194, 199, 214
thon, 186

Qafzeh-Skhul, 71, 74
Quaternary period, 17, 49
Quetzalcoatl, 180, 185, 188, 196, 199

Ra, 178, 187, 196, 213
Ragnarok, 176, 192
Rainham, 154
Rakshasas, 196
Ramayana, 170, 182
Raphael, Max, 123
Ras Shamra, 189
Ravens, 10, 173, 192–3
Reinach, Salamon, 122
Reincarnation, 159
Reindeer, 57–8, 85, 93–4, 99, 104,
    110–12, 118, 122, 124, 129, 133
Religion, 6–7, 16, 73, 124, 126, 134,
    152, 154, 167, 169, 216, 221
Renaissance, the, 3, 219
Reptiles, 11, 22, 30–5, 37, 59, 186
Rhea, 189
Rhine, river, 54, 58, 141, 144
Rhinoceroses, 8, 32, 53, 55, 57–8, 93,
    95–7, 101, 113–14, 207
Rhipidistians, 26
Ridgeway, the, 145
Rietchel family, 230
Rig Veda, 170, 178
Riparo di Vado all'Arancio, 121
Robin Hood Cave, 130–1
Rome, Romans, 4, 78, 90, 99, 105,
    136, 142, 157, 161, 163, 170, 196,
    208, 218
Ronda, 104
Rouffignac, cave, 113–16, 184, 206
Royal family, 158, 216, 225–6
Rudra, 175

Sahelanthropus tchadensis, 44
Saint-Cirq, 117–18
Saint-Gaudens, 43
Saint-Germain, 107, 110, 121, 141
Saint-Savin-sur-Gartempe, 190
Salamanders, 29
Samivel, 126, 155, 186, 238
San people, 62
Santorini, 154
Sarcopterygians, 25–6
Sasquatch, 51
Sassanids, 151
Satapatha, 178
Satyrs, 119
Sauropods, 35
Sautuola, Don Marcelino de, 88–9
Savignano, 107
Saxe-Coburg, House of, 225–6, 231–2
Saxons, 145, 161–2, 216
Schmerling, Philippe-Charles, 55
Scorpions, 24, 27
Scotland, Scots, 26–7, 41, 54, 62, 67,
    87, 104, 154, 157–8, 160–2

Sea cucumbers, 24
Selene, 15
Seleucids, 151
Sellar, W.C., 62
Sely the mammoth, 182–3, 185–6,
    193, 206–208
Serpents, 124, 156, 174, 177, 180,
    182–91, 194, 199, 201, 206–208,
    211, 216
Seth, 217
Sevenoaks, 55
Sforza, Luigi Luca Cavalli-, 66
Shamans, 118–19, 123–5, 134, 154,
    170, 183,185, 193, 210
Shamash, 195
Sheba, Queen of, 218
Shem, 217
Shiva, 152, 175–6, 178, 182
Shrews, 5, 33, 36–7, 41
Sicily, 161
Silbury Hill, 205, 208
Silurian period, 24–5, 27
Simplicity of Creation, The, 7
Sinanthropus, 50
Sippar, 182
Sireuil, Venus of, 107
Sistine Chapel, 9
Sivapithecus, 43
Skye, 41
Snakes, 37, 42, 72, 112, 114, 154,
    173, 184–6, 196, 206–208
Snowball Earth, 21
Snowdonia, 27
SNPs, 67–9, 73, 77, 150
Soerfon Barrows, 156
Solomon Islands, 79
Solomon, King, 217–18
Solutrean culture, 91, 108–109, 111
Sommer, Volker, 48
Songlines, 78, 210, 236–7
Sorcerers, 110, 117–19, 121, 123,
    125
Spartoi, 194
Sphinx, 108
Spiders, 99, 191, 210
Sponges, 21
Stags, 94, 101, 129, 131, 134–5, 149
Standing stones (menhirs), 141–4,
    148, 151
Star Carr, 134, 149
Stavorouni, Mount, 140
Stavrakopoulou, Dr Fransesca, 189
Stegocephalia, 29
Stennes, Stones of, 148
Stoke Newington, 54
Stonehenge, 148, 152–3
Storegga Slide, 135
Strepsirrhini, 42
Stringer, Chris, 50, 72, 76, 95, 99
Sturluson, Snorri, 171, 176
Suffolk, 53–4, 232

Sukuriam, 212
Sumer, Sumerians, 151, 181–2, 195, 212
Sumuqan, 188
Sun, the, x, 14–16, 19–20, 24, 29, 31, 44, 52, 85, 94, 115, 124, 133, 148, 176–7, 179–80, 186, 191–2, 194–5, 199, 216
Sunkenkirk stone circle, 145
Sussex, 35, 53, 95, 145, 147, 156, 207
Swanscombe, 55–6, 85, 227
Sykes, Professor Brian, 91, 135, 150
Symmetrodonts, 33
Synapsids, 31–23, 35, 60

Tacitus, 136
Taittiriya Samhita, the, 182
Tarascon sur Ariège, 100
Targett, Adrian, 135
Tartaros, 174
Tautavel, 54
Teck, Mary of, 232
Tectiforms, 115–17
Tefnut, 188, 196
Teilhardina asiatica, 42
Termites, 46, 48, 138
Terra Amata, 54
Tertiary period, 41
Tethys, 179, 202
Tetrapods, 28–9, 163
Teufelsbrücke, 117
Tezcatlipoca, 180
Thames, river, 43, 54, 58, 99, 206, 237–8
Thamte, 181
Thebes, 194
Theia, 15–16
Theogony, the, vii–ix, 13, 168–9, 174, 179, 189, 214–15, 226
Theosophism, 220–1
Thera, Mount, 154
Therapsids, 31–2
Therianthropes, 118
Theriodonts, 32
Theseus, 114, 154, 207
Thetys, 215
Thomsen, C.J., 154
Thor, 176–7
Thoth, 119
Tiahuanaco, 178
Tiâmat, 181, 188–9, 195, 202, 212
Tigris, river, 151, 181, 195, 200
Tiktaaliks, 28
Tiryns, 154
Titans and titanesses, vii, 15, 27, 179, 194, 196, 214–15
Titicaca, Lake, 179, 199
Tjongerian culture, 133
Toba, Mount, 61, 68, 70–1
Tolkien, J.R.R., 51
Toltecs, 180, 182

Tomnavery stone circle, 147–8
Tonacateuctli, 188
Torres Straits, 78
Torrini, Antonio, 68
Totems, 96, 98, 191, 210
Totnes, 144
Trafalgar Square, 58, 61
Tregaron Neanderthals, 74
Triassic period, 33–5
Trilobites, 23–4, 26, 33
Trottiscliffe, 145
Troy, Trojans, 3–4, 144, 154–7, 159, 161, 171, 214, 218–19, 232
Tuang Child, 48
Tuatha de Danann, 170, 189
Tuc du Audoubert, 123
Turkana Boy, 49
Typhon, 186, 189, 207
Tyrannosaurus rex, 35
Tyre, 207

Ubaid culture, 151
Uffington, 113, 147, 159
Ui Neill clan, 161
Uintatheriums, 41
Ulligarra, 195
Underhill, Peter, 68
Underworld, the, 13, 17, 174, 184
Upanishads, the, 170
Ur, 10, 151
Ural Mountains, 32, 149
Uranos, vii–viii, 27, 179, 189, 215
Uruk, 151, 168, 198–200
Ussher, James, Archbishop of Armagh, 6
Uta-Napishtim, 10, 198, 200, 212–13, 217
Uzamua, 195

Valhalla, 177
Varaha and Varahi, 182
Venus, Venus figurines, 98, 106–108, 111, 112, 116–17, 139, 143, 146–7, 157, 202, 213
Vergil, Polydore, 3–4, 219
Věstonice, 106
Vézère Valley, 56–7, 87–8, 90, 94, 100, 102–104, 107–108, 110–15, 117, 126, 130, 132–3, 206, 230
Victoria, Queen, 225, 232
Vidal, James, 51
Vidar, 176–7, 192
Vigl, Dr Eduard Egarter, 153
Vikings, 86, 161–2, 171, 176, 183, 192
Vimianzo, 142
Viracocha, 178, 194, 199, 216
Virchow, Rudolf, 8
Virgil, 3, 219
Vishnu, 175, 178, 182
Vogelherd, cave, 98
Vogt, Karl, 73

Volcanoes, 6, 16, 18, 20–1, 27, 29, 32, 37, 41, 44–5, 51, 61, 185–6
Voltaire, 6
Voskoboinikov, 183, 238
Vulcanism, 6–7

Wadi Zarqa, 139
Wagner, Richard, 177
Wagner, Sir Anthony, 162
Watson, James D., 65
Waverly Wood, 54
Weald, the, 208
Weidenreich, Franz, 73
Weld-Blundell Prism, 212
Werewolves, 119
Werner, Abraham Gottlob, 6, 17
Wessex, 216
West Kennet long barrow, 145–6, 156
Westbury-sub-Mendip, 54
Westeray Wife, the, 147
Weymouth, 36
Whales, 36, 196
Wilkinson, Toby, 178
Willendorf, Venus of, 106
William, Duke of Cambridge, 232
Williams, Edward, 171
Wilmington, Long Man of, 146
Wiltshire, 35, 132, 145, 148, 205, 20
Windover Hill, 146
Windsor, House of, 232
Winston, Professor Robert, 45
Withypool stone circle, 147
Woden, 145
Wodensbury, 145
Wolphoff, Milford, 73
Wolverine, 112
Wolves, vii–viii, 33, 35, 70, 85, 110–12, 114, 130, 132, 145, 176–7, 193, 206
World shapers, 186–7, 208
Wrangel Island, 136
Wymer, John, 55

Yahweh, 158, 169, 174, 179, 187, 189, 196, 217
Yeatman, R.J., 162
Yeti, 51
Yggdrasil, 192
Ymir, 180, 192
Yoruba people, 182
Yowie, 51
Yudokon, 183
Yupik, 192

Zalgarra, 195
Zeus, vii, 4, 126, 158, 169, 173, 179, 186, 189, 205, 207, 214–15, 218
Zhoukoudian, 50
Ziusudra, 212
Zoroastrianism, 174, 193